Wittgenstein Centenary Essays

EDITED BY

A. Phillips Griffiths

CAMBRIDGE
UNIVERSITY PRESS

Published by the Press Syndicate of the University of Cambridge
The Pitt Building, Trumpington Street, Cambridge CB2 1RP
40 West 20th Street, New York, NY 10011-4211, USA
10 Stamford Road, Oakleigh, Victoria 3166, Australia

Reprinted 1992

British Library Cataloguing in Publication Data

Wittgenstein Centenary Essays.—(Royal Institute of
Philosophy supplement; v. 28).
1. English philosophy
I. Griffiths, A. Phillips (Allen Phillips) *1927-*   II.
Series 192

ISBN 0 521 40947 0 (paperback)

Library of Congress Cataloguing in Publication Data

Data applied for

Origination by Precise Printing Company Ltd, Reigate, Surrey
Printed in Great Britain by the Athenaeum Press Ltd, Newcastle upon Tyne.

Contents

Contents

Preface

This volume of essays is based on the 1989–90 series of Royal Institute of Philosophy lectures given in London to mark the centenary of the birth of Ludwig Wittgenstein (1889–1951).

It was thought that in general the essays should reflect on the degree to which Wittgenstein's influence, in and beyond philosophy, is apparent today; and the degree to which his work is relevant to other areas of thought than the purely philosophical.

While the second question—with regard to for example mathematics, religion, psychology, political thinking—is dealt with by some of the contributors to this volume, the answer to the first question seems clearly to be 'not very much'. This would not have surprised Wittgenstein himself, nor, as far as professional philosophers are concerned, have been unwelcome. ('. . . my work is meant for only a small circle of people (if it can be called a circle)' (CV, 10)). As he wrote in 1947:

> Am *I* the only one who cannot found a school or can a philosopher never do this? I cannot found a school because I do not really want to be imitated. Not at any rate by those who publish articles in philosophical journals (CV, 61).

Indeed he seems to have consciously wished and aimed that this should be so. He wrote of his own work in 1930:

> . . . the spirit of a book has to be evident in the book itself and cannot be described. For if a book has been written for just a few readers that will be clear just from the fact that only a few people would understand it. The book must automatically separate those who understand it from those who do not . .
>
> If you have a room which you do not want certain people to get into, put a lock on it for which they do not have the key (CV, 7).

and he returned to this thought in 1946:

> Yes, a key can lie for ever in the place where the locksmith left it, and never be used to open the lock the master forged it for (CV, 54).

His attitude was much the same to what his effect might be on areas other than philosophy. Thus (1930):

> It is all one to me whether or not the typical western scientist understands or appreciates my work, since he will not in any case understand the spirit in which I write (CV, 7).

And again, in 1947:

> Nothing seems to me less likely than that a scientist or mathematician
> who reads me should be seriously influenced in the way he works. (In
> that respect my reflections are like the notices on the ticket offices at
> English railway stations[1] 'Is your journey really necessary?'. As
> though someone who read this would think 'On second thoughts
> *no*'.) . . . The most I might expect to achieve by way of effect is that I
> should first stimulate the writing of a *whole lot* of garbage and that
> then this *perhaps* might provoke somebody to write something good.
> I ought never to hope for more than the most indirect influence (CV,
> 62).

Was it Wittgenstein's view that we should be provoked to reflect on the
nature of our journeys, rather than look for some justification of them
lacking which we might give them up; and that while he might provoke
us to do this, it would be something we could do only for ourselves?

> In the sphere of the mind someone's project cannot usually be
> continued by anyone else, nor should it be. These thoughts will
> fertilize the soil for a new sowing (CV, 76).

[1] During and immediately after the Second World War.

Wittgenstein: Whose Philosopher?

G. E. M. ANSCOMBE

One of the ways of dividing all philosophers into two kinds is by saying of each whether he is an ordinary man's philosopher or a philosophers' philosopher. Thus Plato is a philosophers' philosopher and Aristotle an ordinary man's philosopher. This does not depend on being easy to understand: a lot of Aristotle's *Metaphysics* is immensely difficult. Nor does being a philosophers' philosopher imply that an ordinary man cannot enjoy the writings, or many of them. Plato invented and exhausted a form: no one else has written *such* dialogues. So someone with no philosophical bent, or who has left his philosophical curiosity far behind may still enjoy reading some of them.

What I call a philosophers' philosopher is one who sees problems, interest in which is the mark of a philosopher, and whose principal thoughts can be derived from his discussion of those problems. When Socrates in the *Phaedo* says he cannot understand how both adding one to one and dividing one can yield two; when in the *Republic* he says that the domain of knowledge is being, of non-knowledge non-being, so that of opinion must be between being and non-being; when he ties Euthyphro into knots because he thinks that the pious pleases the gods *because* it is pious and that the pious is pious *because* it pleases the gods—at least, Euthyphro seems to begin with thinking both and Socrates proceeds to derive a contradiction and to leave the question what piety is in a state of *aporia*; when Plato reproduces arguments of the Sophists to prove that there cannot be such a thing as false belief, because what is false *is not*, and so he who thinks what is false thinks nothing, i.e. does not think anything; when he argues that there must be more than One, Parmenides' *being*, because it has a name and if the name of the one were the same as the one you could just as well call it the one of the name as the name of the one, so the name must be something different; when Socrates argues that if anyone can speak he can be found to know the whole of mathematics, though he has forgotten it and has to be reminded of what in fact he knew before he was born—I will stop because I have given enough examples. When this quite characteristic sort of thing is found argued for in the dialogues, the arguments will say little to interest non-philosophers, but almost always are likely to excite people of philosophical bent.

There is also the fact that where Plato does—or does make Socrates—draw conclusions from discussion of his problems, they do

1

not seem credible. That the Forms are the only really real things; reincarnation and the eternal pre-existence of the souls of men; that it is impossible to want what is bad and all evil-doing is a matter of ignorance that it *is* evil; that there is something called 'the dyad' which makes whatever is two to be two: these and many other Platonic doctrines seldom exercise much appeal to philosophers, though some may appeal to non-philosophers for non-philosophical reasons.

By contrast, Aristotle is not often so much concerned with what are apt to strike non-philosophers as weird or boring problems, and his conclusions very often seem to be down-to-earth and about pretty familiar things. Sometimes this is because he made them familiar: consider the concept of *relation*. Plato had distinguished between what was *per se* (*kath auto*) and what was *to something else*; Aristotle replaced 'to something else' by the simple 'to something', for, as we would now say, a thing may stand in a relation to itself. Again, the concept of *matter* is one we owe to Aristotle: such a concept as is implicit in the reasonings of Lavoisier when he re-obtained mercury by heating mercury calx (as it was then called) in a closed vessel. The same matter but a change of chemical substance and an increase in how much of the matter in the vessel was air.

I will say no more in explanation of my distinction, but will proceed to argue for my main thesis: Wittgenstein is, like Plato, a philosophers' philosopher.

First, however, I will note with sorrow the sad fate that seems to be befalling him. For reasons which I do not understand, there are some philosophers who become cult figures. Plotinus is one, Spinoza another. I know hardly anything about Plotinus; of Spinoza, I know a certain amount—enough to find this vulgar elevation of him incomprehensible. He is a very tough thinker and it is hard work to study him. I doubt very much that *this* fact gives him his spurious aura. Nor would the same facts about Wittgenstein account for the same phenomenon in his case. Having regretfully noticed it, I wave it away from my considerations.

These concern the phenomena of mental life called 'understanding' and 'thinking'. I will begin with *understanding*. Now we (usually) understand the meaning of a word when we hear or say it. Not always: we may think we understand it and not do so. (Think of how some people are fond of using the word 'parameters' in philosophical discussion.) However, we mostly understand words that we hear or say. *When* do we understand them? Well, when we hear them or say them. So is understanding, in that context, an event of a moment? Still more, when we *suddenly* understand a word whose meaning we did not know before. Now Wittgenstein's observation at Part I, section 43 of the *Untersuchungen* (PI) is surely quite correct: 'For a *large* class of cases of employment of the word "meaning"—even though not for all, it can be explained thus: The meaning of a word is its use in the language.' But if the meaning is the use we make of the word, how can I grasp it in a flash? For use is something extended in time. So what I grasp in a flash must, must it not, be something different from use: the whole *use* of a word cannot come before my mind in a flash. And the verb 'to mean' has the same feature. 'When you said 'funny' did you mean queer, or funny like a joke?' And there is such a thing as 'experiencing the meaning of a word'. Suppose I utter the sound *bord* to you. You may be able to answer the question 'what did you hear that as: the word "board" or "bored"—the noun, or the past participle of "to bore"?' and if you say 'the first' did you hear it as meaning something like a plank or something like a group of people with some official purpose? And if you say 'the past participle': was it connected with boredom or with boring holes? Of course, you may say you didn't hear it as anything, you just heard me make that noise and wondered why I did so. But if you do have one of those answers, which you very well may, then haven't you experienced a meaning? However, we cannot say that understanding in a flash is experiencing a meaning.

Suppose you envisaged a plank, the polished leaf of a table round which a board sits—would that prove that you heard the word 'board' as meaning 'plank'? No, the same thing may come before your mind on different occasions when you hear that word and the application still be different. But, once again, application is complicated and extended in time and applications of a word 'in the same meaning' may be various: e.g. in the sentence 'The board was liquidated.' Certainly then, there is such a thing as experience of a meaning and also an experience of understanding a word, but these just by themselves do not, or need not, tell the whole use. (I say need not, because in the case of very idiomatic connectives like the German 'wohl aber' there can be an experience which gives you its whole meaning: or so it has seemed to me. To anticipate, however, this may depend on antecedent circumstances.)

Suppose you are being taught something and are given examples of the kind of thing in question—as it might be a series of numbers, and you have a sudden reaction: 'Now I know what this one is, now I can go on.' 'Various things may have happened here', Wittgenstein says. You may have thought of a formula that fits the bit of the series you have been given; you may have asked yourself 'What is the series of differences between one number and the next?' and got a familiar series; or it may strike you that the series itself is a familiar one which you know how to continue; or you may recognize the series as something and have a mnemonic for going on, like the mnemonic for π: 'How I want a drink, alcoholic of course, after all those lectures confuting Fregean doctrines one by one' or you may simply go on with the series without any device.

But 'understanding the principle of the series' cannot be any of these happenings: it must be more, or it must be something *behind* them.

Here Wittgenstein says:

> If there has to be anything 'behind the utterance of the formula', it is *certain circumstances*, which justify me in saying I can go on—when the formula occurs to me. And further: In the sense, in which there are processes (including mental processes) which are characteristic of understanding, understanding is not a mental process. (PI, I. 154)

'Thus, he continues, '. . . when [the man] suddenly knew how to go on, then possibly he had a special experience . . . but for us it is the *circumstances* under which he had such an experience that justify him in saying in such a case that he understands, that he knows how to go on.'

I will here note that in modern philosophy since Descartes there has been a strong tendency to amplify Descartes' list of *cogitationes* to include memory, even knowledge, probably understanding. I will not pause to consider the inwardness of the limitation of Descartes' list—though I suggest it might be a fruitful enquiry.

However that may be, Wittgenstein now proceeds to a very detailed consideration of *reading*: his purpose, he says, is to make clearer the fact he has just alleged: 'it is the *circumstances* under which he had such an experience that justify him to us in saying in such a case that he understands, that he knows how to go on'.

The choice of *reading* proves to lead us on a very complicated enquiry. It is here that I can most easily justify my thesis that Wittgenstein is a philosophers' philosopher. Non-philosophers are apt to think that there are no philosophical problems about reading: reading is just a special inner experience which you may or may not accompany by utterance out loud of the words you read. And perhaps under the post-Cartesian influence some philosophers too would say this, if they thought about it at all. That understanding and thinking are topics for philosophy none would doubt; that reading might be, it takes a philosophic bent to conceive. The enquiry on reading occupies nine pages of the English edition of the *Untersuchungen*; twelve if we include the corollary enquiry into *being guided*. Not long after Wittgenstein's death I was asked to produce something about him as a BBC programme; I innocently thought: 'This examination of *reading* is a whole and not too long passage and extremely interesting, so I'll read it.' I did, but I heard only rumours of how boring people found it, going on about something not in the least problematic.

Wittgenstein explains that he will give a special restricted—but also partially widened—sense to 'reading'. He will not count understanding what is read as part of reading for purposes of his investigation: it is there the activity of writing from dictation as well as those of rendering out loud what is written or printed and playing from a score.

A reader reads a newspaper: his eye passed along the words; perhaps he says the words; some he takes in as wholes, others he reads syllable by syllable, occasionally letter by letter. Even if he says nothing while reading we would count him as having read a sentence if he could afterwards reproduce it, or nearly so.

A beginner in reading, by contrast, reads the words by laboriously spelling them out. He may guess some, or know some by heart. If he does that the teacher will say he is not really *reading* those words, and perhaps that he is pretending to.

But—Wittgenstein tells us he wants to say as far as concerns uttering any *one* of the printed words, the same thing may take place in the consciousness of the pupil who is 'pretending' to read, as in that of the practised reader who *is* reading it. The word 'read' is applied differently in the two cases.

The first word that someone *reads*—it makes no sense to ask what word that is, unless you stipulate that you are, for example, going to call 'the first word' the first in a series of 50 words that he reads right or something of that sort. But if 'reading' is to stand for a certain experience of transition from marks to spoken sounds, then it does make sense to speak of the first word he really read.

Wittgenstein imagines that someone argues that if only we knew more about the brain and the nervous system, we could look into the pupil's brain and say 'Now the reading connection has been set up.' But why does it have to be like that? If we feel it *must* be, that means that we find that form of explanation very convincing. But we really do not know if it is even probable that there *is* such a mechanism with a 'reading connection'.

If on the other hand we think that the only real criterion is that the 'reader' has a conscious experience of reading, we may be thinking of the contrast with someone who is a conscious fraud, pretending he can read Cyrillic script. He of course knows he is not reading—he knows that he is not having the characteristic sensations that accompany peering, guessing with some confidence, misreading, and so on. The 'and so on' includes the contrast with repeating what you have learned by heart. But now, suppose a practised reader is reading a text fluently—but has the *sensations* of repeating something learned by heart—though he never saw the text before. Or suppose that someone is presented with what look like written characters, but which belong to no known alphabet, and he comes out with words, showing all the outward signs and having the characteristic sensations that go with reading. If he is systematic and consistent in what he does with uttering sounds in connection with the text, there might be disagreement about whether he was reading or not—or, indeed, whether he was making up an alphabet and reading accordingly.

Repeating something you know by heart—is that incompatible with reading? Look at your watch after saying the numbers from 1 to 12 and now *read* the numbers. What did you do, to make it *reading*?

We might want to say: reading is deriving the spoken sounds from the written characters. And we can describe clear-cut cases of such derivation in which a taught rule is used, or a rule for passing from print to handwriting. Such a 'rule' might be a pair of columns with printed letters on the left and written ones on the right; the pupil is to look at a text, check what written letter is immediately to the right of a printed letter, a sample of which occurs in his text, and copy the written letter. Of course he has to have been trained in the practice of using the adjacent columns as a rule, and as *that* rule. If less simple correlations are used, we can describe a series devolving into randomness. This, however, does not mean that there is really no such thing as a clear case of derivation. There is a variety of cases—and this fits in with the fact that a variety of circumstances provide us with cases of reading; from the first, we had to admit that for a beginner and for a practised reader we would apply quite different criteria. A child once said proudly when visiting his grandmother 'I can read!' 'Good', she said, and put a book before him. 'Oh no', he said, 'that's not the right book.'

A 'special experience' or 'words coming in a special way' do not function as explanations of what reading is. A word might come to you in the 'special way', and *any* special way you care to describe otherwise than as 'the way the sounds come to you when you are reading the words' might be found in cases which are *not* cases of reading. As for *that* description, it is useless: one wants to know 'what way *is* that?'

Some generalizations we can make—but they are of a restricted sort. There is a uniformity about reading printed pages when one is familiar with the printed words—for one thing, there is a uniformity in the appearance of many such pages. But reading is not restricted to this class of 'texts'. Wittgenstein remarks on how different the text would look where a sentence was written in Morse code. And if one tries to read our printed lines from right to left, i.e. reading the *letters* from right to left, there is a struggle quite unlike what we experience reading from left to right.

'But when we read do not we feel the word-shapes somehow causing our utterance?'—One would do better to say they grounded it— we would point to the text as a justification for the way we read it out loud—Wittgenstein says 'I would like to say I feel an *influence* of the letters on me'—but he does not want to say that about a solitary letter. The contrast is between a row of printed words and a row of arbitrary printed marks like § , ?, %, *.

We repeatedly have as an argument against explaining *reading*, or *deriving*, or *influence*, or *being guided* in some way that is supposed to apply quite generally, that our cases are particular and that cases vary according to circumstances, and our 'explanation' is not borne out in a different sort of case. In the last example the marks are perfectly familiar, and we would have no difficulty about saying we read them when they occur functionally in appropriate positions. And we might *copy* such an arbitrary row of them—which conforms to Wittgenstein's specifications of what he is counting as 'reading' for his current investigation. One of the other explanations—the use (implicit) of a rule which could be constructed in the form of two columns, one of the printed signs, the other of the written ones—would be more like a justification than an account in terms of 'feeling an influence'.

In short, the whole enquiry in these pages consists largely in rather convincing arguments against generalizing particular expressions that we are inclined to use in highly particular situations and cases.

We must remember the purpose which Wittgenstein claimed for putting his investigation of *reading* at this place in the *Untersuchungen* (PI). It was to help his contentions about *understanding* to become clearer to us. Of these, the principal one was: 'If there has to be anything "behind the utterance of the formula" [a formula you may use to continue a series] it is *certain circumstances* which justify me in saying I can go on—when the formula occurs to me.'

'Now I understand the principle' does not mean the same as 'The formula . . . occurs to me.' The argument that it does not is an argument for a quite clear variety of cases in which one might say 'Now I understand the principle'; the formula . . . occurring to me was just one of the possible cases, and a case in which no such thing happens is not thereby shown *not* to be a case in which I could justifiably say 'Now I understand the principle.' But note this: the formula occurring to me *is* a particular experienced event, and with that we have explained how there can be 'experiences of understanding'. For *that* experience in *that* case is an experience of understanding—though this is true only because of the circumstances, which include much that went before the moment of the formula's occurring to me. That is why 'Now I understand the principle' does not mean the same, even just in this case, as 'The formula occurs to me'. This is illuminated by the discussion of reading: there are experiences connected with reading, but 'reading' is not the name of any of them. Similarly there is a variety of experiences connected with an occasion of understanding, but 'understanding' is not the name of any of them.

G. E. M. Anscombe

Now I do not believe that the investigation into reading which Wittgenstein conducted and compressed into these tight pages is of the sort to appeal to a reader without a philosophical bent. As a contribution to a certain clarifying of the concept of understanding, it plays a part in some major themes of his work—it is not just an eccentric preoccupation with a concept of very marginal importance.

This is my case for saying that Wittgenstein is 'a philosophers' philosopher.'

Understanding was not an abnormal topic for a philosopher: it is the questions, like 'when did understanding take place?' and 'if you understand the integral calculus, when do you do so? all the time, or every now and then?' that surprise. The latter not so much, as it may excite the ready answer: 'Here we are speaking of understanding as something dispositional.' So one also speaks of belief—and of knowledge. Wittgenstein's relevant contribution here was to reject the 'scholastic' suggestion that where there is a 'dispositional' sense of a word like 'belief', there is also and primarily an 'actual' sense of it. I mean as if one could answer a question: 'What are you doing?' by saying, for example, 'Believing that smelling is having molecules hit your smelling apparatus.' 'Believing', Wittgenstein said, has no such 'actual' sense. Clearly *coming to a conclusion*, if it is not just seeing that q follows from p, is arriving at a belief; but belief is not an activity which you can, for example, practise before breakfast every morning. Yet someone can say 'Believe me, it is better to steal than to beg' or recommend you to believe what someone else has said—using an imperative again. Coming to a conclusion, I said, may be arriving at a belief, and certainly is that if it is not finding the implications of a possibly rejected proposition. That means that here at least, thinking, unlike believing, is an activity. (I am not speaking of the usage in which 'I think' *means* 'I believe'.) Anyone might say 'So far, so good: obviously thinking is an activity, which may or may not accompany your utterances and your other actions, but we want to know what this activity, thinking, *is*.' Here Wittgenstein begins to jib—thinking may *be* talking—one does not usually have to think a sentence before saying it—though there may be talking 'without thinking.' So too with other activities: in some cases 'I did it without thinking—I do not have to think about it as I do *that*' claims a practised capacity; in others 'I did it without thinking' explains what sort of mistake in action, psychologically speaking, I committed: I did not deliberately take the wrong turning. So does doing something deliberately involve doing it *with thought*? No, not necessarily, as doing something with practised competence may show us.

We have only scratched the surface, but it is already clear that Wittgenstein was right in saying that the grammar of 'to think' is extremely complicated. To think is an activity, yes, but the activity may

8

be one of, say, sharpening a pencil with a pencil sharpener that requires the pencil to be held in a particular way if the lead itself is to be given a point. Familiarity means that one can do it 'without having to think about it'—but if asked: 'Why are you pressing the pencil sideways like that?' one can immediately give the reason. The activity is one *of* thought (as speech can be) if there is no distinct *accompaniment* of thought.

Our few examples might mislead into thinking that 'thinking' is like 'paying'. If someone claims to have paid some money, the question may well arise 'In what way did he pay it?' For example, was it by cheque, or with money; by post or messenger, or did you in person hand something over, or cancel an equivalent debt? But no: all I have indicated is that certain activities may *eo ipso* be thinking; they may contain moves that have an aim and are decisions, as playing chess or darts do. Here, though, as with *understanding*, a background of human custom is needed to constitute the practices as what they are. Suppose—to take an example from the discussion of *being guided*—I am copying a line that describes a complicated course. Is what I do, in that I draw a line that corresponds to—is in detail *like*—the other, *copying*? That is, is it *eo ipso* copying? We say children copy their parents. Do sheep copy one another? But the case of copying the line is more specialized than these. What do I mean by saying that? I mean that you could *imagine* circumstances, a background in my society, even in the development of people of my ancestry, which would mean that I was not engaged in the activity of copying. This would be decidedly odd—the conception *here* is of a natural regularity like that men grow beards. The construction of such 'philosophy fiction' does not have the purpose of recommending scepticism about whether you can know that I am copying that line; but only of showing what, other than what can be seen to be happening here and now, is involved in the fact that I am doing so.

A lot of things that are not necessarily 'overt actions' are thinkings. Deciding, forming an intention, some exercises of imagination, calculation 'in the head', interpretation. 'Interpreting is thinking, is an action; seeing is a state', Wittgenstein remarks in Part II, section xi of the *Untersuchungen* (PI, p. 340 of the Suhrkamp *Taschenbuch)*. If I say: 'First I thought I would tell him and then I thought I would not', is there a difficulty about understanding such a report? Some have thought that such a 'thought' must *be* sub-vocal movements of the larynx. But how can one know one had such thoughts without knowing anything about such movements? Besides, it seems to hint that that thinking must have been a 'saying within oneself' as one may recite a whole poem 'in one's head'. What, then, did having those two thoughts *consist in*? We have no idea—or no reasonable idea—and we ought to call the question into question. For how does one learn to say such things? Perhaps I can show you the way to saw a plank; I cannot show you the way to have a thought like that—so how do you learn? And what is the relation to its expression in words? Do these constitute a sort of translation as if from one language into another? How could that be, and how could the translation be checked?

One useful method of enquiry would be to construct misuses of these terms, 'thought', 'translation', 'meaning', etc. which show hopeless error about their grammar. 'I know Russian.' 'Right, translate "I'm going out" into Russian.' Silence ensues. 'Well, do it.' 'I did do it, but I can only do it in my head.' I cannot sing in tune—suppose I said that I can think a song in tune, only not out loud.

I will end with a story. I went with my little girl, then four-years-old, to look in on Kanti Shah in Trinity. He was not in his rooms, but there was an offprint on a table. I sat down and picked it up. 'Shall we go now?' asked the child, 'Yes, but first I'll read this a bit.' She waited expectantly and then said 'Read it.' 'I am reading it.' A bewildered silence followed, then she angrily shook my arm, exclaiming *'Read it, read it!'* I could not explain.

'The Darkness of this Time': Wittgenstein and the Modern World

J. BOUVERESSE

In the preface to the *Philosophical Investigations*, written in 1945, Wittgenstein remarks that: 'It is not impossible that it should fall to the lot of this work in its poverty and in the darkness of this time, to bring light into one brain or another—but, of course, it is not likely' (PI, viii). There was quite obviously no question for him of endeavouring to dissipate the darkness of the age itself, but at the most of introducing light into a small number of receptive minds, the existence of which he considered, moreover, as problematical. In a rough draft of the preface to the *Philosophical Remarks* that he wrote in 1930 he says:

> I realize . . . that the disappearance of a culture does not signify the disappearance of human value, but simply of certain means of expressing this value, yet the fact remains that I have no sympathy for the current of European civilization and do not understand its goals, if it has any. So I am really writing for friends who are scattered throughout the corners of the globe. (CV, 6)

It is quite characteristic of his manner that he should have had the conviction of writing for people who like himself were situated outside the main current of European and American civilization which was profoundly antipathetic to him, and that at the same time he should have refrained practically from any explicit indication as to the spirit in which he was writing and hoped to be read, leaving to his writings themselves the care of effecting the discrimination between the few 'friends' to whom they were addressed and the mass of readers incapable of understanding them:

> The danger in a long foreword is that the spirit of a book has to be evident in the book itself and cannot be described. For if a book has been written for just a few readers that will be clear just from the fact that only a few people understand it. The book must automatically separate those who understand it from those who do not. Even the foreword is written just for those who understand the book. (CV, 7)

In 1949 Wittgenstein said to Drury: 'At the present time I do not think people want the sort of ideas I am writing about, but perhaps in a hundred years time it will be what is wanted' (Rhees, 1981, 173). But even though he was, like Nietzsche, persuaded that he was writing but

J. Bouveresse

for a small number of readers of the time and, in fact, of addressing himself essentially to men of another day, for whom his way of philosophizing could finish by becoming completely natural, he energetically resisted the temptation of proclaiming this sort of thing and that of trying to explicate in what his philosophical approach was so untimely. Though, in different places in his manuscripts, he expressed his antipathy for modern civilization and his feeling of belonging to a world which was condemned to disappear, and had practically already disappeared, one would look in vain for some trace of that in the philosophical texts that he intended for publication. Indeed, they contain no explicit judgment about the modern world and no allusion concerning questions of the day: a situation which, it should be said in passing, could but singularly complicate the problem of Wittgenstein's reception in France where, widely during the recent period, philosophy was precisely identified with the adoption of a position concerning questions of the moment and sometimes even explicitly with some form of direct political action.

Wittgenstein was obviously anxious that the problem of his relations with the world in which he found himself bound to live and to work, and to which he considered himself to be profoundly foreign, should remain, as much as was possible, a private affair. It would most certainly not have come to his mind to construct, as others have been able to do, a whole philosophy on such a basis. McGuinness, in his biography of Wittgenstein, remarks that Wittgenstein was attracted by Schubert, amongst other things, for one reason: 'in which the ethical and the aesthetic were intertwined: the contrast of the misery of his life and the absence of all bitterness' (McGuinness, 1988, 124). It is clear that Wittgenstein himself sought to produce a philosophical work which would present the same sort of contrast and would realize the same sort of sublimation, a work the perfection of which would have a quasi atemporal character and would let nothing transpire of the author's personal problems, of the moral misery and the torments of his existence, of his dealings with the modern world and his resentment against the age. In a remark of 1930 he states that: 'The nimbus of philosophy has been lost. For we now have a method of doing philosophy, and we can speak of *skilful* philosophers' (WLL, 21). What is characteristic of an age of declining culture or without culture, such as ours, is, as he remarks, to limit the occasions for the expression of the personality in favour of a methodical and professional approach to all problems, philosophical ones included. He himself most certainly did his utmost to avoid his philosophy appearing to be a direct expression of his personality, at least in the usual meaning of the term 'personality'. It is precisely this sort of temptation which a philosophy that really pretends to be of our age should, to his mind, resist, on pain of being condemned as not genuine.

Musil, in *The Man Without Qualities*, states that the virtues which rendered possible the great scientific discoveries are at bottom of the same type as the vices to which one generally attributes the success of warriors, hunters and merchants:

> Before intellectuals discovered the pleasure of facts only warriors, hunters and merchants, that is to say precisely men of cunning and violent natures, had known it. In the struggle for life there is no place for sentimentalism, there is only the desire to suppress the opponent in the quickest and most effective way; everyone is a positivist. (Musil, 1978, 303)

The 'spirit of facts', as Musil calls it, led, in the realm of the intellect as in all other aspects of existence, to the triumph of a type of man whose dominant qualities are skill, cunning, tenacity, the absence of any scruples and inhibition, the distrust of any sort of idealism, the courage to destroy as much as to undertake, the art of waiting and of profiting from the slightest circumstances. Numerous remarks made by Wittgenstein, of whom the least that one could say is that his vision of the modern world and of human affairs in general certainly did not sin by an excess of sentimentalism, indicate that he was not insensitive to this exigency of the time. In 1930, he said to Drury: 'Yes, I have reached a real resting place. I know that my method is right. My father was a business man, and I am a business man: I want my philosophy to be business-like, to get something done, to get something settled' (Rhees, 1981, 125–126). After having heard a talk which seemed to him to be lacking of any interest, he remarked: 'A bad philosopher is like a slum landlord. It is my job to put him out of business' (ibid., 132).

It is likely that Wittgenstein would later have hesitated more in affirming that he really had found the firm ground on which one can build in all safety, and the appropriate method in philosophy. But the impression that he gives at the beginning of the 1930s is unquestionably that of someone who considers that philosophy had finally found the means of completely resolving its problems with the sobriety and the efficiency which characterize the way in which scientists proceed and, in a more general way, that of the whole age. This will to be 'business-like', even in a domain like philosophy, effectively to end up with concrete results, never disappeared from his preoccupations. Speaking of Lenin with Drury in 1934 he says: 'Lenin's writings about philosophy are of course absurd, but at least he did want something to be done' (ibid., 141). Nothing, of course, proves that he himself considered the fact that philosophy resembles, much more than it did before, a technique enabling the attainment of safely precise objectives, as being a decisive achievement of which our age may be proud. On the contrary everything leads to the belief that he would have preferred to live in an age where philosophy was able to produce something more grandiose and more exalting. He visibly did not consider that philosophy could be the most appropriate expression and the most convincing of the value of an age such as ours. But whether or not he had been influenced by Spengler on this point, he was convinced that in matters of art or of philosophy, an age which is one of decline should not endeavour to produce anything which no longer corresponds to its possibilities, even though there be nothing particularly enthusiastic about them. Drury reports that he had said of the Georgian architecture of the streets of Dublin: 'The people who build these houses had the good taste to know that they had nothing very important to say; and therefore they didn't attempt to express anything' (ibid., 152). In a remark which dates from the 1930s, he notes: 'Architecture immortalizes and glorifies something. Hence there can be no architecture where there is nothing to glorify' (CV, 69). In his view honesty and good taste require that an age such as ours, which probably does not have very much to immortalize and glorify, equally abstains from trying to do it nevertheless.

Musil said of capitalism that it could be considered as 'the most gigantic organization of egoism' (Musil, 1978, 1390). The characteristic of this type of system is precisely that of counting on what is most stable and most sure in man and of constructing what Musil calls 'an order *à la baisse*' based on the rational exploitation of the most inferior of man's capacities, an order remarkably flexible, efficient and creative. Wittgenstein who was the son of one of the founders of the Austrian steel industry, classed by Karl Kraus in the category of 'the steel devouring beasts' (*die eisenfressenden Bestien*), certainly experienced a strong feeling of guilt and considered the fact of being born in a family as rich and privileged as was his own as a sort of original sin that he sought to expiate in one way or another during the whole of his life. But it is most probable that, whatever his feeling of profound dislike for the values and way of life of the people of his social *milieu*, he was none the less sufficiently realistic to recognize that the form of capitalistic organization had at least the merit which Musil attributes to it, namely, of a certain productivity and efficacy. He seems, in any case, to have been much too pessimistic as to the human condition in general to have really believed in the possibility of appreciably improving things by a change in the political organization. Wuchterl and Hübner note, concerning the attitude of the Wittgenstein family towards politics before the First World War:

Even though the grandfather had, in his time, in some of his letters, expressed a keen interest in Austria's foreign policy, his children and grandchildren were at that time living as if politics did not exist at all. It is not by accident that among the family's close friends none were politicians; politics were ignored and politicians despised. So it was that even the war and the developments that had brought it about were received almost as a fatality. (Wuchterl and Hübner, 1979, 56)

It is in like manner that Wittgenstein seems to have accepted the upheavals and political catastrophies which happened later. He reacted towards them as towards things which the situation of the modern world and the perversity of human beings rendered more or less inevitable and against which it would have been perfectly vain to revolt. It is significative that he should have pointed out to Drury in 1936 that the atrocities of the First World War were in fact neither as horrible nor as exceptional as one tended to believe: 'Nowadays it is the fashion to emphasize the horrors of the last war. I did not find it so horrible. There are just as horrible things happening all round us today, if only we had eyes to see them' (Rhees, 1981, 144). Fania Pascal says of Wittgenstein that 'his rarely expressed political opinions could be naïve' (ibid., 57). But his judgments on humanity in general were certainly lacking in any sort of naïvety and romantism. When Drury told him in 1930 that one of his acquaintances was working on a thesis concerning the reasons for the failure of the League of Nations, he replied: 'Tell him to find out first why wolves eat lambs' (ibid., 131). Kraus said that: 'Social politics is the dispaired decision to undertake a corn operation on someone who has cancer' (Kraus, 1974, 70). This is perhaps not far from what Wittgenstein thought of politics in general and of the kind of intervention by which it pretends to heal the incurable and probably mortal illnesses of modern society.

Independently of that which he himself indicated, that is to say the privileged relationship which the review had with Kraus, the reasons for which Wittgenstein chose the review *Der Brenner* and its editor Ludwig von Ficker as an intermediary when, on his father's death, he decided to distribute a sum of 100,000 crowns to Austrian artists in want are not difficult to understand. As McGuinness writes:

The magazine seems to have been an attempt to do in a less personal and individualistic manner—in a less fastidious one too—what Kraus also was attempting; something very Austrian, and something, we can now see, very Wittgensteinian, to achieve a moral reform of life and thought without attempting to alter the conditions of life. The unworldliness can be seen as a reflection of the actual political impotence of the intellectuals of the time, or as a reflection more generally of the rottenness of the Austrian–Hungarian Empire, but it can also be seen as an important discovery, the discovery that the revolution needed (however impossible it might be) was not one in institutions, but one in the thinking and the sensibility—Kraus would say, in the language, of men. (McGuinness, 1988, 205–206)

In an article in *Der Brenner* in November 1920 entitled 'Revolution', Theodor Haecker begins by announcing that:

there must currently be some metaphysical decision of European peoples by which they allow themselves to be governed not by kings, but by parliaments, ministers and presidents, and reject monarchies recognizing henceforth 'democracy' as salvation. (Haecker, 1920, 481)

But he concludes by remarking that:

The revolution of our day must be taken seriously only because it does not come from God, it has only been allowed by him in order to punish those who made it and those against whom it was directed; it cannot, as a 'revolution', be taken seriously by us who recognize but He, who are waiting for the only one, that which will destroy worlds and build the heavens, we who await with the unquiet preoccupation of being that day amongst those who can proclaim with innocent heart or delivered of his sins and in complete openness: Blessed be he who comes in the name of God! (ibid., 503)

On reading this kind of thing one understands better why, and whatever his sympathies for *Der Brenner* may have been before the war, Wittgenstein wrote to Englemann in 1921: 'Ficker keeps on sending me *Der Brenner* and I keep on wanting to write to him to stop it, as I believe *Der Brenner* is nonsense (a Christian journal is intellectual make-believe)—but I never come down to sending the notice of cancellation to Ficker, as I cannot find sufficient peace and quiet to write a lengthy explanation' (Englemann, 1967, 43–44). Wittgenstein was certainly convinced that the real revolution could not be that which simply overturned institutions: 'That man will be a revolutionary who can revolutionize himself' (CV, 45). But he was also undoubtedly closer to Kraus' individualism and little disposed to according superiority to a particular form of religious organization rather than to others. As he said to Drury in the 1930s: 'As if nowadays any one organization was better than another' (Rhees, 1981, 129). He also said to Drury in 1929: 'Make sure that your religion is a matter between you and God only' (ibid., 117). The revolution of which he was thinking could but be a strictly personal affair between the individual and God or between oneself and the world. As convinced as he said he was that the real reform, the only one which was susceptible of really changing something, had to be an internal reform, he always received with repugnance and scepticism the idea of trying to create it by some form of predication. In the talks with the Vienna Circle, he says, employing, in a modified form, a formula from Schopenhauer: 'Preaching morals is difficult, founding it impossible' (McGuinness, 1967, 118). In a letter written in 1912, Russell speaking of Wittgenstein remarks: 'He abominates ethics and morals generally; he is deliberately a creature of impulse and thinks one should be' (McGuinness, 1988, 70). It is clear that what Wittgenstein detested was in reality much less ethics itself than the efforts undertaken to found it on a theoretical discourse of the philosophical or religious type. More generally, he considered the pretension of giving reasons there, where there are none, as a blunder or characteristic dishonesty.

* * *

It is difficult to determine what exactly could have been Wittgenstein's position on what Musil called the problem of 'Buridan's Austrian' divided between two bales of hay, those of the Danubian Federation and Great Germany, the latter being definitely richer in calories and the former emitting a much more inviting spiritual perfume. But it would certainly be no exaggeration to say that some of the virtues that he appreciated the most were of a typically Prussian character and that he did not have a very high opinion for the most reputed of Austrian deficiencies, those that the autochtons strove to pass as qualities. We know, in any case, that he had a great admiration for Bismark and was fond of talking of him (cf. Fann, 1967, 62). Drury remarks that in 1949, at a time when the books that he was fond of reading were historical works, he had at his disposal a personal copy of Bismark's *Gedanken und Erinnerungen* (cf. Rhees, 1981, 175).

It always seems, at first sight, somewhat surprising that a man as unconventional as Wittgenstein should have been so profoundly patriotic and have felt so bound to his country's destiny. Like many other Austrian intellectuals of his time, his relation to Kakania was certainly quite ambivalent. But it is obvious that he had been considerably affected by the decline and the disappearance of the Austro–Hungarian Empire, even though it is true that he would not have been tempted into giving the sort of idealized and even somewhat idyllic representation of pre World War One Austria that one finds in Stefan Zweig's *The World of Yesterday* (Zweig, 1943). When the First World War broke out, Wittgenstein accepted military service as a civic duty. But he did it in a frame of mind that had nothing to do with the bellicose enthusiasm and even sometimes hysteria that the opening of hostilities gave rise to nearly everywhere. Whereas the servicemen of the different countries enlisted in the war with the certainty of a rapid victory, Wittgenstein

J. Bouveresse

did not think that Germany was in a position to win the war. On 25 October 1914 he wrote in his Notebooks:

> It makes me feel today more than ever the terribly sad position of our race—the German race. Because it seems to me as good as certain that we cannot get the upper hand against England. The English—the best race in the World—*cannot* lose. We, however, can lose and shall lose, if not this year, then next year. The thought that our race is going to be beaten depresses me terribly, because I am completely German. (McGuinness, 1988, 211)

McGuinness remarks that at this time Wittgenstein was: 'an admirer of much in English patterns of behaviour and personal relations' (ibid., 120). Later, in 1940, when England found itself threatened with annihilation by Hitler's Germany, he said to Drury: 'You have often heard me speak of my dislike of many features of English life. But now that England is in real danger, I realize how fond I am of her. How I would hate to see her destroyed' (Rhees, 1981, 159). He did not, at that moment, however, believe that Hitler's opponents were really capable of winning the struggle: 'England and France between them can't defeat Hitler. But if Hitler does manage to establish a European empire, I don't believe it will last long' (ibid., 158). It is at the least interesting that he should have ignored Hitler's projects for Austria to the point where on the eve of the Anschluss he reacted to the news that Hitler was preparing to invade his country saying to Drury: 'That is a ridiculous rumour. Hitler doesn't want Austria. Austria would be of no use to him at all' (ibid., 158).

Though he certainly had no liking for Hitler and everything that he represented, Wittgenstein seems to have been persuaded, like many German and Austrian intellectuals, that the existing democratic governments, after having by their inability and their inefficiency rendered fascism almost inevitable, would not be capable of presenting Hitler with any real resistance. It is a fact that many people, estranged *a priori* from everything in Hitler's ideas, unhappily did not believe sufficiently in the virtues and chances of democracy in order to take its side against the threat that the rise of fascism represented. Musil expressed a feeling which was probably widespread when he wrote:

> One should make the thought experiment which consists in asking oneself whether one could imagine national socialism replaced politically by something else. A sensation that is independent of desires and fears, that would even often go against them, generally replies after all that such a change can no longer be accomplished simply as a return to the old state or to an even older one. This sensation should most probably not be interpreted otherwise than as signifying that national socialism has its mission and its hour, that it is not a flurry

18

but a step in history. (Quoted by Wilfrid Berghahn; cf. Berghahn, 1963, 125)

When the Nazis took the power in Germany, Wittgenstein said to Drury: 'Just think what it must mean, when the government of a country is taken over by a set of gangsters. The dark ages are coming again. I wouldn't be surprised, Drury, if you and I were to live to see such horrors as people being burnt alive as witches' (Rhees, 1981, 152). But Wittgenstein considered precisely that the indignation of the democrats was powerless against the gangster type methods that Hitler had chosen to use. To him they visibly resembled a form of inefficient gesticulation, the sort of thing that according to him should be avoided at all price in all clashes of this kind: 'The difficulty is: not to make superfluous noises, or gestures which don't harm the other man but only yourself' (ibid., 225). Rhees, in connection with this, says the following:

> A month or two before the Nazis entered Prague in 1939 a German refugee paper printed *en face*: a page giving a statement by Benes of what is essential to a liberal regime showing respect for individuals, and opposite this a page from Hitler's *Mein Kampf* on the need for ruthlessness and Realpolitik. It was meant to honour Benes. I thought it was well done, and I showed the two pages to Wittgenstein. When he'd read them he paused and then, nodding, reflectively: 'At the same time, this (pointing to the *Mein Kampf* page) is much more *business-like* than that one.' (ibid., 225)

We know, in any case, that just like Kraus, who declared that all in all he dreaded much less the misdeeds of censorship than those of the sacrosanct freedom of the press, Wittgenstein was not, by any means, an unconditional partisan of the liberal political system. Manifestly, he had always been convinced that a political system could be reproached with more serious matters than the limitation or the suppression of individual freedom; and the recourse to methods of government of a more or less authoritarian type did certainly not seem to him to be *a priori* inadmissible. Near the end of the Second World War he said to Rhees that the essential problem after the war would be that of everyone being able to find work. The question of the means to be used for that and the price to pay in order to attain this result seemed to him to be relatively secondary:

> He thought the new regime in Russia did provide work for the mass of people. If you spoke of regimentation of Russian workers, of workers not being free to leave or change their jobs, or perhaps of labour camps, Wittgenstein was not impressed. It would be terrible if the mass of the people there—or in any society—had no regular

work. He also thought it would be terrible if the society were ridden by 'class distinctions', although he said less about this. 'On the other hand, tyranny . . .?'—with a questioning gesture, shrugging his shoulders—'does not make me feel indignant'. (ibid., 226)

* * *

Karl Kraus more or less adopted as a motto for the life long battle that he led against the scandals, the perversions and the atrocities of the time a sentence from Kierkegaard: 'A man cannot alone help an age nor save it, he can only express the fact that it is waning' (*Tagebücher*, ed. Th. Haeker, 332). One could ask oneself whether Wittgenstein did not already consider the attempt of *saying* to his age that it was going toward its end as impossible or absurd. In a remark written in 1931 he wonders whether there were not problems in the Western intellectual world with which people like Beethoven (and to a certain extent, Goethe) had been confronted but which no philosopher had ever encountered. It is possible, he remarks, that 'Nietzsche passed by them'. These problems, which are perhaps lost to Western Philosophy, are linked to the presentiment of the death of a great culture at a time when it is precisely still a culture and not a civilization (in Spengler's sense), a time at which its decay and its end can be but obscurely felt and described in the epic mode by a few of its greatest creators. At the time at which a culture is really disappearing there is no one to write the Epic of this disappearance, as had been (or could have been) done before:

> It might be said that civilization can only have its epic poets in advance. Just as a man cannot report his own death when it happens, but only foresee it and describe it as something lying in the future. So it might be said: If you want to see an epic description of a whole culture, you will have to look at the works of its greatest figures, hence at works composed when the end of this culture could only be foreseen, because later on there will be nobody left to describe it. So it's not to be wondered at that it should be written in the obscure language of prophecy, comprehensible to very few indeed. (CV, 9)

Though the tone adopted by Spengler in *The Decline of the West* resembles much more that of an inspired prophet than the rigorous and imperturbable scientist which he pretended to be, he was quite obviously not in the position of someone who was attempting to write something like the Epic of the disappearance of his own culture. Firstly, he came too late for that, at a time when this culture had already entered its terminal phase, that of decline and death; and, secondly, he expresses himself in a language that has nothing to do with that of more or less obscure feelings, but which, to the contrary, is that of certainty based on unquestionable 'scientific' data. Spengler begins *The Decline of the West* by announcing that 'in this book the task is undertaken for the first time of attempting to predetermine history' (Spengler, 1972, 3). According to him one can already see 'in the words youth, ascension, zenith, decline, which until now, and today more than ever, were regularly the expression of subjective evaluations and of very personal interests of a social, moral and aesthetic nature, finally, the objective designations of organic states' (ibid., 36). Spengler considers that it is already possible to adopt towards the present itself, the phase of historical development which is presently in course and in which one is involved, a perfectly distanced and objective attitude:

> One could . . . perhaps say, and it will be said one day, that in a general way there has until now lacked a real vision of history of a Faustian style, that is to say a vision which possesses sufficient distance to consider even the present—which *is* but relatively to one and one only among the innumerable human generations—as something infinitely remote and foreign, as an interval of time that weighs no heavier than the others, without measuring it to the falsifying standard of some ideals, without regard for oneself, without desire, anxiety and internal personal implication, such as practical life demands; a distance which consequently allows—to say it with Nietzsche, who was far from possessing as much as he would have needed—to overlook the fact of Man being completely from an enormous distance; a view on cultures, even on one's own, as on the line of the summits of a mountain range on the horizon. (ibid., 125–126)

Wittgenstein notes that all these problems, those that concern doubts, anxieties and finally the anguish that a culture can, at a given moment, begin giving birth to as regards its future are not part of his philosophical universe, and that, in a general way, tragedy is absent from the world which is his. The result of his work could be described as consisting in putting the world with the infinite diversity that it contains and which engenders the conflict and the tragedy to one side: 'The whole outcome of this entire work is for the world to be set on one side. (A throwing-into-the-lumber-room of the whole world.)' (CV, 9). The will to be finished with the world considered as an amorphous, transparent and more or less indifferent mass seems to be characteristic of his philosophical attitude.

Just like Heidegger, who said in *Was heisst denken?* that the Spenglerian idea of the decline of the Western World was but the negative, yet correct, consequence of Nietzsche's 'The desert is growing', Wittgenstein certainly found spontaneously enlightening the idea that Western culture was already, and had been for some time, engaged in an irreversible process of decline. A number of remarks in his manuscripts clearly indicate that the ideal world from his point of view, the one to which he would have liked to belong, was not that to which he belonged but one which had disappeared and had ended near the middle of the nineteenth century:

> I often wonder whether my cultural ideal is a new one, i.e. contemporary, or whether it derives from Schumann's time. It does at least strike me as continuing that ideal, though not in the way it was actually continued at the time. That is to say, the second half of the Nineteenth Century has been left out. This I ought to say, has been a purely instinctive development and not the result of reflection. (CV, 2)

Then again it is clear that just like Spengler he was convinced that an age must not try and do something other than that which corresponds to its possibilities and was quite opposed to the voluntarist illusion which consists in imagining that, in a period of decline, one can will and in spite of everything realize things which were possible in an age of great culture, but which, from a given moment, ceased to be once and for all.

It is, however, no less obvious that whatever the instinctive sympathy that Wittgenstein felt for it he could not use the idea of decline in the manner in which Spengler had done. For in order to do so, it would in effect have been necessary for him to believe, like the author of *The Decline of the West*, in a rigorous historical determinism that allows the prediction of, if not the details, at least the general form of future evolution; and in the possibility for an historian who at the same time as he is himself an actor in the historical process in course, can treat the present with the same kind of detachment and objectivity as the past. Spengler says that one can but wish that which will happen in any case or nothing at all. He concludes *The Decline of the West* with a quotation which perfectly summarizes the spirit of the work: *'Ducunt fata volentem, nolentem trahunt'*. Wittgenstein's reaction toward the historical events which overwhelmed the world in which he was living was on the whole most certainly closer to resignation or (purely and simply) fatalism, than to the desire of openly opposing the unacceptable, even when externally it presents all the appearance of the inevitable. Wittgenstein said of Hitler in the year 1945: 'It isn't sensible to be furious even at Hitler; how much less so at God' (CV, 46). But perhaps he could have also said: 'One cannot be angry with God nor with History nor with Humanity, and consequently not with Hitler either.' Whatever his admiration for Kraus, the absurdities and horrors of the present age, to which he was certainly as sensitive as Kraus, never led him to the sort of revolt which is expressed by the will to combat, in all possible ways, the intolerable, without taking into account the fact that the battle is perhaps vain and already lost. If indeed he effectively opposed the spirit of the time, he did it in an indirect way and with what he believed to be the only weapons that a philosopher has at his disposal today. In philosophy he gives the impression of behaving like someone who was working for a hypothetical distant future, the realization of which depends on factors over which neither he nor philosophy in general has any real hold, and who has renounced intervening directly in the present situation.

Nevertheless, he manifestly did not, contrary to Spengler, believe that the limits imposed on the will, power and duty of individuals by the characteristics of the age to which they belonged could be plotted with the kind of 'scientific' precision that the author of *The Decline of the West* believed himself capable of attaining. He was to the contrary convinced that the course of history remains today, as it did in yesteryears, fundamentally unpredictable and uncontrollable. The reality of an age is, by definition, never the realization of the anticipations and dreams of the preceding age. As he remarked 1929: 'When we think of the world's future, we always mean the destination it will reach if it keeps going in the direction we can see it going in now; it does not occur to us that its path is not a straight line but a curve, constantly changing direction' (CV, 3). In another remark, in 1947, he notes that the behaviour of historical agents is not determined by laws of development the knowledge of which could permit both to explain the events and to orient them in such or such a way:

> A man reacts *like this*: he says 'No, I *won't* tolerate that!'—and he resists it. Perhaps this brings about an equally intolerable situation and perhaps by then strength for any further revolt is exhausted. People say: 'If *he* hadn't done *that*, the evil would have been avoided.'. But what justifies this? Who knows the laws according to which society develops? I am quite sure they are a closed book even to the cleverest of men. If you fight, you fight. If you hope, you hope.
>
> You can fight, hope and even believe without believing scientifically. (CV, 69)

In accordance with a general tendency of his philosophy which sees in instinct and will, and not in judgment and the intellect, what is foremost and fundamental. Wittgenstein rejects any intellectualistic interpretation of history and maintains that the evolution of societies results essentially from desires, hopes, beliefs, refusals and acceptances, which are anything but scientific, and the awaited consequences of which are for the most as different from those that will effectively happen as are dreams from reality. In a remark written in the same year, he speaks derisively of the kind of verbiage that one can read on cause and effect in books on history: 'There is nothing more stupid than the chatter about cause and effect in history books; nothing is more wrong-headed, more half-baked. But what hope could anyone have of putting a stop to it just by *saying* that? (It would be like my trying to change the way women and men dress by talking.)' (CV, 62).

At one moment, Wittgenstein asks himself what in fact distinguishes his conception from Spengler's: 'But then how is a view like Spengler's related to mine? Distortion in Spengler. The ideal doesn't lose any of its dignity if it's presented as the principle determining the form of one's reflections (*Prinzip der Betrachtungsform*). A sound measure (*eine gut Messbarkeit*)' (CV, 27). One cannot apprehend this age under the category of decline but by reference to an ideal which one has fixed. But this ideal must function only as an object of comparison or a standard of measure. One must at all costs avoid conceiving it as 'the preconception to which everything *must* conform' (CV, 26), an attitude that Wittgenstein qualifies as 'dogmatism' and which Spengler did not escape from. For Wittgenstein it is there that lies the danger *par excellence* in philosophy: 'The ideal, as we think of it, is unshakeable. You can never get outside it; you must always turn back. There is no outside; outside you cannot breathe. Where does this idea come from? It is like a pair of glasses on our nose through which we see whatever we look at. It never occurs to us to take them off' (PI, I, 103). The ideal must not be something to which we aspire or something which was once realized and is so no longer, something which would justify a depreciatory judgment of reality, whether it concerns language, as it is, or in another style, the age in which we live.

The dogmatism and injustice that Wittgenstein reproaches Spengler with apparently did not prevent him from having an unquestionable sympathy for the distinction between culture and civilization and the cyclic conception of the evolution of any culture, including that of the Western world:

Perhaps one day this civilization will produce a culture.
When that happens there will be a real history of the discoveries of the 19th and 20th centuries, which will be deeply interesting. (CV, 64)

In his talks with the Vienna Circle, Wittgenstein in 1931 formulated an extremely negative judgment as to the future of European culture: 'What should one give to the Americans? Could it be our half-rotten culture? The Americans don't yet have a culture. But they have nothing to learn from us. . . . *Russia*. Passion is promising. The chatter that is said against that is powerless' (McGuinness, 1967, 142).

One could incidentally remark that Spengler, in *The Decline of the West*, had predicted that Russia was going to shortly give birth to a new culture. Universal history in the higher sense of the term, that is to say the history of great cultures, should continue, which constitutes a relative consolation for the historian who is obliged to resign himself to the idea that Western culture is near its end. Spengler never believed that the triumph of technology would survive the disappearance of the Faustian world. He thought that technology would be adopted provisionally by other peoples as a means of opposing the domination of the West whose spectacular development of science and technology assured, for the moment, its superiority; but that as soon as the West ceased to play an historical role, the peoples who at the moment were in a position of inferiority compared to it would quite simply abandon the technology. The civilization of machines would disappear with the Faustian man; it will one day be destroyed and forgotten.

Neither the theme of the West's decline nor the interest in Soviet Russia and the conviction that something really new and promising was probably there in the making constituted for Wittgenstein at that time particularly original elements, for equally one encounters them among a good number of European intellectuals and they were, in a certain sense, even part of the *Zeitgeist*. As Fania Pascal remarks: 'It must be a matter of comfort for some of us that, however unusual and autonomous a man he was, Wittgenstein still belonged to his time and place' (Rhees, 1981, 57). One could suppose that his idealization of Russia was concerned more with the Russian spirit, the virtualities of which the influence of Faustian civilization had not succeeded in smothering, than with the political system that issued from the Revolution of 1917. He could even have thought just as Spengler did that Bolshevism merely corresponded to an episode relatively superficial and misleading that would be overcome by the only really significative thing: the rebirth of Russian Culture.

> To my mind, (writes Fania Pascal), his feeling for Russia would have had at all times more to do with Tolstoy's moral teachings, with Dostoïevesky's spiritual insight than with any political or social matters. He would view the latter, which certainly were not indifferent to him in terms of the former. His rarely expressed political opinions might be naïve. (ibid., 57)

What is clear is that it is unnecessary to suppose that Wittgenstein felt any particular enthusiasm for what was newly emerging in Russia or elsewhere. His reactions seem to have been more those of someone who considered the attempt of assuring the survival of things which had had their day useless, and even to speak as Nietzsche, who had a propensity to push that which is already falling. But someone who thus takes the side of things which have a future against those which do not can do so in a frame of mind that is finally nearer to the resignation to things which in any case will happen sooner or later than to a personal adhesion, even a mitigated one.

* * *

Wittgenstein, as we have seen, considered that when the vision that a man has of the culture of his time is determined, as was the case for his, by an idea of decline, it must not be used as a norm which could allow of formulating objective judgments of value. In a remark written in 1949 he says: 'My own thinking about art and values is far more disillusioned than would have been *possible* for someone 100 years ago. That does not mean, though, that it's more correct on that account. It only means that I have examples of degeneration in the forefront of my mind which were not in the *forefront* of men's minds then' (CV, 79). A representation of things from the aspect of decline which was not possible 100 years ago can become possible and even natural today. That does not for all that mean that it is correct.

It has become common, in particular in literary and artistic circles, for Wittgenstein to be considered as a more or less typical representative of the Viennese modernist movement. This is something which on first sight is very surprising, and for at least two essential reasons. Firstly, it is easy to realize that he had practically no link with the milieu to which he is supposed to be attached. McGuinness for example notes that:

> Ludwig gave little sign of any period of interest in contemporary literature. Hofmannsthal was a distant family connection and his idea of a return to the Baroque as a refuge from the decline of culture in his own day had some attraction. At any rate Ludwig liked to quote his saying:
>
> 'One has to behave decently
> Some day, somehow, somewhere, it will pay off.'
>
> But on the whole he was a stranger to Young Vienna and he hardly knew the names of the writers Ficker selected for his benefaction in 1914: Musil with whom he has often been compared he probably never read: there could have been no question of that before 1906 in any case. The chief exception to this disregard for contemporary literature—an exception proving the rule—was his respect for Karl Kraus, one of the chief influences on his thought, he said in the 1930s, listing those influences in the order Boltzmann, Hertz, Rus-

sell, Kraus, Loos, Weininger, Spengler and Sraffa. (McGuinness, 1988, 37)

Secondly, it is quite obvious that his literary and artistic tastes were, just like Kraus', altogether extremely classical and even in some cases openly reactionary. He most certainly shared Kraus' cultural pessimism and his conviction that the great cultural works are already behind and not in front of us, his cult of tradition and his scepticism with regard to the future of the forms of art the most representative of the spirit of the age. Wittgenstein, like Kraus, had the distinct tendency to use the great classics, especially Goethe, Schiller, Lessing, and Mörike, as an antidote to the literary production of his time which, with rare exceptions, he did not appreciate—it is the least that one could say— very much. As to music his opinions were not very different. In 1930 he told Drury: 'Mendelsohn's Violin Concerto is remarkable in being the last great concerto for the violin written. There is a passage in the second movement which is one of the great moments in music. Music came to a full stop with Brahms; and even in Brahms I can begin to hear the sound of machinery' (Rhees, 1981, 127).

After having, in the rough draft of the preface to the *Philosophical Remarks*, opposed the spirit of his book to that of European and American civilization, he continues:

This is not a value judgment. It is not, it is true, as though he accepted what nowadays passes for architecture as architecture or did not approach what is called modern music with the greatest suspicion (though without understanding its language), but still the disappearance of the arts does not justify judging disparagingly the human beings who make up this civilization. For in times like these genuine strong characters simply leave the arts aside and turn to other things and somehow the worth of the individual man finds expression. Not, to be sure, in the way it would at a time of high culture. A culture is like a big organization which assigns each of its members a place where he can work in the spirit of the whole; and it is perfectly fair for his power to be measured by the contribution he succeeds in making to the whole enterprise. In an age without culture on the other hand forces become fragmented and the power of an individual man is used up in overcoming opposing forces and frictional resistances; it does not show in the distance he travels but perhaps only in the heat he generates in overcoming friction. But energy is still energy and even if the spectacle which our age affords is not the formation of a great cultural work, with the best men contributing to the same great end so much as the unimpressive spectacle of a crowd whose members work for purely private ends, still we must not forget that the spectacle is not what matters.

> I realize then that the disappearance of a culture does not signify the disappearance of human value, but simply of certain means of expressing this value, yet the fact remains that I have no sympathy for the current of European civilization and do not understand its goals, if it has any. (CV, 6)

We could here think of what Nietzsche said about the concept of 'decadence':

> It is shameful for all socialist systematicians that they should think that there could be circumstances, social combinations, in which vice, illness, crime, prostitution, destitution would no longer develop themselves . . . But that would mean *condemning* life. A society does not have the freedom to remain young. Even at the height of its force it must create rejects, refuse. The more it proceeds in an energetic and audacious manner the richer it will be in badly-formed beings, failures, and the nearer it will be to decline. One does not eliminate age by institutions; illness neither nor vice. (Nietzsche, 1979, 799)

Nietzsche maintains that: 'what has until now been considered as *the causes of degeneration* are in fact *its consequences*' (ibid.).

I do not, of course, wish to suggest that the concept of 'decline' as used by Wittgenstein could be usefully compared to the Nietzschian concept of 'decadence'. Wittgenstein, as we have seen, precisely refuses to envisage the idea of decline other than as a principle to which one can decide to submit the form of one's examination of things, but which has nothing obligatory or correct about it. But it is obvious that he too considers that it is not within the power of a society to remain young, and that it would equally be absurd to reproach an aging one with the fact that it no longer has the possibilities or the means of youth. One can neither rejuvenate a society by institutional changes nor be indignant that it suffers from the illnesses of its age.

Spengler maintains that cultures decline and finally perish by the impoverishment of their vital force. Musil proposes a different hypothesis which is that, despite appearances, the quantity of spiritual energy available at any moment remains to a considerable extent the same: it is simply distributed otherwise. It could quite simply be that modern societies are by their dimensions and the extreme complexity of their mode of organization condemned to divert a greater and greater part of this energy simply to maintaining the minimum of order, stability and security, indispensable to daily existence and normal relations between men. What diminishes is not the total quantity of energy but the quantity of useful energy. The difference between culture and civilization is probably that one must:

speak of culture there where reigns *an ideology* and a form of life still unitary, and on the other hand define civilization as the state of culture which has become scattered. Every civilization was preceeded by the expansion of a culture which disaggregated in it; every civilization is distinguished by a technical mastership of nature and a very complicated system—that requires, but at the same time absorbs, a very large amount of intelligence—of social relations. (Musil, 1978a, 1057)

Musil considers that civilization, as opposed to culture, does not suffer from a fundamental lack of spirituality, idealism or generosity, but rather from the fact that due to the excessive complexity of the forms of economic, social and political organization there is greater difficulty for the guiding and organizing impulses to be transmitted and for them to act. Correlatively, the individual finds himself placed in a situation of uncertainty which he no longer succeeds in dominating:

What we call civilization, in the poor sense of the term, is, in fact, essentially, nothing more than the fact that the individual finds himself laden with the burden of questions of which he hardly knows the first word (just think of political democracy and newspapers). Consequently it is quite normal that he should react in a completely pathological manner, today we impute any shopkeeper with decisions in which a conscientious choice would not be possible even for a Leibniz. (ibid., 1367)

Wittgenstein himself, in the first version of the preface to the *Philosophical Remarks*, also seems to reason within a framework of what one could call a principle of conservation of spiritual energy, which is why all ages could be considered as equivalent as regards the total sum of energy they mobilize. As he says, 'energy is energy'. The difference resides in the distribution and the smaller or greater fraction of energy that is spent simply in resisting contrary forces and in overcoming the friction. In an age where culture is lacking, individual forces are not expressed as the quantity of real and useful work in the sense of the whole, but are spent in the effort made in order to get the better of the frictions and are manifest only in the heat thereby produced. From Wittgenstein's point of view, an age of this kind is characterized by its incapacity to impose a common direction on the individual efforts, the consequence of which is that they are condemned to be dispersed and opposed. The dissolution of the traditional organic relations consecrates the triumph of individualism, and instead of a differentiated and hierarchical system in which each individual works at his assigned place, one obtains a more or less amorphous mass in which, as he says, the best themselves can pursue only objectives that are essentially private.

J. Bouveresse

Just like Nietzsche, Wittgenstein saw in the disappearance of the will of tradition and the triumph of disorganizing principles the essential characteristic of the modern age:

> What is most deeply attacked today is the instinct and the will of *tradition*; the modern age finds distasteful all the institutions that owe their origins to this instinct. At bottom, one thinks and does nothing the goal of which would not be the pursuit of the tearing-up with the roots of this sense of tradition. Tradition is taken as fatality: one studies it and knows it (as 'inheritance'), but it is not *wanted*. The tension of a will over long temporal distances, the choice of states and evaluations that allow one to dispose of the future over centuries—that is precisely, and to the highest degree, anti-modern. The result of this is that the character of our age is given by the *disorganizing* principle. (Nietzsche, 1979, 644–645)

Wittgenstein is also close to Nietzsche when he expresses his incomprehension of the aims of a society that seems to have given itself the programme of eliminating constraints and suffering in whatever form, or more precisely that of proceeding as if they did not exist. He remarks for example:

> I think the way people are educated nowadays tends to diminish their capacity for suffering. At present a school is reckoned good if the children have a good time! And that used *not* to be the criterion. Parents moreover want their children to grow up like themselves (only more so), but nevertheless subject them to an education *quite* different from their own.—Endurance of suffering isn't rated highly because there is supposed not to be any suffering—really it's out of date. (CV, 71)

Since Wittgenstein himself manifestly did not believe that we are on earth essentially 'to have a good time', it is not surprising that he felt but little sympathy for a type of civilization in which the only thing that gives the impression of still bringing individuals together, and at the same time can, by definition, but constantly divide them, is constituted by aspirations of a purely egoist and hedonist type. It nevertheless remains that, as Musil said: 'never again will a unitarian ideology, a culture, give birth to itself in our white society; even if they existed in former times (though as regards this things are probably much too embellished), water comes down from the mountains and does not go back up.' (Musil, 1978b, 176).

In spite of his obvious predilection for societies of a traditional type, strongly organized and hierarchical, even when they function in a more or less authoritative manner, Wittgenstein reacts towards this in the same way as Musil did. It would be of absolutely no use to advocate something like a return to a former state; and even if the spectacle that the present civilization offers us is, from the aesthetical point of view, much less grandiose than one could wish, in any case much less than the sublime and heroic philosophical conceptions *à la* Spengler would like it to be, the aesthetic aspect is none the less not the most important thing and does not, from a moral point of view, authorize any condemnation of the value of this civilization and even less that of the individuals who belong to it.

Wittgenstein, just as Musil, considered that due to the absence of any efficient organizing and guiding impulses the individual, abandoned to himself, is today regularly confronted with problems much too complicated for the capacities at his disposal:

> Earlier physicists are said to have found suddenly that they had too little mathematical understanding to cope with physics, and in almost the same way young people today can be said to be in a situation where ordinary common sense no longer suffices to meet the strange demands life makes. Everything has become so intricate that mastering it would require an exceptional intellect. Because skill at playing the game is no longer enough; the question that keeps coming up is: can this game be played at all now and what would be the right game to play? (CV, 27)

Older people generally finish, of course, by resigning themselves simply to playing the game, as it is. But this ceased a long time ago to appear as the only possible and legitimate one to the young generations, who must if possible not only acquire the mastership of it, but also resolve for themselves the question as to whether it is the right one or not.

Wittgenstein's remarks as to the future of scientific and technological civilization remind one, in many regards, of Kraus' apocalyptic conception. In a note written in 1947 he describes, in the following way, what he calls the 'apocalyptic conception of the world':

> The truly apocalyptic view of the world is that things do not repeat themselves. It isn't absurd, e.g. to believe that the age of science and technology is the beginning of the end for humanity; that the idea of great progress is a delusion, along with the idea that the truth will ultimately be known; that there is nothing good or desirable about scientific knowledge and that mankind in seeking it, is falling into a trap. It is by no means obvious that this is not how things are. (CV, 56)

Kraus precisely had the tendency to see in the advent of scientific and technological civilization the probable beginning of the end of humanity. In a text entitled 'Apocalypse', he says:

> It is my religion to believe that the gauge is at 99, gases are escaping from all parts of the pus of the world's brain, culture no longer has

the possibility of breathing and in the end there is a dead humanity laid next to the works that cost it so much spirit to invent that none was left to use them.

We were complicated enough to construct the machine, and we are too primitive to make it serve us. (Kraus, 1908, 11)

In Kraus' view, the First World War was essentially that of technology and industry themselves. Moreover, modern technology is in itself already of warlike essence. It is a form of war against nature which will in the end probably lead to the destruction of humanity itself. Kraus says: 'The soul is dispossessed by technology. This has made us weak and warlike. How do we make war? By transferring the old sentiments to technology' (*Die Fackel*, 445–453, 1917, 4).

One could, however, also imagine an issue other than that of apocalypse, but which is not necessarily more heartening than the perspective of humanity's final disappearance. In another remark written in 1947 Wittgenstein suggests the following possibility:

Science and industry, and their progress, might turn out to be the most enduring thing in the modern world. Perhaps any speculation about a coming collapse of science and industry is, for the present and for a *long* time to come, nothing but a dream; perhaps science and industry, having caused infinite misery in the process, will unite the world—I mean condense it into a *single* unit, though one in which peace is the last thing that will find a home.

Because science and industry do decide wars, or so it seems. (CV, 63)

As we saw, this is a possibility which Spengler prevented himself from envisaging, and yet it is that which seems to be realizing itself today. It is not obvious that for Kraus this compared to the pure and simple annihilation which he dreaded would have made a great difference. As he says:

The real end of the world is in the destruction of the spirit, the other depends on the indifferent attempt that can be made to see whether, after the destruction of the spirit, there can still be a world. It is the reason why I believe that I am, to a certain extent, justified in the extravagant pretension that the continuation of the 'Fackel' represents a problem whereas the continuation of the world is simply an experience. (Kraus, 1908, 16)

It is sure that Wittgenstein, given the destructions and the miseries that would be the consequences of it and the fact that the united world that would perhaps finally be so produced would be anything but pacific, could not consider the perspective of the unlimited continuation of scientific and technological progress as a comforting one either.

* * *

That Wittgenstein was more than sceptical toward the idea of progress itself is something which is beyond doubt. Rhees reports that in 1943 at a meeting of the College Philosophical Society at Swansea he remarked in the discussion that:

> When there is a change in the conditions in which people live we may call it progress because it opens new opportunities. But in the course of this change, opportunities which were there before may be lost. In one way it was progress, in another it was decline. A historical change may be progress and also be ruin. There is no method of weighing one against the other to justify you in speaking of 'progress on the whole'. (Rhees, 1981, 222)

According to him, it is in this way that even the change which gave birth to modern science should be considered, despite all the new possibilities which it created: 'Science: enrichment and impoverishment. *One* particular method elbows all the others aside. They all seem paltry by comparison, preliminary stages at the best. You must go right down to the original sources so as to see them side by side, both the neglected and the preferred' (CV, 61). Carnap, in his Autobiography, says of Wittgenstein: 'I sometimes had the impression that the deliberately rational and unemotional attitude of the scientist and likewise any idea which had the flavor of 'enlightenment' were repugnant to Wittgenstein' (Fann, 1967, 35).

The phrase from Nestroy that Wittgenstein chose as an epigraph for the *Philosophical Investigations*, 'it is in the nature of every advance that it appears much greater than it actually is' (*Der Schützling*, Act IV), was also one of those that Kraus was fond of quoting. McGuinness remarks (1988, 251) that the passage from Kürnberger that Wittgenstein used as an epigraph for the *Protractatus*, 'And anything a man knows, anything he has not merely heard rumbling and roaring, can be said in three words.' (PTR), was also quoted by Kraus and could have been borrowed directly by Wittgenstein. McGuinness says that:

> It . . . seems likely that he knew Kraus from adolescence on. The little brochures (*Die demolierte Literatur, Sittlichkeit und Kriminalität* and so on) are to be found in their original editions on the shelves of family libraries and his sister Gretl (perhaps other family members too) had a complete set of *Die Fackel*, despite its fierce attacks on her father. (1988, 37)

Wittgenstein's and in general his family's relations with Kraus are effectively, at first sight, somewhat paradoxical since the father, Karl Wittgenstein, had, on a number of occasions, been the target of Kraus' polemics and sarcasms in *Die Fackel*. It is quite easy to realize that, in fact, he occupied exactly the sort of position particularly susceptible of being designated for Kraus' verdict, for whom he represented one of the most typical examples of the collusion between the major industries, unscrupulous dealings on the stock exchange and the lies of the liberal press, in particular those of the *Neue Freie Presse* for which Karl Wittgenstein wrote articles in economics. In *Die Fackel* No. 56 (1900), Kraus states that 'The Vienna Stock Exchange fears God, Taussig, Wittgenstein and outside them nothing in the world' (p. 6). The reproaches he formulated against the methods of 'the American Wittgenstein' ranged from falsified balance sheets to the most shameful manipulations on the Stock Exchange and the blackmailing of the newspapers. The Wittgenstein family's paternalism and the money spent in charitable activities (what Kraus calls the 'Lumpengeld') constituted in Kraus' view, of course, but an aggravating circumstance. As to the father's activities as a patron of the arts, such as, for example, the support given, at one time, to the artists of the Secession, they were evidently not of a nature to really impress the author of *Die Fackel*.

I do not know whether the Wittgenstein family was in a position or not to acquire from time to time sufficient distance as regards everything it represented from an economic, social, and cultural point of view in order to understand and really appreciate Kraus' irony. But, as I have already remarked, Wittgenstein himself, who, quite obviously, amply shared Kraus' point of view on industrial civilization and on the clear conscience and the progressive well-meaning intentions of the enlightened upper-class, could, from this point of view, not but have been placed in a somewhat embarrassing position. Wittgenstein's vision of the world, and his conception of philosophy itself, unquestionably contain, whether their presence should or should not be attributed to Kraus' direct influence, the most significative elements of the Krausian *Fortschrittskritik*.

When Kraus, in 1899, published the first number of *Die Fackel*, he recognized that the review's political programme could seem somewhat poor: 'It is not a resounding "What we bring" (*Was wir bringen*) but an honest "What we kill" (*Was wir umbringen*) that has been chosen as its motto.' Even if Wittgenstein himself probably had the tendency to exaggerate the aspect of his philosophy, which is at first sight purely destructive, it is perhaps not quite incongruous to say that he too could have chosen a like motto for his philosophical enterprise. In 1912, when he began an attentive reading of philosophers, he expressed, according to Pinsent, his 'naïve surprise' in noting that those that he had 'worshipped in ignorance' were finally 'stupid and dishonest and make disgusting mistakes'. One can therefore suppose that he had initially approached philosophy in a frame of mind which at bottom was not very different from that of Kraus, with the will to settle at least those things that were neither credible nor respectable, without necessarily feeling obliged to replace them by something else. He seems, at the same time, to have considered that men such as Kraus and himself found themselves confined, by the very nature of the age, to tasks that were essentially negative and which were in a way subaltern compared with what is possible in an age of great culture. Kraus states that: 'What tortures someone are the lost possibilities. To be sure of an impossibility is a gain' (ibid., 170). In philosophy as elsewhere, the problem of an age such as ours is, in Wittgenstein's view, that it must understand that certain things are not possible, on pain of ridicule or characteristic dishonesty, and be able to give them up. But the difficulty is precisely that of perceiving as a gain what at first sight seems to be an essential loss.

McGuinness may be right in affirming that Kraus' influence on Wittgenstein was on the whole secondary and indirect. For it is difficult to determine to what extent the remarkable concordance that exists between the appreciations that they both formulated as regards the situation of the modern world is the result of a real influence rather than a simple chance encounter. The two essential things that Kraus really worshipped and which he passionately defended on every occasion were Nature, attacked by technological progress, and language, attacked by journalism and bad literature. Evoking the 'cosmic discontent' and Nature's justified revolt against the excesses of human stupidity, a revolt which is manifested in earthquakes, tempests and the sinking of technological wonders such as the Titanic, along whose route Nature had forgotten to remove the icebergs, he says: 'It procures one a certain tranquillity to feel Nature's fury against civilization as a pacific protest against the devastation which it has provoked in Nature' (Kraus, 1908, 53). Kraus reproaches modern man with having, with the complicity of the press, become a simple voyeur of progress, who appreciates in it but the performance and the spectacle, without bothering to ask himself of what use it can be: 'The feelings of man's superiority triumphs in the expectation of a spectacle to which only modern people have access' (Kraus, 1914, 11). In *The discovery of the North Pole*, Kraus suggests that in reality it was stupidity that conquered the North Pole and that it is *its* flag which victoriously flies there in order to indicate that the world belongs to it.

In his view, the modern religion of progress represents exactly the sort of inversion of values which precisely constitute real decline. Progress as it is conceived today is nothing more than an inordinate and paranoiac affirmation of humanity's will of power to the detriment of what he calls the 'will of essence' (*Wille zum Wesen*), that is to say the will of the essential, it has put the mean (*Lebensmittel*) above the ends

(*Lebenszweck*): 'Civilization is the subservience of the aim in life to the means of living. It is this ideal that progress serves and it is to this ideal that it furnishes its weapons. Progress lives to eat and from time to time shows that it can even die in order to eat' (Kraus, 1914, 11).

I do not know whether Wittgenstein would or would not have approved the sarcastic judgments that Kraus formulates with regard to some of the most remarkable performances of modern science and technology; what is obvious is that his doubts concerning the reality and the usefulness of what is called 'progress' were at the least as serious as those of Kraus and it is on this very point that he considered himself as being far from and almost at the antipodes of the spirit of his time:

> Our civilization is characterized by the word 'progress'. Progress is its form rather than making progress being one of its features. Typically it constructs. It is occupied with building an ever more complicated structure. And even clarity is sought only as a means to this end, not as an end in itself. For me on the contrary clarity, perspicuity are values in themselves.
>
> I am not interested in constructing a building so much as having a perspicuous view of the foundations of possible buildings. (CV, 7)

Of course, the fact that progress is the form of our time, and in any case the form under which it is perceived and represents itself, does not necessarily mean that it really progresses. It could properly be a formal property more than a material one. Perhaps, when it believes that it is progressing, it makes the kind of mistake that Wittgenstein denounces in the *Philosophical Investigations*: 'We predicate of the thing what lies in the method of representation' (PI, I, 104). Kraus said that: 'Progress is a standstill and has the air of being a movement' (Kraus, 1909, 197). The question that is posed concerning progress is the following:

> How does it reveal itself in daylight? In what form does it show itself when we imagine it as a more agile servant of the age? For we have bound ourselves to a representation of this kind, we would like to render account of progress; and we simply lack the perception of something of which we are convinced. We see, of everything that walks, runs and rolls but feet, hooves and wheels. The tracks fade away. (Kraus, 1909, 197–198)

Progress, Kraus says, is a representation that we have imposed upon ourselves, but we still do not know and in some respects we know less and less as to what it resembles. Musil, who, unlike Kraus, protests against the temptation of prematurely dispairing of the rationalist and progressivist ideal that we inherited from the age of the enlightenment, is led to the same sort of finding. Remarkable discoveries and advances certainly occur in each field of science, culture and art, envisaged separately, but the addition of all these things no longer succeeds in being really perceived as a progress. Progress which is something that we believe by obligation is at the same time something that we do not or no longer 'feel'.

Failing progress, we do have, of course, at least movement. We are living in an age where there is, in any case, no question of staying where one is. One must, as Musil said, stir oneself and advance or, as Wittgenstein said, participate in the construction of more and more elaborate and complicated devices. This is exactly what men such as Kraus and Wittgenstein, who chose to stay put, refused to do.

Kraus, in the poem 'Zwei Läufer' ('Two Runners'), opposes the optimists who believe in an unending progress, who despise tradition, who come from nowhere and who pursue an aim that forever escapes them to those who come from the origin and for whom 'the origin is the goal', those of whom one can say that, in a certain way, they have already arrived there where they wished to go. The opposition between the two types of runners could easily be found in the field of philosophy itself. A philosophy that wishes to conform to the spirit of the time, as Wittgenstein perceives it, would see in the conjectural method and the progressive approach of the empirical sciences the ideal to which philosophy should set itself. The misunderstanding between Wittgenstein and Russell and later between Wittgenstein and the Vienna Circle arose mostly because he had always been, in Kraus' sense, a runner of the second type and had never shared this kind of rationalist and optimistic conception. For him, philosophy's approach is fundamentally different from that of the sciences and does not consist in formulating hypotheses and explications that one can hope to improve progressively, but rather in the indefinite deepening of things already known. As he says in a passage which is strongly reminiscent of Kraus:

> I might say: if the place I want to get could only be reached by way of a ladder, I would give up trying to get there. For the place I really have to get to is a place I must already be at now.
>
> Anything that I might reach by climbing a ladder does not interest me. (CV, 7)

* * *

McGuinness, in his biography of Wittgenstein, characterizes the position of the *Tractatus* as regards science as having for its central element 'the rejection of any claim by science to *explain*, if (that is) explanation is taken to be anything other than presenting the phenomena in some clear and easily grasped form. Of course, Mach had already effected this reaction: but Wittgenstein's position is of special interest in that it proceeds from purely logical considerations, not from any empiricist prejudice' (McGuinness, 1988, 314–315). Wittgenstein thinks that we owe to modern science, or perhaps more exactly to the spirit in which it is practised, some of the most characteristic superstitions of our time, in particular that which consists in believing that everything has been or will be explained one day or another. In the *Tractatus*, he wrote:

> The whole modern conception of the world is founded on the illusion that the so-called laws of nature are the explanations of natural phenomena.
>
> Thus people today stop at the laws of nature, treating them as something inviolable, just as God and Fate were treated in past ages.
>
> And in fact both are right and both are wrong: though the view of the ancients is clearer in so far as they have a clear and acknowledged terminus, while the modern system tries to make it look as if everything were explained.' (TR, 6.371–6.372)

It is because science accustoms us to the misleading idea that everything has been, or in any case, can be explained that we have the tendency to consider propositions such as 'It is God's will' or 'It is Fate' as being essentially the expression of ignorance and impotence, whereas what they express is above all another attitude, another way of behaving toward events:

> In the sense in which asking a question and insisting on an answer is expressive of a different attitude, a different mode of life, from not asking it, the *same* can be said of utterances like 'It is God's will' or 'We are not masters of our fate'. The work done by this sentence, or at any rate something like it, could also be done by a command. Including one which you give yourself. And conversely the utterance of a command such as 'Don't be resentful' may be like the affirmation of a truth. (CV, 61)

Another of the most characteristic superstitions of our time and which is as it were constitutive of the spirit of the age is, in Wittgenstein's view, the illusion that scientific and technological progress, or at the least progress in general is capable of providing a solution to all the fundamental problems of humanity. It is quite possible that the usual discourses on humanity's progress are finally of the same kind as 'the chatter about cause and effect in history books'. They probably were at any rate in Wittgenstein's opinion. But he most certainly did not believe that one can hope to change them by merely saying and repeating that they are absurd. The ideology of progress has been denounced over and over again and the modern scientific and technological civilization has given rise to a great number of radical philosophical critiques. But, to speak as Wittgenstein, the whole problem here is to know whether philosophy, in so doing, has not done itself more harm than it did to the type of civilization that it was attempting to combat. One of Wittgenstein's essential preoccupations was, as I have said, to avoid—and especially in philosophy—gestures that risked being useless and inefficient. As he used to say, 'Nur kein Geschwätz!' or 'Stop gesticulating!' Bouwsma records a conversation with Wittgenstein in July 1949:

> He made such remarks as that some people are interested in a system; others are interested in preaching. He makes the distinction clear between something up in the air—using his hands—the talk of philosophers, and now someone saying: Don't be revengeful; let not the sun go down on thy wrath, etc. This is the distinction between nonsense and exhortation. (Bouwsma, 1986, 7–8)

In a time such as ours, it is particularly difficult for philosophy to recognize and to follow the narrow path that passes between nonsense and predication. The greatness of Wittgenstein is, it seems to me, to have passionately looked for it and probably to have found it.

Wittgenstein and the Transmission of Traditions

ANTHONY O'HEAR

In this country, we tend to look at Wittgenstein in a rather ahistorical way. We see his concerns as fundamentally logico-linguistic, following on first from the work of Frege and Russell, and then referring back indirectly to the concerns of the British empiricists, to those of Locke and Hume, say, on such matters as the reference of our talk about sensations and scepticism about the external world. Recently there has been considerable discussion of the extent to which Wittgenstein's own analysis of the private language and of rule-following might not itself be a new version of a fundamentally Humean scepticism: according to Saul Kripke, Wittgenstein's arguments amount to a demonstration that there is no more reason for speakers of a language to follow the rules governing the concepts of that language in the same way than on the Humean account there is any reason for an effect to follow its causes (Kripke, 1981).

I do not want to claim that seeing Wittgenstein in the context of British empiricism is wrong, or to assert that the arguments in his later philosophy do not have a precise and devastating bearing on the philosophical assumptions of empiricists such as Locke and Hume. They certainly do, but it is worth remembering that Wittgenstein was Viennese, and that before the fall of the Empire there was in Austro-Hungarian thought a particular tradition which is also relevant to Wittgenstein's concerns in his later philosophy. I want to suggest that it might also be fruitful to see Wittgenstein within the context of Austro-Hungarian conservative thinking, as well as within the tradition of British empiricism, and, ultimately, to see his philosophy as a synthesis of elements from both traditions.

One needs only to consider the Austrian conservative philosophical tradition and the philosophical anthropology they engendered to see the bearing Wittgenstein's later thought has on them. Christophe Nyiri has summed up these concerns in terms of the following:

What does it mean to view a man as a creature bound by traditions? What is the relation of reason to tradition, of subjective thought to intersubjective language, of individual creativity to handed-down rules, of aesthetic judgment to training and habit? (Nyiri, 1989).

The Austrian conservative tradition stands in stark contrast to the individualism implicit in much seventeenth- and eighteenth-century philosophy, and the more modern philosophies influenced by them.

For Descartes, by contrast, truth was to be sought in the light of natural reason, which flickers fitfully in the soul of each individual, and only able to shine when the individual withdraws from the hub-bub of human opinion and worldly exchange. For Hobbes, language was primarily a means for the individual to label the contents of his mind, and only secondarily a means of interpersonal communication. For Locke, we each build up our picture of the world on the basis of the simple ideas of sensation each of us has: 'knowledge is founded on and employed about our ideas only' (Locke, Bk. IV, Ch. II, Sect. xv). In Hume it is, if anything, even more clear that Locke's 'our' is really 'my': or rather, some stream of experience so private that it is prior to any distinction between mine and ours, and arguably unable to provide any grounds for the conceptions which underlie the actual distinctions we make between myself, and the external world, conceptions which can only be retrieved by forgetting philosophical argument altogether. Kant, of course, saw that I could not categorize my own sensations on the minimal assumptions allowed us by Hume, but even in Kant the relation between the individual synthesizing subject, with all his categories and forms of sensibility, and his fellows is unclear. Is it just chance that we all synthesize in the same way, that my phenomenal experience coincides with yours? And in ethics, it is Kant more than anyone who emphasizes and elevates the autonomy of the individual ethical agent, beyond the deliverances even of the Holy One of God.

Against this tendency to base everything on the individual and his reasoning powers and experiential input, conservatism will emphasize the way reason (including the reason of the individual) is based on communal behaviour and habit, the extent to which the experience of the individual, far from being a pristine datum on which all else may be based, depends for its shape and structure on pre-existing linguistic and sensory forms, and the ways in which linguistic and social forms develop spontaneously, and, even where theoretically guided by human reason and intention, as much despite as because of the intentions of agents and policy-makers. Thoughts of these sorts form an interconnecting thread through five generations of Austro-Hungarian thinkers; from Klemens Maria Hofbauer, Ferenc Széchényi and Friedrich Schlegel at the turn of the nineteenth century, through Franz Grillparzer, Istvan Széchényi, Jozsef Eötvös, and Carl Menger, down to Thomas Masaryk, Robert Musil, F. A. von Hayek and, arguably, Wittgenstein himself in our own century. Despite his well-documented dislike of many of the tendencies of his time, particularly its scientism and what he saw as the 'disappearance of a culture', I do not have textual evidence that Wittgenstein was directly influenced by any of these figures, although equally it would be hard to find more than a handful of references in his work to Descartes, Locke or Hume. But I do think that it might be fruitful to see his later work in the context of Austro-Hungarian conservative thought as many of his themes, and, more importantly, that in his later work, he supplies us with arguments which might support the kind of conservative anthropology we find in these thinkers, and also, incidentally in Burke, Acton and Oakeshott in this country (cf. Nyiri, 1982).

The arguments which Wittgenstein uses to support what I am calling a conservative anthropology are the very arguments which he uses to construct his picture of the mind and of its relationship to our language of the mind. The basis of these arguments and of the conception of mind which they support is to be found in what is known as the private language argument and the analysis of rule following. The private language argument is designed to show that the private linguist is bound to fail in his task. The private linguist may be seen as the lone Humean individual attempting to classify and sort out his experiences prior to any grasp of an objective world of public language. All such an individual has to go on in his attempt to describe his sensations is the sensations themselves and his memories of them. How then can he be sure that what he is calling by a certain term today is similar to what he called by that term yesterday? More radically, how can he know that his use of the term 'S', let us say, is the same today as it was yesterday? All he can do is to summon up his memory of how he used 'S' yesterday. But this is no check at all, for his current use of 'S' today just is what he remembers 'S' to have referred to yesterday. And what if he remembered wrong? It would make no difference to what he decided, for there is no effective contrast for him between remembering rightly and remembering wrongly. Whatever seemed to him to be right would be right. And a language in which we could not verify the correctness of our terms, and in which we could not distinguish between correct and incorrect judgments would be no language at all, no better than mere animal noise.

The private language argument certainly shows that there cannot be a language which is in principle private, which refers to things which can only be known to one person. But that is not the same as thinking that thought and language require an actual public language, in which the individual speaker and reasoner engages in linguistic practices already established within a community. After all, might we not, as A. J. Ayer (1954) once did, conceive of a Robinson Crusoe born on some isolated island, away from all human kind, who nevertheless devises a primitive language for the classification of birds and plants and stones on his island? There would be nothing intrinsically private about this classifactory scheme. The islander would be speaking about publicly identifiable objects. He would not then be open to the same objection as the private linguist. If he wanted to check his current use of a term, for a plant say, he could return to the original exemplar and see if the current use corresponded to the first use. A plant is not like a sensation in that it persists through time and can be returned to if the need arises. The islander will not necessarily be using the same memory to check itself, as the sensation namer is in an analogous case; the islander may remember that the plant he originally referred to as 'T' was the plant nearest to the mouth of his cave, and this is a different memory from that involved in calling up an image of the look of the thing.

But if our Crusoe avoids the particular and peculiar problem of the private linguist, more is required in Wittgenstein's view for Crusoe to succeed in speaking a language. The private language argument shows that any language speaker must exist in a world of publicly observable objects, but it leaves it open that a solitary individual by chance born and raised in isolation in a world whose objects could in principle be observed by others might, nonetheless, succeed in speaking to and for himself about his world. It seems clear to me that Wittgenstein's analysis of rule-following is designed to rule out just such a possibility. This is a claim which is not only striking in itself; it is so striking a claim that some commentators have been inclined to deny—partly on grounds of what they take to be common sense—that Wittgenstein could have held such a thesis (e.g. McGinn, 1984, 200). Wittgenstein does not deny that someone who is already a member of a linguistic or rule-following community could follow a rule privately. Indeed, he explicitly envisages such a case:

> Certainly I can give myself a rule and then follow it. But is it not a rule only for this reason, that it is analogous to what is called 'rule' in human dealings? (RFM, IV, 41)

A question clearly expecting the answer 'yes'.

Wittgenstein's claim, then, is that only a member of a rule-following community can follow a rule. Only such a being can prescribe to himself a rule which he then follows privately. This, to stress, is something over and above the private language argument, and would apply to rules dealing with enduring, re-identifiable and potentially public objects, which would seem to escape the strictures of the private language argument. As it is so striking a claim, at least two sets of commentators have striven hard to deny that Wittgenstein ever made it (McGinn, 1984; Baker and Hacker, 1986). I think though that anyone who reads section 6 of the *Remarks on The Foundations of Mathematics*, or Norman Malcolm's recent paper 'Wittgenstein on Language and Rules' (Malcolm, 1989; cf. Malcolm, 1986, 154–181), would find it hard to deny that Wittgenstein is claiming that rule-following for an individual always requires a background of a rule-following community to which that individual belongs, even and perhaps especially where what is at issue is a rule an individual has newly devised and has not yet communicated to anyone else or perhaps never will. Wittgenstein, in other words, denies what Colin McGinn calls 'the natural idea' that facts about that person alone determine what concepts a person possesses (and, in so far as concept-possession depends on rule-following, whether he can be credited with concept-possession *simpliciter*). On what I take to be Wittgenstein's view (and what McGinn takes to be so absurd that it could not be Wittgenstein's view)

> nothing you can do in the construction of an individual can justify the assertion that he has concepts or means anything *until* you create other individuals: Adam had, so to speak, to wait for Eve before he could follow rules (in particular, have thoughts). But how could the creation of other individuals wreak such a momentous change in the first created individual? (McGinn 1984, 191n)

How indeed, *if* rule-following and thinking were seen simply in terms of the psychology of an individual? But this is not how Wittgenstein sees it. Wittgenstein denies that the powers of an individual psychology are sufficient to found an activity of rule following even for an individual.

Wittgenstein asks the following rhetorical questions (RFM, VI, 45):

> Could there be arithmetic without agreement on the part of calculators?
> Could there be only one human being that calculated? Could there be only one that followed a rule?

And he says

> Are these questions like, say, this one:
> 'Can one man alone engage in commerce?'

It seems to me clear that one man alone cannot engage in commerce, and that Wittgenstein does take these other questions to be analogous to that one, an impression which is reinforced by the next remark:

> It only makes sense to say 'and so on' when 'and so on' is understood, i.e., when the other is as capable of going on as I am, i.e., does go on just as I do.

I shall return to the full significance of this remark shortly, but its import is clearly to reinforce remarks elsewhere in Part VI of the *Remarks on the Foundations of Mathematics*, such as:

> The phenomenon of language rests on regularity, on agreement in acting.

> The agreement of human beings is a presupposition of logic.
> The phenomenon of agreement and of acting according to a rule are interdependent.[1]

Part of the burden of Wittgenstein's argument here is certainly to insist that rule-following is what McGinn refers to as a *diachronic* concept. That is to say, when we grasp a rule at a certain time, we envisage its repeated application over a period of time. In Wittgenstein's example, a man logically could not just once in the history of mankind follow a sign-post, whereas it would make sense to say that just once in the history of mankind someone walked parallel with a board. The contrast is between rule-following, which depends on custom, practice and use, and activities which can be described purely by reference to the physical circumstances obtaining at one moment in the history of the world. To emphasize this difference, Wittgenstein says that following a rule relates to a custom, that obeying a rule is a practice, that a word has meaning only in the practice of a language, that a language itself relates to a way of living, and that a rule is an institution. In order to make out his individualistic interpretation of Wittgenstein's analysis of rule-following, McGinn has to regard custom, practice, institution and way of living as things an individual could construct for himself, as possibly referring to regularities in individual behaviour. How true this is to Wittgenstein's meaning and to his use of such terms, I will leave the reader to judge; but even if McGinn is right in his individualistic interpretation of these key terms, he is going to have problems with Wittgenstein's assertions that

> the phenomenon of language is based on regularity, on agreement in action.

and that

> here it is of the greatest importance that all or the enormous majority of us agree in certain things. (RFM, VI, 39)

The context in which Wittgenstein makes these remarks is crucial, for, although he goes on immediately to discuss language as a means of communication, the remarks just quoted are offered as an answer to the individualistic question

> How can I follow a rule, when after all whatever I do can be interpreted as following it? (RFM, VI, 38)

and immediately following the observation that

> It is true that *anything* can somehow be justified. (RFM, VI, 39)

[1] These remarks are quoted in his own translation by Malcolm (1989), 22.

Wittgenstein and the Transmission of Traditions

It is my contention that Wittgenstein introduces the practice of a community into his analysis of rule-following in order to put a stop to the difficulties that arise from the insight that on some interpretation, anything can be seen as following from a rule, difficulties which would dog my individualistic attempt to follow out the implications of a self-imposed rule, whether or not I was interested in communicating my understanding of the rule to others.

We can approach this problem in a way which will be familiar to devotees of Goodman's paradox, but which is also raised by Wittgenstein in his many treatments of people who calculate differently from the norm. Let us call some plant 'T' if it is the same or similar to the plant we previously called 'T'. But what is to count as being the same as or similar to the earlier T? Similar in what respect? The same in what way? Transposing slightly what Goodman says regarding his paradox, similarities are 'where you find them, and you can find them anywhere' (cf. Goodman, 1972, 388)). That is to say, the fact that I place a certain number of objects in a certain category does not in itself determine which objects I ought to put in that category in the future. This, of course, is the lesson Goodman derives from his consideration of green and grue, but it is a point emphasized by Wittgenstein in what he says in the *Philosophical Investigations* about rule following. As he puts it 'whatever I do is, on some interpretation, in accord with the rule' (PI, I, 198), a point he emphasizes again and again in the *Remarks on the Foundations of Mathematics*.[2] Where the rules are those governing the future applications of concepts, this means that—with sufficient ingenuity—any future objects can be made to fall or not fall under a given concept, however tightly we have circumscribed the concept in the past. And so it seems that language itself could fall apart at any moment, with formerly linguistically united people going off in wildly different directions in their use of words, a point again stressed by Wittgenstein by means of his examples of people who seem to be calculating like us, but who then at a certain point generalize on the basis of the examples we all agreed on in a way which seems quite illogical to us.

But language does not in fact fall apart, with all sorts of different applications of concepts and the rules governing them because there already exist publicly recognized customs in the use of concepts. These customs we, as language users, through our education and training learn and grasp and apply in the main unthinkingly. There is no

---

[2] Part of Wittgenstein's point here and at PI, I, 201 is to emphasize that rule-following is not to interpret a rule, with all the indeterminacy that implies, but to act on it. This is the basic reason why commonality of action must underlie concept-possession.

question of multiple interpretation of rules; indeed we do not interpret most rules at all. We just act on them. It is because there is a publicly established use of concepts or way of acting on them, on which my fellows and I agree on the whole, that there is a distinction between what is right and what merely seems to me to be right. In following a rule embedded in a public language, then, I will be wrong when my usage of a term does not fit the communally accepted and established use.

The putative private rule follower, however, does not have recourse to any public correction or corroboration in his future use of a rule he has set himself. McGinn (1984, 179–180) says that he will know what his concept is and what is logically entailed by it because he will be able 'to appeal to remembered facts about past meanings [etc.] and hence justify [his] conviction that today [he is] using words correctly'.[3] But this is to underestimate the force of the Goodman–Wittgenstein point. McGinn rightly insists that what is here at issue is not a general scepticism about memory. We can remember as well as we like what our past uses of a given term are, how a rule was applied in the past. But whatever content these rememberings may be taken to have, the point Goodman and Wittgenstein will insist on is that this content will always underdetermine future applications of the rule. If, to use Wittgenstein's example, I obey the instruction 'add 2' by going 994, 996, 998, 1,000 up to 1,000, there may be nothing in my past behaviour or thoughts or which will preclude my continuing the series 1,004, 1,008, 1,012, . . . It may just seem to me that that is the natural way to go on, when I reach 1,000, and I may insist that going on in the same way means just that for me. It will be very much a case here of whatever seems to me to be right to be right.

My instructor may say that in teaching me how to add up to 1,000, he had *meant* me to go on 1,002, 1,004, 1,006, . . . But, as Wittgenstein says to the instructor

> you should not let yourself be misled by the grammar of the words 'know' and 'mean'. For you don't want to say that you thought of the step from 1,000 to 1,002 at that time and even if you did think of this step, still you did not think of other ones . . . (PI, I, 189)

The assumption is rather that if he had been asked what came after 1,000, he would have said '1,002', and in like manner for other as yet unenvisaged steps, and that what is being reported here is a *reaction* of the same kind as 'If he had fallen into the water then, I should have jumped in after him'.

[3] I erroneously argued in a similar way in O'Hear (1980), 83–84 and O'Hear (1984), 207.

Looking at my own case, when I conceive myself following a given rule, I will in the end react in this sort of way, blindly and without thought, as Wittgenstein constantly emphasizes. For obeying a rule is not a matter of interpreting it—which is giving another verbal account, which could itself be variously interpreted—but a matter of acting, as when I go to the left when someone points to the left: in the end, I can no longer justify what I do, I just do it. I obey the rule blindly (PI, I, 219). And it is because rule-following in the end means a *blind* reaction, that there is no difference in the individual case between what seems to be right, and what is right. There is just the unjustified action, which, whatever it is, can be made consonant with the rule, which in turn is tantamount to acting without a rule. Only against the background of a socially accepted custom can one bit of blind obedience be judged correct and another incorrect, and this is why rule-following cannot be a purely individual matter, and why Wittgenstein says that I can properly say 'and so on' about some series I have started to construct or some rule I have devised only when some other would go on just as I do.[4]

[4] Cf. RFM, VI, 45. Crispin Wright (1980), 32–38 argues, correctly in my view, that one of Wittgenstein's prime targets in his analysis of rule-following and elsewhere is the idea that the subject has privileged access to the character of his own understanding. Not at all, Wright construes Wittgenstein as saying. All the subject can do is to intend sincerely to follow his initial use of a term. But it is always 'conceivable that while seeming to myself to be using (a) word in a consistent way, my employment of it might actually be quite chaotic and irregular' (p. 37). That is, I will take as right whatever seems to me to be right. Wright himself wants to reject this. He argues (pp. 381–384) that there is a crucial difference between the individual attempting in isolation to name his sensation and his attempting to follow rules about publicly observable enduring objects, such as in a game of chess. In the latter type of case, the individual can return to some written representation of his game and reason with himself about some possible failure to follow a rule, just as someone else will do if the individual belongs to a chess playing community, drawing attention to things a deviant rule-follower has overlooked and so on. I agree with Wright that there are important differences between sensations and enduring public objects. But to think these differences by themselves can lead to some account of private rule-following in the enduring object case is to overlook the extent that rule-following is based in blind reaction and not in reasoning, appraisal or reflective judgment. It seems to me that once one concedes to Wittgenstein that reaction comes before reasoning, the troubling conclusions he draws follow. And Wittgenstein surely is right in thinking that reasons in whatever field, including the logical and semantic, must come to an end. All we are left with is shared reaction, or the possibility of shared reaction.

Regularities in behaviour and perception and reaction obviously occur in pre- or non-linguistic creatures, and can be envisaged in individuals reared in isolation. In Wittgenstein's view the existence of natural given regularities of this sort in our behaviour form the basis of our shared language and rule-following. We all tend to act the same way, to walk the same way, follow pointing fingers in the same way, respond to colours and tastes in the same way. But neither regular behaviour nor selectivity and directedness in perceptual classification yet constitute rule-following. As Wittgenstein puts it, my being trained to follow a sign-post in a given way and the physical behaviour that ensues does not tell us what 'going-by-the-sign' really consists in (cf. PI, I, 128). It is the failure to see what is involved in the difference between regular behaviour alone and rule-following proper that prompts the resistance to Wittgenstein's essentially communitarian view of rule-following, a failure which is compounded by a lot of the current talk of information-processing in cognitive psychology. As Grant Gillett (1989) has usefully argued, we need to distinguish in this area between 'thin' informational processes and 'thick' ones. The former are

> transactions in cause and effect or dispositional terms and they involve steps which mechanically follow one another or interact with one another; no notion of validity or groundedness is involved (ibid., 85).

Thick informational processes are those in which, in addition to the results of these causal processes and transitions, there is a question of a norm, a rule or a standard, which may or may not have been met by these results. As Gillett puts it, 'in this conceptual milieu the notion of what *ought* to follow from what (and not merely what the system is disposed to do or what tends to happen) is of central importance' (ibid.). The rule-follower, then, is not just an information-processor, however sophisticated; but a being who strives to meet certain norms or standards in his activity, cognitive or otherwise, a being who understands and can make an effective distinction between what he does or believes, and what he ought to do or believe, and to whom we accordingly may credit a degree of self-consciousness as the introspective concomitant of this distinction. It is Wittgenstein's view that it is only public standards of correctness (linguistic or behavioural or both) which can give sense to a distinction between what *is* right and what seems to be right. An isolated individual would not be able to draw any such distinction because, owing to the inherent indeterminacy in the applications of rules, such a being would have no grounds for distinguishing between what seemed to it to be right and what really was right in the future application of a rule or a concept. And in so far as thinking depends on the use of concepts, it would not be able to think either, as opposed to processing information as a step in some causal interaction with the world.

It is not, as Kripke (1981, 268) tends to suggest, that the Wittgenstein–Goodman argument makes concept possession and hence language impossible, or even unintelligible. In Wittgenstein's hands at least the indeterminacy thesis is used to show that the possibility of a language cannot be based solely in the existence of abstract rules or structures in our minds or elsewhere, for such rules or structures will not serve to rule out a host of deviant uses. Indeed, by themselves, they will not be able to base a distinction between deviant and non-deviant applications of a rule. What this distinction requires, over and above natural tendencies to react in various ways and formulations of rules of various sorts, is the existence of a community, united in education, training and judgment and at one in the application of rules and the use of concepts. Against such a background, a deviant calculator will be corrected by the reactions of others to his deviance and we can also envisage people individually devising new rules, drawing as it were on the communal experience of rule following. Failing such a background, though, our calculating procedures and much else would collapse. As Malcolm (1989, 27) points out, it is Wittgenstein's view that if as a matter of empirical fact widespread and irremovable differences appeared in the results achieved by different calculators, then what they were doing would no longer be called 'multiplication'. Multiplication requires consensus (Malcolm, 1989, 27). That Wittgenstein is quite prepared to go along with the implications of the view is confirmed by what he says in Vol. II of *Remarks on the Philosophy of Psychology* (RPP), about my own knowledge of tastes I experience depending on the fact about 'the outside world' that in the main I and my fellows agree with each other in making such judgments. A 'confusion of tastes' in which people disagreed about sweetness and sourness would undermine my own ability to classify tastes privately. The background against which I could make sense of the distinction between a correct and incorrect use of 'sweet', 'sour' and so on would have vanished.

It is not that the result of a calculation or my describing what something tastes like is some kind of prediction about public opinion. Rather, what Wittgenstein calls 'peaceful agreement' regarding similarities of length, colour, quantity, taste and so on form 'the characteristic surrounding' of our use of concepts, practices of calculation, and so on (RFM, VI. 21). Such unspoken agreement and consensus in reaction forms the basis for the standards of correctness in judgment and the following of rules which allows us effectively to distinguish between what is right in a particular instance, and what merely seems to be right.

If this basis presupposes a community, what follows about the nature of the mind? What follows, I think, is this. We are not to look at mental activities, such as thinking, categorizing, reasoning, judging, willing simply in terms of the contents of the mind or the brain. Such contents, whether conscious or not, will always underdetermine the rules which underlie our activities of thinking, categorizing, reasoning, and the rest. For these, and hence for what is involved in these activities, we also have to look to the communal activities from which I, as an individual thinker, judger, categorizer, derive my standards for these activities, and against which my activities are themselves assessed. These considerations about rule following take us far beyond a Burge-style objection to the thought that thoughts cannot be analysed purely in terms of the contents of a mind or brain, but require reference to the world outside to know just what is being referred to by our referring terms. They also provide something of the background to the anti-reductionist stance taken by Wittgenstein in *Zettel* (Z, 608–612), where it is suggested that a mental order of thought and so on might well arise out of a chaos at the neurological level, so precluding any enlightening physiological investigation of the psychological.

The essentially communal aspect of much of our mental activity does not, of course, justify this anti-reductionism of Wittgenstein, even for those who might on other grounds find it congenial. Wittgenstein himself says only that he finds his denial of psychophysical parallelism natural. By contrast, though, Wittgenstein's views of the communal nature of standards of thought and reasoning have some direct and profound implications for epistemology and the forms of our knowledge, implications which we must now examine.

If what I have said about the private language argument and the analysis of rule-following is correct, we would expect to find a similar emphasis on the community in Wittgenstein's treatment of questions of epistemology and value. Reasoning, like rule following, will be seen in terms of the way we all go on in response to problems or questions we are confronted with. If what *really* follows from a proposition or a set of premises—as opposed to merely seeming to follow—is marked out in terms of the way people spontaneously agree in their conclusions (RPP, II, 699), we should expect the same to be true for our conceptions of what it is reasonable to believe and value, for what calls for doubt and further explanation and for what counts as settling a doubt or providing an explanation. The individual mind, in its epistemic and axiological aspects will be a product of the community to which its owner belongs, as much as in its logical aspects. Such a conception is indeed what we find in *On Certainty* and elsewhere. What determines our mentality is never the inner workings of individual minds, but always the participation of the individual in communal practices of action, thought and reasoning.

In *Zettel* (pp. 387–388), Wittgenstein says that an education quite different from ours might also be the foundation for quite different concepts. In such a case life would run on quite differently. In a different way of life concepts different from our own would no longer be unimaginable. This is important. Wittgenstein does not think that we could actually make deviant calculations intelligible to ourselves, precisely because of our intuitively, blindly making the ones we do. But in different circumstances we might have different intuitive responses. If our circumstances changed, we might abandon our current practices (cf. OC, 616–617).

In a similar way, in *On Certainty*, Wittgenstein insists that in learning to live with us and in learning our concomitant forms of expression, the child learns what is to be investigated and questioned, and what not. In a striking passage, he writes that he wants

> to regard man here as an animal; as a primitive being to which one grants instinct but not ratiocination. As a creature in a primitive state. Any logic good enough for a primitive means of communication needs no apology from us. Language did not emerge from some kind of ratiocination. (OC, 475)

Reason, then, builds on instinct, reaction, prejudice even, and depends on a context of unthinking assent and judgment. Children learn to fetch books, sit in armchairs and so on before they learn that books and armchairs exist, or are in a position to start raising questions about the existence of things. The child learns first to react and not to know anything; knowing comes later (OC, 538). The language-game in which all this takes place is not itself reasonable or unreasonable. It is simply there, 'like our life' (OC, 559). In learning to live with us, the child learns to act in accordance with a lot of things. 'Bit by bit there forms a system of what is believed'; so some things in that system stand 'unshakeably fast', not because they are intrinsically obvious or convincing, but because they are held fast by what surrounds them (OC, 144).

For a child not to accept what is unshakeable (though groundless) in our system is for it not to judge in conformity with mankind. But this would not be a sign of its superior intelligence or reasoning powers, because failure to accept the fundamental beliefs of our system will make reasoning impossible. Reasoning can occur only against a background of what it is to count as reasonable, while doubting has any force only in contrast to and in the context of what is not doubted.

Wittgenstein himself gives an account of the way in which teaching, learning and doubting are connected in sections 310–317 of *On Cer-*

tainty. He envisages a pupil who will not let the teacher get on with teaching and explaining, but is constantly interrupting with factitious doubts. The boy starts questioning everything in a history lesson, and even whether the earth really existed a hundred years ago. 'Here it strikes me as if this doubt were hollow. But in that case—is not *belief* in history hollow too?' (OC, 312). No, says Wittgenstein, because so much else connects with it.

Or again, imagine that the boy starts doubting whether the table is really there when he turns round, or whether nature is uniform, or induction justified.

> The teacher would feel that this was only holding them up, that this way the pupil would only get stuck and make no progress—And he would be right. It would be as if someone were looking for some object in a room; he opens a drawer and doesn't see it there; then he closes it again, waits and opens it once more to see if perhaps it isn't there now, and keeps on like that. He has not learned to look for things. And in the same way the pupil has not learned how to ask questions. He has not learned *the* game we are trying to teach him. (OC, 315)

Doubts such as these are not in our game, says Wittgenstein, adding, significantly, 'but not as if we *chose* this game!' (OC, 317).

The picture then is of what we know and believe forming an interconnected system or picture within which first we act and only subsequently ratiocinate. The system itself, being grounded in our way of life is prior to reasoning and therefore cannot be grounded in reasons. From the rational point of view, it is groundless, and the learner simply has to accept it as and when he accepts other things about our life. Within the system, he learns to doubt and to reason, but his doubts and reasons will always be constrained by what can be doubted and what counts as a reason within the system. To attempt to step outside these limits is actually to attempt to step outside our shared way of life; this is not primarily an intellectual or cognitive matter, but one reaching deep into our affective and emotional lives, and one which we are unlikely to waste time idly reasoning about if, for example, we are about to be burned by a fire or are suffering pangs of guilt or jealousy (cf. PI, I, 473).

In *On Certainty*, Wittgenstein is at pains to emphasize the groundlessness of our believing. As with our rule-following, we can sometimes give reasons, but these reasons run out. Judgments like 'This is my hand', 'The earth has existed for a long time', 'I have never been on the moon' are not, in normal circumstances, further justifiable. They form the context in which we live and serve to set the standards by which other, less certain judgments are assessed. In our lives, nothing could be more certain than them, although that does not make them immune to sceptical doubts. But part of the point, indeed, of *On Certainty* is to suggest the practical and moral uselessness of such doubts. The sceptic is right to stress the epistemological groundlessness of our basic beliefs about the world, and the way in which they do not simply copy or picture a reality already categorized and intelligible apart from our interests and schemes of classification. But he is wrong to suppose that the doubts he raises about these basic beliefs are ones which ought to detain us or which can be entertained in any substantive way while we continue to live as we must, so long as we remain human beings in the community to which we belong.

Our standards of epistemic reasonableness, then, are given to us as and when we learn (as children and students) about the world and its various facets. And this learning and teaching obviously presupposes a community in which a particular picture of the world and concomitant standards of rationality are transmitted to the learner. Deviant judgments will be punished and correct ones reinforced as we saw in the example of the teacher and the pupil, and much in the same way as other practices of rule-following are implanted. It is, though, at this point that certain doubts about the Wittgensteinian picture begin to emerge, doubts arising from the suspicion that the Wittgensteinian picture is fundamentally relativistic both about rule-following and systems of belief.

Wittgenstein himself, it must be admitted, does little to allay these suspicions when, for example, he discusses the physicists and the natives in *On Certainty* (OC, 608–612). It is not wrong, apparently, for us to be guided in our action by the propositions of physics, but we must realize the groundlessness of our doing so. Natives who consult oracles instead of physicists would be considered by us to be primitive, but we must remember that we are simply using our language-game as a base from which to combat theirs. Reason only goes so far, 'at the end of reasons comes persuasion'. Think, says Wittgenstein, of what happens when missionaries convert natives.

Despite the way this passage sounds and the way it is often interpreted, I want to suggest that the Wittgensteinian perspective, while deeply conservative, need not and should not be taken in a relativistic way. In the first place, immediately after the remark about missionaries, Wittgenstein goes on to state that

> certain events would put me into a position in which I could not go on with the old language-game any further. In which I was torn away from the *sureness* of the game. (OC, 617)

This is in line with the thought in the *Remarks on the Foundations of Mathematics* that certain physical and psychological facts underlie our calculating practices, and also with the passage in the *Philosophical Investigations* (PI, I, 142) in which Wittgenstein argues that our normal language-games would lose their point if certain regularities did not obtain, if there were not, for example, characteristic expressions of pain, of joy, of fear, or if when we attempted to weigh them in order to price them, lumps of cheese began to grow or shrink for no obvious reason. So, while our language-games do not passively mirror the world, they do presuppose certain empirical facts both about the world and about us, and the continuation of certain regularities in the world or us. On the former point, the sceptic has a grain of justification. For while our language-games do not enable us to express doubt about certain things in an intelligible way, our previous certainties could let us down if the world changed radically. As Wittgenstein says, it is always by favour of nature that we know something.[5] On the latter point, in *Zettel*, Wittgenstein says that it is 'an extremely important fact of nature' that if we teach a human being such-and-such a technique by means of examples, he then proceeds in one way rather than another in a new case, or regards something as not the natural continuation of a series (Z, 355). The world and our psychology, then, constrain our language-games at the limit.

Moreover, in *On Certainty*, Wittgenstein speaks of a game we play 'proving its worth', adding that 'that may be the cause of its being played, but it is not the ground' (OC, 474). This idea is one which could be found in a host of conservative thinkers in both British and Austrian traditions, of whom we need only mention here von Hayek. It is the idea that successful human practices survive, but that our reason for playing them is not that they survive or indeed the reason that they emerged in the first place which has more to do with the fact that some people initially found them plausible on their own terms. The thought that a language-game proves its worth, though, is a further non-relativistic strand in Wittgenstein's thinking, suggesting as it does that practices which do not in some sense prove their worth, or which come up against worthier competitors will be modified or eliminated. So long as we do not interpret proving their worth in terms of foundational reasons or in terms of mirroring and remember that proving the worth of a language-game may imply a wider notion of fit than is used in most standard epistemologies, this would not be entirely inconsistent with the physicists and natives passage.

[5] OC, 505. On the whole issue of the connection between our normal objective certainty and what would remain true in any imaginable alterations in circumstances, cf. Norman Malcolm's very perceptive essay 'Certainty' (Malcolm, 1986).

Be that as it may, I now want to follow Hilary Putnam and suggest rather radically that whatever Wittgenstein himself may or may not have said on occasion, there is something deeply anti-relativistic about the Wittgensteinian analysis of the private language and of rule following (cf. Putnam, 1961). The key point of both these analyses for Putnam and for me is the working out of the distinction between one's being right and one's merely thinking that one is right. It is in order to get some purchase on this distinction that Wittgenstein insists in the case of the private language that inner processes stand in need of outward criteria and that we need to see rules in the context of a community of rule-followers. The aspect of Wittgenstein's thought brought out by Putnam is that without the ability to distinguish between being right and thinking one is right (which is what relativism amounts to), one can make no distinction between 'asserting or thinking on the one hand, and making noises or producing mental images on the other'. In actually thinking and asserting, one must really and non-relativistically be using one's words and concepts according to rules, or the words and concepts will be liable to bend and tack in a random way; it will then become impossible to make objective and consistent judgments with them, judgments that are actually *about* anything, judgments which clearly delimit the range of things which fall under the concepts involved and which fit in with the rest of our lives in a stable way. Such judgments are, of course, in Wittgenstein's view judgments or ultimately based on judgments on which I and my linguistic community will unthinkingly and intuitively agree. The thinker not based in a community has no community to provide him in his judgments with the required standards of objectivity—his mental images or whatever do not determine the consistent future development of his concepts, and, so in a sense, he has no concepts as opposed to pre-conceptual dispositions to respond to stimuli in various ways. These responses determine his map of the world and his behaviour, but of their consistency he himself lacks the conceptual resources to judge. For the later Wittgenstein logical necessity is not a kind of super-physical hardness but something based in communal human response.

Following Putnam's lead, however, I want to bring out another and perhaps more basic way in which the idea of rule-following is inherently anti-relativistic. The very distinction between being right and thinking that one is right, which rule-following is invoked to uphold, is one which implies that there are standards which, if I am rational, I have to uphold in my acting and speaking and thinking. The Wittgensteinian analysis is clearly not relativistic as far as deviant calculators or thinkers within a given community go. They are firmly dispatched as being unreasonable, blind, even insane. The problem arises from Wittgenstein's stress on the community, together with his insistence that the logical and epistemic standards of a given community are in the end groundless. So what happens when we get two *communities* with different basic concepts and beliefs?

Here I think we have to focus the very idea of a standard of belief or consistency, rather than on the particular community from which one initially derives the idea. The distinction that is so important is between being right and thinking that one is right. Wittgenstein's insight is that this distinction is initially communicated to an individual in and through his membership of an epistemic community. But it is crucial to see that once an individual realizes that such a distinction exists—and is brought in this way to a specific type of self-consciousness in which he sees that his beliefs and reasonings may not be correct—the possibility is also raised for that individual that some of the beliefs widely held in his community may also be wrong. Sometimes this can happen, of course, without any very shattering implications for the epistemology of the community, when, for example, a widely-held belief in the community is demonstrated to fall short by the standards of that community. That something about the standards themselves may be suspect, or that some basic belief is questionable, though, is in abstract a mere possibility, and one which, as *On Certainty* teaches, we need not entertain unless and until it comes under an effective challenge.

Wittgenstein's point in *On Certainty* is that philosophical scepticism of the traditional sort does not amount to an effective challenge, and that the mere possibility of practices other than our own should not lead us to weaken our allegiance to our own practices. But he does not say that there are no effective challenges, or that community-wide beliefs or standards may not be revised on occasion. Indeed, he says that they can be, and denies any hard and fast distinction between the waters and the river bed in our system of knowledge and belief (cf. OC, 97).

It is plausible to suggest that contact with an alien system of belief which is actually in place, embedded in an actual form of life (with natives in other words) might present such an effective challenge to formerly unquestioned beliefs we hold. There may naturally be problems about resolving such a challenge or even understanding it, but these problems do not in themselves provide any support for relativism. Wittgenstein is certainly very aware of the difficulties of resolution and intelligibility in considering challenges to our fundamental beliefs, more so than many rationalist or foundationalist philosophers, but there is nothing in what he says to suggest that he believes such challenges to be impossible in principle or not amenable to some sort of reasoned assessment. Despite Wittgenstein's belief in common threads linking all humanity—threads which make communication between different cultures possible—he does not see human nature as static or unhistorical. He sees change and development in our practices and behaviour, and is not averse to criticizing well-embedded practices at times.

I want to close this paper by suggesting that far from acquiescing in ethnocentric relativism or leaving deep differences of belief to mere persuasion, Wittgenstein himself was very concerned to demonstrate problems and inconsistencies in certain of the most cherished presuppositions of the contemporary world. In a characteristic passage from *Culture and Value*, Wittgenstein writes that

> It isn't absurd to believe that the age of science and technology is the beginning of the end for humanity; that the idea of great progress is a delusion, along with the idea that the truth will ultimately be known; that there is nothing good or desirable about scientific knowledge and that mankind, in seeking it, is falling into a trap. (CV, 56)

Wittgenstein also wrote that

> the spirit of this civilization makes itself manifest in the industry, architecture and music of our time in its fascism and socialism and it is alien and uncongenial to the author. (CV, 6)

His dislike of empirical psychology is well known and his rejection of reductionism regarding the mind has already been mentioned. Both these tendencies he saw as part of the increasing scientism of his time. He also, perhaps more strikingly, regarded Cantorian set theory, with its talk of completed infinities and comparisons of such sets in terms of magnitude as hocus-pocus, and as part of the sickness of our time. Von Wright comments on this claim that

> to Wittgenstein set theory was a cancer rooted deep in the body of our culture and with distorting effects on that part of our culture which is our mathematics.[6]

So Wittgenstein's insistence that we are rooted in the way of life and concepts of our community did not preclude the criticism of aspects of our way of life and our concepts. His conservatism in matters of reasoning and belief in no way meant that arguments could not be offered against even deeply-rooted aspects of one's own culture. These criticisms could be sharp, detailed and precise, or they could amount to an attempt to shift the way one views a whole segment of one's life. Wittgenstein engages in both types of criticism of aspects of our thinking and our activity, often I believe with considerable conviction.

So Wittgenstein did clearly think that it was possible to criticize aspects of one's own time. His conservatism about beliefs and rule-

---

[6] G. H. von Wright, 'Wittgenstein in relation to his Times' (McGuinness, 1982), 112.

following did not imply conformism to whatever existed. Against what he saw as the shallow rationalism of his time, he was clearly conservative in an ideological, cultural sense, a point nicely illustrated by the well-known story of his reaction to the pictures of Beethoven, Schubert and Chopin on the one hand and those of Russell, Freud and Einstein on the other. (He thought that a century that took the latter trio as spiritual leaders was immeasurably inferior to one that produced the former.) But—and here we return to another and perhaps deeper sense in which he was conservative in the sense adumbrated at the start of this paper—he was not at all optimistic about the effectiveness of argument and reflection in counteracting the abuses inherent in a civilization. The sickness of set theory is cured not by thought but

> by an alteration in the mode of life of human beings, and it was possible for the sickness of philosophical problems to get cured only through a changed mode of thought and of life, not through a medicine invented by an individual. (RFM, II, 23)

And he goes on to say that sicknesses caused by the motor-car will persist until mankind abandons the habit of driving. The rationalist would, of course, say that reason and reflection are sufficient to get people to change a practice and the thought that goes with it. But this was not a view open to Wittgenstein who saw thought and the way we follow the rules governing our thinking as parasitic on our forms of life. On this point though Wittgenstein himself might well seem closer to the economic determinism of a Marx than to the rather more open attitude to thought and society of characteristically conservative thinkers such as Burke or Oakeshott who would have held no *a priori* views about the priority of behaviour over thought in effecting social or ideological change.

Wittgenstein's Influence: Meaning, Mind and Method

A. C. GRAYLING

In the first and shorter part of this essay I comment on Wittgenstein's general influence on the practice of philosophy since his time. In the second and much longer part I discuss aspects of his work which have had a more particular influence, chiefly on debates about meaning and mind. The aspects in question are Wittgenstein's views about rule-following and private language. This second part is more technical than the first.

I

In *The Legacy of Wittgenstein* Anthony Kenny (1984) laments the degree to which Wittgenstein's thought has failed to influence contemporary philosophy. Georg von Wright (1982), by contrast, says that Wittgenstein is the most influential philosopher of the twentieth century. In his study of Wittgenstein's philosophy of language Charles Travis (1989) says that Wittgenstein's views, particularly on questions of meaning and understanding, have had 'little influence'. But J. N. Findlay (1975) describes Wittgenstein's philosophy as immensely consequential. What can such diversity of opinion mean? Is Wittgenstein an influential philosopher, or is he not?

An answer to this question presupposes an answer to another. What should the measure of Wittgenstein's influence be? An unsatisfactory candidate is the number of publications about him which have appeared since his death. There are many, ranging from memoirs to exegesis and critical discussion. But Wittgenstein is not alone in being much discussed—Frege and Russell afford comparable examples—and there is anyway no direct relationship between the quantity of published discussion about someone and that individual's influence. Much has been written about, for example, the twentieth century's dictators, but that betokens the *reverse* of their possessing influence over our thought and ways, except negatively.

A much better measure of Wittgenstein's influence would be the degree to which he has shaped philosophical concerns, and therefore the philosophical debate, since his death. As a first step to determining this we can ask ourselves four questions. Do we share Wittgenstein's views about the nature of philosophy? Do we share his opinion about which problems are the right ones to tackle? Do we agree with him about what the philosopher's task should be? Are we guided in our thinking about philosopical problems by his attitude to them? When we consider that to the first and third of these the answer is 'no' (except for the Wittgensteinian 'school', membership of which is defined by acceptance of Wittgenstein's commitments on these heads: more later), and that to the other two the answer is 'on certain matters, occasionally', the reason for Kenny's and Travis's pessimistic assessment of Wittgenstein's influence becomes clear.

But this suggests we are concerning ourselves with a distraction. I think this could be the fault of some of Wittgenstein's more energetic admirers: they have made Wittgenstein's influence, indeed his 'greatness', an issue, as though philosophy were something like a beauty contest; and I suspect that, sometimes, part of the motive people have for persuading us of someone's stature is that they wish it to be a reason for accepting his views. And that is a fallacy with a severe Latin name.

To get the picture more into focus, and to isolate some of the respects in which Wittgenstein's thought has contributed to philosophical debate, one must assemble a few reminders.

For much of its history philosophy has been conceived as the attempt to clarify, and if possible to answer, questions about a range of matters which seem central to our understanding of ourselves and the world we inhabit. These include, among other things, questions about our concepts of reality, knowledge, reason, truth and value. Attempts at an understanding of some part of some or all these matters have ranged in character from the systematic to the piecemeal. On one view of the history of these endeavours, especially since the seventeenth century, the discovery of the right questions to ask, and of promising ways to answer them, has resulted in much progress (this might be part of a story about the development of natural science, psychology, sociology and linguistics; and, under our very noses, artificial intelligence and cognitive science).

But Wittgenstein does not accept this picture of philosophy. His opinion is that it is not the philosopher's task to engage with the questions mentioned, but rather to show that those questions are spurious, and arise in the first place only because we misunderstand the workings of language. This view is central both to his early and his late philosophies. The difference between the early and late philosophies lies in his views about how language works, and therefore the character of the misconceptions about language which give rise to philosophical problems. In the later philosophy—representing Wittgenstein's preferred views—this diagnosis of philosophical problems entails something definite about the task of the philosopher: which is to cure people of their 'urge' to misunderstand language.

What makes someone a *Wittgensteinian* is his or her adherence to this account of philosophical problems as pathological, and accordingly of the philosopher's task as therapeutic. Anyone who does not accept these views is not in the strict sense a disciple. Perhaps those who mourn the failure of Wittgenstein to be influential, or influential enough, have in mind the fact that few people working in philosophy are or have been disciples of Wittgenstein in this sense.

Two points need to be noted briefly here. One is that it would be a mistake to characterize the Wittgensteinian position as *distinctively* 'anti-philosophical'. The reason is that all philosophy is anti-philosophical, in the sense that all philosophers wish to bring philosophy to an end. They wish to do this by solving the problems of philosophy; often, by showing that they are problems of another kind, to be solved by the techniques of natural science, say, or some other special pursuit. Some problems remain obstinately conceptual, but even here it might be hoped that philosophical investigation can bring to an irenic conclusion the quest either for understanding or clarification.

There is therefore little difference of ends between the philosophical tradition and Wittgenstein, only one of means. He sought—and he is not alone in the history of philosophy in this respect—to bring philosophy to an end by arguing that it should never have begun. His approach represents an attempt at a shortcut, for if one adopts it one disposes of all the problems of philosophy in one blow (as with the tailor and the flies) without having to become involved in analysis of its various problems. Felling a tree at its root is more economical of effort than bringing it down branch by branch. This approach to philosophy is clearest in the *Tractatus*; in the later philosophy Wittgenstein tacitly acknowledges that matters are not so straightforward, even if the goal remains the same.

The second point arises from the first. To say that few people working in philosophy share Wittgenstein's attitude to it is to say that on this fundamental matter he has failed to persuade. The reason is simple. To claim that philosophical problems arise from misunderstandings of language just seems implausible as a diagnosis of the causes of philosophical perplexity. Many philosophers from Plato to Russell have cautioned against the beguilements of language, and with good reason. But to say that all philosophical problems arise from that source goes too far. Wittgenstein has to attribute to language users an 'urge' to misunderstand their language at precisely the points at which one would suppose them struggling to do otherwise; and one would have paradoxically to resort to deliberate muddle if one were trying to get someone to see the perspectives from which, say, one of our most entrenched and fundamental concepts appears problematic. But *obviously* matters are not like this. Language is an instrument capable of subtlety and precision, and some of its most refined applications are to be found exactly where, on Wittgenstein's view, our philosophical concerns are supposed to emanate from confusion. There may indeed be confusion and puzzlement present, but the point is that they are the cause of the urge to understand, not the effect of an urge to misunderstand.

But the chief implausibility arises from the fact that careful attention to our uses of language, for example our employment of expressions containing the terms 'good', 'true' and 'know', have not resolved our difficulties over goodness, truth and knowledge. Were matters that straightforward philosophy would have no history because it would have needed none.

An upshot of these remarks is that Wittgenstein's thought has not been a major influence in philosophy if the mark of its being so is that philosophers agree with, and act in accordance with, his view of philosophy as pathological and of philosophical investigation as therapy. Here, therefore, he has quite failed to convince. Indeed philosophy since Wittgenstein has continued to involve exactly what he opposes, and by means he proscribes; namely, systematic attempts to understand reality, knowledge, truth, and the other central concerns. It is because his followers believe that this constitutes a perpetuation of the evils Wittgenstein was most anxious to combat that a sharp separation exists between them and what might still be called the mainstream. Once again, it is this which explains the regret felt by some of his admirers at the unWittgensteinian character of philosophy since his time.

But this is not at all to deny that there are aspects of Wittgenstein's thought which are powerfully suggestive and which have prompted insights and debate. The philosophical community at large has treated Wittgenstein's work as it does all philosophical work: it profits where profit is to be had, and ignores the rest. Despite the fact that Wittgenstein's method of doing philosophy is crucial to the nature of his views about mind and meaning, his method has on the whole been repudiated, but some of his views about mind and meaning have entered and nourished the wider debate. What has attracted most attention are his views about rule-following and the possibility of private language. Much of his genuine influence, negatively and positively, lies here. To certain points about these matters I now, and in more detail, turn.

II

I wish to raise three points about Wittgenstein's views on rule-following and private language as these are set out mainly in the *Philosophical*

Investigations. They all revolve upon the same consideration, which I discuss in connection with the first point. The other two points, accordingly, I treat of more summarily. In all three I engage only with one aspect of the rule-following considerations, which are a larger and more complex matter than can be dealt with fully in this essay.[1]

The first point concerns what it is to follow a rule. In discussing this matter Wittgenstein is at great pains to establish that someone's following a rule does not involve his being in an internal mental state, or going through an internal mental process, which constitutes 'understanding' the rule in the sense in which a standard intentionalistic psychology would have it. Someone follows a rule, says Wittgenstein, as a result of being trained to do so (cf. PI, I, 208); acting in accordance with that training exhausts what it is to follow the rule. There is, he says, nothing to be appealed to, beyond the agreements which ground our practices, in explaining what goes on here. I wish to suggest a reason for being dissatisfied with this view.

The second point concerns a corollary of a question about the degree of indeterminacy there can be in rules which are supposed to be constitutive of meaning. Some of what Wittgenstein says implies that this degree may be high. I wish to suggest that his motives for saying this, even if the suggestion itself is correct, are misplaced. I only touch upon the substantive issue of how high such indeterminacy can go before there is a failure to preserve stable public senses in language.

The third point concerns the connection between the rule-following considerations and the private language argument. Here there may be certain awkwardnesses, perhaps even—on one reading—a conflict: the possibility of which, at least, needs to be identified, together with the possibility of a solution.

I take each point in turn.

In what has been called the 'rule-following chapter',[2] that is, from about PI, I, 80, but especially from I, 143–242, Wittgenstein has several important concerns in hand at once. One is to repudiate the notion that, although language is clearly a rule-governed activity, the rules in question are those of logic—something Wittgenstein had himself argued in the *Tractatus* but had come to regard as mistaken. Another, closely connected, concern is that the rules governing language-use should not in any sense be thought of Platonistically, that is, as existing independently of our observances of them, and as imposing objective standards of correctness from without. A third, and equally

---

[1] The fuller picture demands a treatment of points raised by Kripke, McDowell, McGinn, Wright, Pears and others; see e.g. Kripke, 1982; McDowell, 1984, McGinn, 1984; Wright, 1986b; and Pears, 1989.

[2] Wright's phrase. Pears calls it the 'Anti-Platonist chapter'.

closely connected, concern is the denial that following a rule involves understanding as an internal mental process: rather, Wittgenstein says, what it is to understand a rule is exhausted by the rule-following activity itself.

Wittgenstein's reasons for denying that understanding a rule involves internal mental states or processes are clearly in view at PI, I, 151–156. The picture he wishes to combat is the familiar one that anyone who follows a rule does so because he has grasped what the rule demands, and knows how to recognize the circumstances in which those demands are to be met; to say which is to employ an intentionalistic vocabulary referring to entities or events of a sort Wittgenstein thinks we should understand quite differently. Accordingly he argues that to say someone understands a rule is not to attribute anything *cognitive* to him, in the sense of an internalized awareness of a rescript by reference to which he can keep track of a rule through all its applications in novel cases. His argument later adds to this denial the claim that even if understanding a rule were indeed an internalized cognitive state, we would be in a quandary over how that state could be supposed to enable us, on each occasion for the rule's application, to recognize what it requires of us (cf. PI, I, 198, I, 209–213; RFM, VI, 38, 47). This is a species of regress argument, for it suggests that even if understanding a rule were an internal cognitive state, one would still need to interpret the rule to judge its applicability in a given situation; but then the problem of how to interpret it correctly arises, and so one might have to know something else, a further rule perhaps, which tells one how to apply it in that case. Both components of Wittgenstein's argument are in view in the considerations I shortly advance.

It is first necessary to note that Wittgenstein has a highly restrictive view of what a mental state or process is. As his remarks in for example PI, I, 154 show, he takes mental states to be *phenomenological* in character—the paradigms are pains felt, noises heard—and that therefore anything mental has to have a felt quality. Consistently with this he talks often, and without displaying any sense of the oddity of doing so, of having a 'feeling' or an 'experience' of, variously, reading (PI, I, 157, 169, 170), deliberating (PI, I, 174), or being guided or influenced (PI, I, 175, 176). He even talks of having a 'sensation' that something is easy to do (PI, I, 151). And he seems to take it that the class of mental states can be delineated by establishing whether one can give an answer to questions about *when* one did something. You can say when you felt a pain, or felt that you were being influenced; but you cannot say when you know how to play chess or understand a rule. By restricting the concept of a mental process to what is datably occurrent and phenomenological Wittgenstein rules out explanations of understanding and other cognitive notions in intentional terms, that is, as representational states of which the paradigm is the propositional attitude. It is of course precisely the possession of such states which seems most distinctive of language-using creatures, for whereas one must, by the meaning of 'sentient', suppose all sentient creatures to enjoy phenomenological states, there is usually much debate about where in the scale of nature to allow attributions of intentionality. The problem is felt most sharply in connection with intelligent-seeming creatures like dogs and chimpanzees, whose behaviour demands description in propositional–attitude-ascribing terms, but within narrower limits than we feel bound to impose in the case of language-users. One is reminded of Wittgenstein's own remark about the dog which expects its master home, but cannot be said to expect its master home next week. This seems to be a remark about the extent of a dog's intentional capacities. One cannot say, with the Wittgenstein of PI, I, 154 (and PI, I, 544–545), that expecting someone home is entirely a kind of feeling; for what *different* feeling yields the 'next week' dimension? (Is there another feeling for 'next month', a third for 'next year'? How different does 'I expect him in two hours' feel as against 'in two hours ten minutes'?) The restriction to datable phenomenological states and processes is accordingly implausible from the outset, not least because of the explanatory impoverishment it promises, if we accept it, in the kinds of contexts just mentioned. This point recurs more fully below.

In line with this restrictive view Wittgenstein claims that the explanation of what it is for someone to understand a rule has to turn on the idea of his being coached in its use by means of examples and practice (PI, I, 208). The learner does not thereby come to grasp anything more than his teacher knows; what his training does for him is to enable him to apply the rule in novel cases in ways which agree with the practices of his community. Indeed it is, as PI, I, 242 and elsewhere shows, the existence of agreements in judgments and practices upon which rule-following (generally: any institutional activity) is grounded. To understand a rule, then, is to satisfy the two conditions embodied in behaving in conformity with the community's practices, as one is trained to do by other members of that community.

It is fruitful to look at the view Wittgenstein attacks, and his alternative to it, in terms of two possibilities for *explaining* rule-following. One explanation appeals to an intentional psychology for which understanding is an internal cognitive state in possessing which a rule-follower is aware of a rescript for carrying out certain procedures in cases identified by criteria given, in the standard case, with the rule he therefore obeys. The other explanation—Wittgenstein's—is that by example and practice trainee rule-followers are coached to act in ways conforming with the ways others in their community act, there being nothing more to rule-following than the conformity arrived at, and in particular no psychological state in which a content (a message, pre-scription, or specification), grasped as a result of this training, serves as a possession of the trainee which guides him. The practice itself is all there is. The whole weight of the explanation is borne by generalizations about conformities in behaviour, the possibility of which, in turn, is attributed to primitive agreements in judgments and practices. It is important to note that these are not intended merely as platitudes we should expect to hold true in virtue of the fact that it is a commonplace social phenomenon we are discussing: *they are* the explanation itself, and there is no more to it.

Put in terms of this contrast it seems hard to see why Wittgenstein's views should be taken seriously. They invite us to accept as an explanation something wholly mystifying: that someone can, on the basis of examples, extrapolate to new cases, but not because of anything he 'understands' in the old, unreconstructed sense. He just goes on, and his going on counts as a rule-following because it conforms to community practice. Wittgenstein is fond of saying that explanation has to come to an end: the problem here seems to be that it is absent. The impression of explanatory vacuity is reinforced by a more detailed comparison with the idea that understanding is a cognitive state on the familiar intentionalist model Wittgenstein repudiates; as follows.

On the intentionalist model we say of someone who understands a rule that he knows what it requires in the cases to which it applies, and knows how to recognize these later. This is to say that in addition to awareness of the kind of requirement the rule's being a *rule* imposes, one who understands it has relevant recognitional capacities and mastery of a relevant procedure. This procedure has to be finitely specifiable but potentially unbounded in the number of occasions it is applicable. This requirement, despite serving as one of the sticking-points for Wittgenstein and many in the subsequent debate, is unproblematic. Wittgenstein appears to hold that if one understood a rule in the intentional sense, one would have to have all its future applications traced out for one (RFM, VI, 31); as if in the 'add 2' example every number at which one might arrive by adding two to any other must somehow be present to one in grasping the rule. But this is a caricature; in understanding 'add 2' I have only to grasp that given any number I am to respond by giving its next but one successor. To grasp *this* I do not have to have, *per impossibile* and least of all occurrently, the thought that 1002 is arrived at by adding two to 1000, and so for all other possibilities. I do not need any particular number in mind at all. And part of the point is that to be in a *position* to understand 'add 2' one has to know enough arithmetic: there are holisms of understanding for a region (for a practice, say) which the teacher can draw upon in explanations of what is to be done, and the learner in vindications of what he is doing. The point is yet clearer in the case of chess or culinary recipes: the rule determines the move or mixture as it were abstractly; it only demands a grasp of the *type* of circumstances in which its application is required, not a simultaneous grasp of all, or indefinitely many, *token* circumstances.

If a defender of Wittgenstein's position says that this begs the question, by supposing that the type–token distinction here at work is clear when it is in fact part of the problem (the conception of a *type* of situation in which a rule applies is intimately—in some cases constitutively—connected with the notion of the rule itself), he misses the point about *explanation*. On the intentional view of understanding we find ourselves equipped with a powerful apparatus for description, prediction and clarification of what people do when we attribute to them understanding of what they do. (Prediction, in particular, is a persuasive feature.) This is shown by our having tests for whether someone understands a rule. At the simplest level, where Wittgenstein locates his criterion, understanding is established by a subject's success in applying the rule in novel cases. But more searchingly, where we wish to challenge a subject's capacities to recognize applications in hard cases, or to manipulate its applications creatively, we do so by tests designed to elicit *more* than mere conformity, aimed at distinguishing three importantly different cases: accidental conformity to a rule, mechanical or incomprehending conformity to a rule (as when a school pupil applies a mathematical formula knowing *that* it works but not why), and grasp of a rule in which the rule-follower has a conception of why he follows it as he does.

Our being able to distinguish these cases, and especially to identify the third, connects in perspicuous ways with our understanding of how rules are bent, broken or changed, creatively varied, or honoured in the breach; and of how some are to be accounted prudential, some obligatory in the presence of sanctions, and some constitutive of given practices. In what ways can Wittgenstein's account provide comparably rich explanations and sortings of these kinds? In each case we appear bound to invoke a notion of intelligent grasp of the rule to be bent or changed, of the sanction to be risked or of the practice constituted, if we are to make any sense of the rule's being a rule for those to whom it applies. And it provides us with something else Wittgenstein's view cannot: it explains how correcting someone's mistaken application of a rule works. On Wittgenstein's model, resuming a training with new examples as a way of correcting a mistaken rule-following cannot be distinguished from introducing a new rule. It seems indeed pointless trying to articulate a notion of *correcting* rule-following error on Wittgenstein's principles when it is hard to see where they provide room for a notion of rule-following error itself: for it is a corollary of one of Wittgenstein's sceptical suggestions—namely that almost *any* interpretation of a rule could be said to be conformable with it—that little or nothing counts as error in the first place. But this implausible result follows only if, in line with Wittgenstein's main thesis, we take it that nothing counts, *beyond* the fact that conformity of practice occurs, as settling whether a rule is being correctly applied. Given the sceptical suggestion, indeed, there may be a problem in settling how conformity is itself to be established in the first place.

The distinction between accidental, mechanical and intelligent rule-following trades upon witholding or attributing possession of contentful cognitive states to rule-followers, and they enable us to bring talk of these practices and what explains them into the broader matter of describing, predicting and explaining intentional behaviour in general. So we wish to say that there is nothing puzzling about the capacity we have for understanding rules as the familiar intentionalist model says we do, for this account connects in illuminating ways with other and more general accounts of our abilities: especially, our ability to recognize patterns, to make comparisons and draw distinctions, to remember, to repeat ourselves with exactness, and to vary our practices creatively. Appeal to these attributes of mind is constitutive of the intentionalist account of how rules are grasped and applied. In what sense are we massively astray in interpreting our behaviour according to these categories? In Wittgenstein's terms, either such talk not only fails to explain anything, but actually creates philosophical perplexity where there should be none; or it needs wholesale reinterpretation into third-person descriptions of conformities between ways in which members of a community behave. The point I am urging is that either option, in comparison to the intentionalist view, is explanatorily impoverished to a degree.

There is a well-known case for arguing that appeal to intentional concepts of the kind at issue is irreducible. The behaviour of Fodor's cat, for a famous example, with its expectations of food and its appropriate choice of a place to curl up, cannot, on this view, be explained adequately unless it has attributed to it, in non-trivial ways, such states as having a representation of how things are in its environment, and therefore certain beliefs and desires with determinate content. But one does not have to make out the case for this here. To challenge Wittgenstein in the present instance it is enough to pose a question: because one is looking for a place for explanation to end, why have it end in the mystery of how the trainee succeeds in just going on in ways that in fact conform with the community's practices, rather than ending instead with the available and familiar set of psychological concepts which affords such a powerful network of description and prediction?

This is by no means a merely rhetorical question, for, as the foregoing discussion implies, if rule-following is not to be seen as a cognitive achievement then it cannot be seen as rule-following. It would not be the following of a *rule*, which in virtue of being something regulative describes limits and demands a certain pattern of conformity to them, such that the limits and the pattern have to be appreciated as such by a rule-follower in order for the rule to function as such. And it would not be the *following* of a rule, which excludes accidental, haphazard, random or variable conformity, but has to consist in a determinate respect for what it is that the rule says is constitutive of observing it. On both counts therefore we should expect that if it really is rule-following we are dealing with, the rule-follower must at least in principle be able to cognize the requirements of the rule and be conscious of meeting them.

According to Wright (1989, 303) one of the main reasons why Wittgenstein resists the intentionalist picture is that it prompts the regress difficulty already mentioned, namely, that thinking of the rule as being situated 'in mind' does not explain how it helps to have it there; for the further matter of recognizing what it requires of one is not settled, so Wittgenstein has it, by the mere fact that it *is* 'in mind'. Wright puts the point in the form of a question: How is it possible to know what the rule which I grasp requires of me here?' (ibid.) From the perspective of the intentionalist resource for explaining rule-following this question must appear absurd: for what else could be meant by saying that one has a grasp of a rule other than that one knows what it requires? If one did not know what the rule requires one cannot have grasped it. It is the simple but powerful observation that grasp *consists in* knowledge of what is required—is a cognitive state—that marks the explanatory superiority of that account over the bare notion that facts about conformity to community practices is where explanation of rule-following ends.

It should, I think, be noticed that among the reasons Wittgenstein has for resisting an intentionalist account are certain points which could only arise from a misunderstanding of what it involves. For one thing, nothing in the intentionalist account says that public constraints on the learning of rules and their correct use are dispensable. On the contrary, the very idea of 'internalizing' a rule supposes its take-up from a training, or at any rate from observation of what happens in the public domain. Similarly, if we are to have conceptions of getting the rule right and wrong, and correcting the latter, that too supposes the availability, indeed the necessity, of public checks. Therefore as to acquisition and manifestation of rule-following competency, the community requirements Wittgenstein insists upon as fundamental are satisfied. Wittgenstein's move, from recognizing the constitutive importance of these facts to saying that they are *all* the facts, is what the intentionalist account finds incoherent.

A related point is that the intentionalist account does not, despite Wittgenstein's claims otherwise, entail that rules have the kind or degree of autonomy which understanding them Platonistically would suggest. On the contrary, the intentionalist view depends upon the idea of their conventional origin and support in the way just described, and this is every bit as anti-realist an attitude towards them as Wittgenstein's own. On this, indeed, the two views are one. As noted earlier, Wittgenstein seems to attribute to intentionalism the corollary that understanding a rule would have in some sense to be infinitary in character, so that all possible applications of the rule are somehow present to the rule-follower in his grasp of its requirements; and this is what prompts Wittgenstein to interpret the view Platonistically, for it suggests that one cognizes the rules as rails running forever into the future, and therefore as antecedently and independently fixed. But as also noted, cognizing a rule is no such infinitary matter, and therefore the intentionalist view does not imply Platonism.

This leads naturally to the second point I wish to raise, concerning a corollary of a question about the degree of indeterminacy there can be, before shared understanding of expressions is threatened, in rules which are constitutive of meaning. The problem here is suggested by the fact that Wittgenstein insists upon the normative character of language, and the requirement that the rules which in general govern language use should be based upon agreements in judgments and practices (PI, I, 99, 107, 240, 242; RFM, VI, 39), and yet, in other places, he says that the use of expressions is not everywhere bounded by rules (cf. e.g. PI, I, 79–80). One wishes to know whether there can indeed be language use which is not governed by rules. Wittgenstein's own claim that one would be prevented from recognizing the vocalizations of a group of aliens as a language if these vocalizations lacked sufficient regularity (PI, I, 207) suggests that such latitude itself must have limits. But where do they lie?

Wittgenstein describes a group of people playing various ball-games (PI, I, 83). They start, say, with football, and after a while change to netball, then rugby, and so on. Between starting and abandoning recognized games they throw the ball about aimlessly, chase one another, and bombard one another with the ball. Wittgenstein says that it would be a mistake to think that every stretch of this activity is rule-governed. The thought is that there are, familiarly enough, games without rules. They are games because of their family resemblance to games with rules. And the implication is that language-games are analogous.

But why should we accept that language-games are analogous to games in this way? The pressure for refusing to accept that there can be uses of words which are not rule-governed comes from the requirement imposed by the bare fact that language is a public instrument of communication. At very least this imposes the requirement that anything which can count as an expression of the language must have a role specifiable by what is or can be done with it in the language. And this is to bring it under rules.

Wittgenstein does not in fact go so far as to say that a language-game as a whole might be non-normative. It is rather that the application of an expression may not in *every* case be bounded by a rule (PI, I, 80, 84). We may concede that language is *in general* rule-governed, but allow that the sense of an expression could still, in certain uses or circumstances, 'leave this or that open' (PI, I, 99). What Wittgenstein wishes to resist is the demand expressed by the claim that 'it isn't a game if there is some vagueness in the rules', or at very least that it is not a 'perfect' game (PI, I, 100). And his motive is that if we thought that language-games have to be everywhere bound by rules we would be re-admitting the *Tractatus* idea of fixed rules underlying language, or more generally a notion of the sense of expressions being objectively determined, independently of the use to which they are put by speakers of the language. This species of view is, broadly speaking, Fregean; it comes down to saying that what confers sense on expressions transcends what speakers know about using them.

The Fregean idea might be put as follows: for the sense of expressions to be publicly available to all speakers of the language they must be determinate, and therefore cannot consist in what individual speakers subjectively understand by them. When a speaker acquires mastery of an expression he does so by grasping its objective sense and thereafter employing it, if he does so correctly, according to its objective sense-conditions. Only in this way is communication possible, because only in this way can each speaker understand by the expressions of the language what all the others in his linguistic community understand by them.

From Wittgenstein's point of view both the notion of sense transcending use and the appeal to an intentionalist account of speaker understanding are deeply uncongenial. For Wittgenstein the link between the two theses is close and works like this: if you grant the intentionalist account of speaker understanding you thereby grant that grasp of an expression can be the internalization of an objective sense, something fixed by conditions which are independent of speaker practices and community agreement. The denial of the Fregean objectivity of sense is thus made to turn on the supposed inadequacy of the intentionalist psychology which underlies it. The key to Wittgenstein's views in this connection is PI, I, 205. Here he contemplates the thought that the mental process of *intention* does not depend on the existence of a custom or technique. This suggests that on the intentionalist account there could be an understanding of an expression or a following of a rule which only ever happened *once*. (The example he gives is of a game of chess only ever once played—or begun, but interrupted.) And this of course he rejects outright: rule-following is a custom, a practice (PI, I, 198, 202); it would be nonsense to say that in the history of the world a rule was followed (a game played, a sentence uttered) *just once* (RFM, 332–328).

But if we recall what was suggested in connection with Wittgenstein's attack on the intentionalist interpretation of understanding, the connection he supposes between such an account and a Fregean theory of the objectivity of sense (and hence—more broadly—Platonism about rules) just does not exist. For one can, with perfect propriety, jointly assert the following two claims: that sense is conferred ultimately by agreement, and therefore is a function of or is constituted by use, and that it is the awareness of the pattern of use thus grounded which constitutes a speaker's grasp of the expression. Indeed it is hard to see why it should be thought that the existence of a capacity to understand an expression in the way described by the intentionalist account should entail, or even merely license, the view that a rule need not be a custom. Nor indeed—but this is an aside—does one see why a one-off rule has to be, in virtue of being one-off, Platonistically understood.

It seems that Wittgenstein's use of observations about the slack there can be in the rules governing expressions is intended as a defence against the kind of objectivism he had himself espoused in the *Tractatus*. Now we can note that he can be right about the existence of such slack despite the fact that an appeal to facts about it is not required for such a defence. But what does his observation come down to? As masters of our language we recognize in non-standard uses of expressions such phenomena as perturbations (in the grammarian's sense), change of meaning, figurative and poetic uses, puns, jokes, and plain mistakes. Does Wittgenstein mean more than this? I think if he does mean more there is the prospect of a tension between whatever it is he means and his own insistence, correct as most would agree, on the requirement for public constraints on sense, something demanded for successful communication and supplied by agreements. I might suggest, but shall not argue the case here, that among those constraints could be ones which say: if something is a language it is such that an alien linguist should be able to recover from observation of its users' practices their language's grammar, and an alien anthropologist should be able to recover from those same practices the bulk of their mundane beliefs. These represent indeed quite demanding constraints, but it is hard to see how what the alien investigators are studying could otherwise be a language. And I note in passing that the reference to 'beliefs' is, in line with the preceding argument, to be taken at face value.

The thought that on an intentionalist account there might be just one following of a rule or playing of a game naturally and immediately suggests a connection with the private language argument. This is the third and final point I wish to touch upon.

Wittgenstein's private language argument is an attack on the idea that there can be a language which can *only* be understood by its user, that is, a logically private language. It has been noted that this attack, if successful, not only blocks a certain way of thinking about how we talk—and learn to talk—about our own mental states and processes, but also generalizes to wider epistemological concerns, where it shows that the 'Cartesian' approach to questions about knowledge is open to particularly sharp challenge. This perspective, familiarly, has it that in determining what one knows one is to begin with the private data of one's consciousness, from which one is to build outwards to conclusions about what might exist beyond them; the idea being that in this way one at least starts with something incorrigible and indubitable. On the Cartesian view first-person knowledge of psychological states is unproblematic, because we enjoy direct and transparent access to them, whereas both third-person knowledge of them, and knowledge of whatever we standardly take them to represent, is highly problematic, as the sceptical arguments show. One powerful effect of a private language argument is to suggest a reversal in this order of difficulty.

Wittgenstein, however, is led by his argument against the possibility of logically private language to conclude that, as Wright puts it, 'there cannot be such a thing as a first-person privileged recognition of the dictates of one's understanding an expression' (Wright, 1986a). If there were, so the implication goes, one could recognize that one were using an expression (or more generally, following a rule) correctly from one's own cognitive resources. But part of the case in the private language argument is that since there would be no independent check on one's employment of these internal cognitive resources, one would not be in a position to recognize their use as correct, and so could not be said to be using the expression (following the rule) at all. The point here is one that Wittgenstein particularly stresses: that in order for rule-following to take place there has to be available a distinction between following a rule and only *thinking* one is following a rule; in the absence of such a distinction the possibility of rule-following collapses. But this is precisely how it is from the point of view of the private would-be rule-follower: the distinction is not available to him, and therefore neither is the practice.

A. C. Grayling

What seems right about these thoughts is the denial that an individual can name his internal states by an act of inner ostension, and on that basis attach sense to a discourse about his own psychological history which is logically impenetrable to all but himself. It also seems right to extend this to the general epistemological case, with all that this implies for the Cartesian perspective. Both points turn on the need for public constraints which underwrite the essential distinction—the distinction between following a rule and only thinking one is—and these Wittgenstein refers, familiarly, to a basis in agreement. But what is wrong with these suggestions is the supposition that the private language argument entails that there can be no such thing as first-person privileged recognition of the dictates of one's understanding an expression. From the fact that mastery of an expression is and can only be learned in a public setting, and that its proper use has to be controlled by public checks, nothing follows as to the impossibility of an understanding of an expression, thus acquired and controlled, consisting in a cognitive state of its user. The anxiety which prompts Wittgenstein to claim that first-person possession of cognitive states is inconsistent with community constraints on acquisition and correct use, is the same as that identified earlier in connection with Platonism. Wittgenstein seems to think that if understanding is an inner cognitive state, a rule could be followed once only, and therefore there can be a private language. But neither of these two last follows from the first, nor do the reasons for denying these two last entail the impossibility of the first.

This, together with the parallel points made in the two earlier connections, suggests that one might detach Wittgenstein's view that the meaning of expressions in a language, in general constituted by the rules for their use, must be public in character, from his view that it cannot be the case that anyone's understanding of an expression or a rule consists on an inner cognitive state of that person. Wittgenstein thinks that these two commitments hang or fall together: but the argument here is that they are independent. Several things follow, of which two are immediately relevant.

First, one ground for refusing to accept Wittgenstein's rejection of intentionalist psychology is, as we saw, the enormous superiority it has as an explanatory system of concepts over the bare gesture towards the fact of conformity in behaviour based on 'agreement in judgments' upon which Wittgenstein's account of rule-mastery turns. That account makes what *enables* anyone to follow a rule a mystery, and not even of the sort that patient investigation might reduce: for that is where, we are told, explanation is to end. But intentionalist psychology, which not only provides a familiar account of understanding but brings it into relationship with the whole repertoire of our psychological concepts—a repertoire, one notes, employed with such enormous daily success—constitutes a far better place to bring explanation to an end. And this point, to repeat, leaves undiscussed a much stronger one: that appeal to such concepts is in any case strictly irreducible. It is easy to see why someone who takes this latter view, namely Fodor, can say that he finds it 'appalling' (his word) that Wittgenstein has no theory of cognitive processes, and that it is 'painfully obvious' (his words again) that Wittgenstein never succeeded in shaking off behaviourist inclinations (Fodor, 1987). I think one possibility is that what seems most right in Wittgenstein's views in this area, namely the requirement for public constraints on the acquisition and employment of rule-following competency, could be obscured by its connection with these implausible concomitants.

Secondly, and connectedly, one cannot fail to notice that in the literature on these matters there has been a surprisingly unhesitating acceptance of the philosophical psychology which Wittgenstein thought was particularly germane to the rule-following considerations and their connection with the private language argument. The odd situation has arisen that a strong case has persisted in the philosophy of mind for the irreducibility of intentional notions, while among many of those who write about Wittgenstein there has remained a readiness to think that what often look—to other eyes—like quasi-behavioural reductions of intentional phenomena are in no need of scrutiny. Wittgenstein's influence on this important area of research may accordingly strike one as negative.

A point that has to be made briefly here is that if one is willing to accept an intentionalist account of understanding together with the view that acquisition and employment of what is thus understood is necessarily public, one is thereby accepting what is sometimes called a 'thick' notion of content, but not one in which mental contents are to be individuated by objectively-conceived states of the *world*, that is, states existing independently of what is made of them by the community from whom the content in question is acquired and by whom its employment is constrained. Rather, the thick end of content lies just there—in the public conditions specified. This suggests (one can only offer it as a hint here) something like an anti-realist picture of thick content suitable for an intentionalist psychological account of publicly governed rule-following. I mention this to show that the connections established by Wittgenstein in this area may fall interestingly apart if one refuses to accept the enervated account of understanding he offers.

A concluding point, also on the connection between the rule-following and private language considerations, is this. If the sense of expressions in language is constituted by the rules for their use, and if these are only possible on the basis of agreements within a community, it follows that language is *necessarily*, that is *logically*, public. This might at first sight seem to be a corollary of the private language argument, but it is not. For the private language argument says that language cannot be logically private, that is, knowable only to its user. The claim that language cannot be logically private is not the claim that it is logically public, for it leaves open the possibility of contingent privacy—that is, the possibility of a Robinson Crusoe figure abandoned from birth on an island who nevertheless survives and, as he grows, develops a language. All that is required for it to be a *language* that he uses is that it should admit of being shared by others. (We are not concerned with the entirely trivial examples of 'private language' which, like Pepys's code, are merely public languages in cypher.) Wright has argued that it is a condition on the cogency of any argument against private language that it should allow for contingent privacy, for otherwise, he says, far too much will be established, and we will not be able to make sense of what a Robinson figure does who, for example, teaches himself how to play with a Rubik Cube washed up on his beach (Wright, 1986a).

But if we reconsider the demands of the rule-following argument we see that the community constraints on what can count as rule-following conflict with the idea of contingent privacy. They do so at both major points. First, the rule-following considerations make it a condition that rule-following must start with training in a community's practices in a public setting. Secondly, they make it a condition that public checks by the community should be available so that a rule-follower can distinguish between following a rule and only thinking he is doing so. Neither condition is satisfied by Robinson Crusoe. He cannot start, and if *per impossibile* he could, he could not go on. He therefore cannot be a language user in *any* sense.

In having it that language is *logically* public the rule-following considerations constitute a far stronger thesis than does the private language argument. Given that there is a conflict, which should give way? *Pace* Wright, I see no difficulty in saying that it is contingently private language that has to go. This if right is an important matter, because it suggests—even promises—a range of philosophically interesting possibilities. One might mention the refutation of scepticism as traditionally conceived, and indeed the displacement of the whole set of Cartesian considerations which make that scepticism possible. That has been implicit all along in the concept of following a rule.

Perhaps it is here—in his contribution, along with others in the twentieth century, to the undermining of the Cartesian perspective— that later generations will locate Wittgenstein's greatest contribution.

Wittgenstein on Mathematical Proof

CRISPIN WRIGHT

To be asked to provide a short paper on Wittgenstein's views on mathematical proof is to be given a tall order (especially if little or no familiarity either with mathematics or with Wittgenstein's philosophy is to be presupposed!). Close to one half of Wittgenstein's writings after 1929 concerned mathematics, and the roots of his discussions, which contain a bewildering variety of underdeveloped and sometimes conflicting suggestions, go deep to some of the most basic and difficult ideas in his later philosophy. So my aims in what follows are forced to be modest. I shall sketch an intuitively attractive philosophy of mathematics and illustrate Wittgenstein's opposition to it. I shall explain why, contrary to what is often supposed, that opposition cannot be fully satisfactorily explained by tracing it back to the discussions of following a rule in the *Philosophical Investigations* and *Remarks on the Foundations of Mathematics*. Finally, I shall try to indicate very briefly something of the real motivation for Wittgenstein's more strikingly deflationary suggestions about mathematical proof, and canvass a reason why it may not in the end be possible to uphold them.

I

Euclid is credited with the first proof that, among the series of positive whole numbers, the occurrence of prime numbers is endless. His reasoning, as many readers doubtless recall, was based on what is often called the Fundamental Theorem of arithmetic—the lemma that every number has a unique prime factorization: i.e., can be represented as the product of a multiplication sum in which only prime numbers occur as factors. [Thus 28 is $7 \times 2 \times 2$; 273 is $3 \times 7 \times 13$; and so on.] The proof then proceeds by *reductio ad absurdum*. Suppose there were a last prime—call it N. And consider the corresponding N!+1—the number we get by cumulatively multiplying N by each of its predecessors in turn and adding 1 to the total. If N is the greatest prime, as we have assumed, then this number is not prime but composite. Hence, by the Fundamental Theorem, it is the product of a unique set of prime factors. But what are they? They cannot comprise any number *smaller than or equal to* N, for, given the way that N!+1 is constructed, none of

Crispin Wright

those numbers divides into it without a remainder—they all leave remainder 1. So the prime factors of N!+1 must be *greater* than N—but then that contradicts our hypothesis, that N is the greatest prime, which is therefore refuted. If there were a greatest prime, then, by the Fundamental Theorem of arithmetic, there would have to be prime numbers greater than it; so there is no greatest prime number— the primes run on without end.

It is natural and attractive to view this pleasantly economical reasoning as constituting a *discovery*. The basic concepts of number theory— the branch of pure mathematics that deals with zero and the positive whole numbers that succeed it—are very accessible: they include the concept of zero itself, the idea of one number succeeding another, the idea of an endless array of such numbers getting larger and larger *ad infinitum*, and elementary operations upon them such as addition, multiplication, exponentiation and so on. In terms of this basic and easily intelligible set of notions, all the concepts and operations of pure number theory can be defined and all the statements which exercise the interest of the number theoretician can be formulated. And because of the accessibility of the basic concepts, and the straightforward character of many of the consequential definitions, some of these statements are extremely easy to understand. That the primes are infinite is one such; Goldbach's Conjecture, that every even number is the sum of two primes, and the alleged 'last theorem' of Fermat, that the equation $X^n + Y^n = Z^n$ has no solution among the natural numbers for values of n greater than or equal to 3, are two famous examples of readily intelligible statements which remain unresolved to this day.[1]

Confronted with such examples, our inclination is to think that they raise interesting questions which must have answers but to which we do not at present know the answers. It would be quite possible, before I knew anything of Euclid's proof, to wonder about Goldbach's Conjecture and then realize that, if true, it would require the infinity of the primes, and to proceed to wonder about that. Euclid's proof would then naturally present itself as a discovery that at least one necessary condition for the truth of the Goldbach Conjecture was met. And it would remain to wonder whether a similar but, no doubt, more complex feat of human ingenuity will some day disclose that the Conjecture itself is indeed true, or whether, rather, far out into the series of natural numbers, occurs an even number which is the sum of no two of its prime predecessors.

A striking aspect of this intuitively natural way of thinking is the separation it effects between the concepts of truth and proof in mathe-

[1] For n=2, of course, there are "Pythagorean" solutions—for instance, 3, 4 and 5; 5, 12 and 13; and so on.

matics. We wonder whether the Goldbach Conjecture will ever be proved or refuted. But the statement of the Conjecture is so easily grasped, and its meaning so apparently sharp, that we are not at all inclined to doubt that it must be, determinately, either true or false. For the series of natural numbers itself, we conceive, is a perfectly definite structure, in which the even numbers are a sharply defined sub-series. And of each particular even number it is, surely, a definite question with a definite and (in principle) ascertainable answer, whether it is the sum of two primes or not. And now, how can the question whether *all* items of a certain kind have a certain characteristic fail to have a determinate answer—even if we cannot know what the answer is—if the items in question are a sharply defined class and the characteristic in question is something which *each* of them determinately either possesses or not?

We are thus instinctively drawn, at least in the case of number theory, to *mathematical realism*. According to mathematical realism, the number-theoretician is a kind of explorer. His project arises because, whereas the natural numbers are infinite, the capacities and opportunities possessed by the human mind are finite. Perhaps a deity could somehow mechanically check each even number and determine whether it was the sum of two primes or not—and then remember whether, in the course of this infinite labour, any counter-examples to the Goldbach Conjecture had been turned up. But *we* can do no such thing. For us, the only way of determining the truth or falsity of such a statement is, as it were, indirectly, by cunning. So proof comes to be seen as merely a kind of cognitive auxiliary, a method of investigation which we are forced to use because, in dealing with infinite totalities, our finiteness leaves us with no other recourse.

To conceive of the truth of number-theoretic statements in this way invites, of course, the question: what, when such a statement is true, *makes* it true? And it is no answer to say: the way things are with the natural numbers. What the questioner is requesting is advice about how, in general terms, the states of affairs which—perhaps quite independently of any possibility of human knowledge—confer truth on number-theoretic statements, should be conceived as constituted. A very ancient answer is that the world contains numbers and other kinds of mathematical objects much as it contains mountains and seas; that there is an abstract substance to the world as much as a physical one. Such a view is, remarkably, still a topic of ongoing professional debate.[2] But the view of most contemporary philosophers of mathematics would

---

[2] Kurt Gödel is widely regarded as endorsing the ancient answer in his (1947), pp. 483–4. Penelope Maddy is also a staunch champion of it; see her (1980).

be that it is no more than a metaphor for the kind of objectivity which, driven by the sort of intuitive realist thinking which I briefly sketched, we would like pure mathematics to have. What, I suspect, with our realist hats on, we really think about the constitutive question is something more anthropocentric. Kronecker said, famously, that whereas all the rest of pure mathematics was the work of man, the natural numbers were created by God. But no realist need think anything of that sort. It is enough if we are capable of creating, in thought, a sufficiently definite concept of the series of natural numbers to give substance to questions about its characteristics which we may not know how to answer. And is that so puzzling an idea? The rules of Noughts and Crosses, for instance, are perfectly definite, yet it is not totally trivial to show that the second player can always force a draw; and it is possible to understand the rules perfectly yet be unaware of the point. Is it not, nevertheless, a perfectly objective feature of the game which, when it finally dawns on one as a child, it is proper to think of oneself as *finding out*? And is not Noughts and Crosses a human invention for all that? As the small child with Noughts and Crosses, so the adult mathematician with number theory; the difference is only that there is, in the case of Noughts and Crosses, no analogue of the infinity of the number series to set up the possibility that truth and verifiability, even verifiability 'in principle', might come apart.

We now have on display almost all the ingredients in our intuitive thinking about pure mathematics against which Wittgenstein's later philosophy reacts. The conception of mathematics as a kind of investigative science; the notion that it explores a special domain of states of affairs, which are constituted by acts of human concept formation yet somehow acquire the autonomy to outstrip what is transparent, or even in principle accessible to the human subject; the view of proof as an exploratory tool, albeit a kind of cognitive prosthetic on which we are forced to rely because of finitude—each of these ideas is roundly criticized throughout Wittgenstein's later writings on mathematics. It remains only to include our sense of proof as somehow excluding all rational options but assent to its status as proof—what Wittgenstein famously characterized as the 'hardness' of the logical 'must'—and the associated idea, which even Descartes' scepticism did not prompt him seriously to call into question, that proof in mathematics is a source of an especially sure and certain genre of knowledge—add these and we have both a thumbnail sketch of the lay-philosophy of mathematics which we find most attractive and an inventory of the principal confusions to which Wittgenstein regarded our thought about these matters as prone.

For Wittgenstein, pure mathematics is not a project of exploration and discovery; mathematical proof is not an instrument whereby we find out things; conceptual structures cannot have the kind of auto-nomy to allow their characteristics to outstrip what can be ratified by human thought; there is no external compulsion upon us when we ratify proofs—we are driven, but not by cognition of an external, normative constraint; and in so far as there is a special sureness about at least some mathematical propositions, it does not amount to a superla-tive genre of knowledge—such propositions do not enjoy a *cognitive* certainty at all.

Here are some passages illustrative of each of these deflationary lines of thought. On mathematics as an investigative science in which we explore the characteristics of our own conceptual constructions and rules, Wittgenstein writes:

> What, then—does [mathematics] just twist and turn about within these rules?—It forms ever new rules: is always building new roads for traffic; by extending the network of the old ones.
>
> But then doesn't it need a sanction for this? Can it extend the network *arbitrarily*? Well, I could say: a mathematician is always inventing new forms of description. Some, stimulated by practical needs, others from aesthetic needs,—and yet others in a variety of ways. And here imagine a landscape gardener designing paths for the layout of a garden; it may well be that he draws them on a drawing board merely as ornamental strips without the slightest thought of someone sometime walking on them.
>
> The mathematician is an inventor, not a discoverer. (RFM, I, 165–7)

He speaks with suspicion of the idea of

> Arithmetic as the natural history [mineralogy] of numbers. But *who* talks like this about it? Our whole thinking is penetrated with this idea. (RFM, III, 11)

And in the Appendix on Cantor's Diagonal Argument he remarks:

> 'Fractions cannot be arranged in an order of magnitude'.—First and foremost, this sounds extremely interesting and remarkable.
>
> It sounds interesting in a quite different way from, say, a proposi-tion of the differential calculus. The difference, I think, resides in the fact that *such* a proposition is easily associated with an application to physics, whereas *this* proposition belongs simply and solely to mathematics, seems to concern as it were the natural history of mathematical objects themselves.
>
> One would like to say of it e.g.: it introduces us to the mysteries of the mathematical world. *This* is the aspect against which I want to give a warning.
>
> When it looks as if . . . , we should look out. (RFM, II, 10)

Against the conception of proof as an instrument of conceptual discovery, Wittgenstein urges a quite different picture:

> I am trying to say something like this: Even if the mathematical proposition seems to point to a reality outside itself, still it only expresses acceptance of a new measure (of reality). . . . we have won through to a piece of knowledge in the proof? And the final proposition expresses this knowledge? And is this knowledge now independent of the proof (is the navel string cut)?—well, the proposition is now used by itself and without having the proof attached to it.
>
> Why should I not say: in the proof I have won through to a *decision*? . . .
>
> The proposition proved by means of the proof serves as a rule . . . (RFM, II, 27, 28)
>
> I go through the proof and say: 'yes, this is how it *has* to be; I must fix the use of my language in *this* way'.
>
> I want to say that the *must* corresponds to a track which I *lay down* [my emphasis, C.W.] in language.
>
> When I said that a proof introduces a new concept, I meant something like: the proof puts a new paradigm among the paradigms of the language . . . the proof changes the grammar of our language, changes our concepts. It makes new connections, and it creates the concept of those connections. (It does not establish that they are there; they do not exist until it makes them.) (RFM, II, 30, 31)

Proofs do not draw to our attention what must be the case, nor is it right to think of them as commanding our assent:

> What is the transition that I make from 'it will be like this' to 'it *must* be like this'? I form a different concept. One involving something that was not there before. When I say: 'if these derivations are the same, then it *must* be that . . .', I am making something into a criterion of identity. So I am recasting my concept of identity. . . .
>
> Can I say: the proof induces us to make a certain decision, namely that of accepting a particular concept formation?
>
> Do not look on a proof as a procedure which *compels* you, but as one which *guides* you.—And what it guides is your *conception* of a (particular) situation. (RFM, III, 29, 30)
>
> *What* is unshakably certain about what is proved?
>
> To accept a proposition as unshakably certain—I want to say— means to use it as a grammatical rule: this removes uncertainty from it. (RFM, II, 39)

And again, on mathematical (logical) compulsion:

> We say: 'If you really follow the rule in multiplying, you *must* all get the same results'. Now if this is only the somewhat hysterical way

of putting things that you get in university talk, it need not interest us overmuch.

It is however the expression of an attitude towards the technique of calculation, which comes out everywhere in our life. The emphasis of the *must* corresponds only to the inexorableness of this attitude both to the technique of calculating and to a host of related techniques.

The mathematical Must is only another expression of the fact that mathematics forms concepts. (RFM, V, 46)

Finally, on a mathematical problem structurally similar to that posed by the Goldbach Conjecture—the question whether seven consecutive '7's occur in the decimal expansion of Π—Wittgenstein writes

The question—I want to say—changes its status when it becomes decidable. For a connection is then made which formerly *was not there* . . .

However queer it sounds, the further expansion of an irrational number is a further expansion of mathematics . . .

I want to say: it looks as though the ground for the decision were already there; and it has yet to be invented. (RFM, IV, 9)

It does indeed look as though the 'ground for the decision were already there'. How could it not be? For is not the decimal expansion of Π determined by rule at every step? So how can there be any indeterminacy, before we get any mathematical result on the matter, about what is the correct answer to the question? Either, we want to say, seven consecutive '7's do occur—and necessarily so, since their occurrence, where they occur, is built into the identity of Π—or, again necessarily, they do not. The question could be indeterminate—'the ground for the decision' not yet exist—only if there were some indeterminacy in the proper expansion of Π. But there is, surely, none. Yet Wittgenstein challenges these intuitive and seemingly unassailable thoughts head-on.

Might I not say: if you do a multiplication, in any case you do not find the mathematical fact, but you do find the mathematical proposition? For what you *find* is the non-mathematical fact, and in this way the mathematical proposition. . . . a mathematical proposition is the determination of a concept, following upon a discovery . . .

The concept is altered so that this *had* to be the result. I find, not the result, but that I reach it. And it is not this route's beginning here and ending here that is an empirical fact, but my having gone this road, or some road to this end.

But might it not be said that the *rules* lead this way, even if no one went it? For that is what one would like to say—and here we see the mathematical machine which, driven by the rules themselves, obeys only mathematical laws and not physical ones.

I want to say: the working of the mathematical machine is only the *picture* of the working of a machine. The rule does not do work, for whatever happens according to the rule is an interpretation of the rule. (RFM, III, 47, 48)

What drives Wittgenstein to these implausible-seeming and unattractive views?

II

Ten years ago, in a systematic study of Wittgenstein's later philosophy of mathematics (Wright, 1980), I was, I think, the first to offer and develop in print the suggestion that the critical examination of the concept of following a rule, pursued both in the *Remarks on the Foundation of Mathematics* and the *Philosophical Investigations*, is central to the interpretation not just of Wittgenstein's later thought about mathematics but of his later philosophy as a whole. This perspective seems to have been an idea whose time had come. Subsequently Saul Kripke published his highly influential *Wittgenstein on Rules and Private Language* (Kripke, 1982) outlining a vivid 'Sceptical Paradox' which it presents as the heart of Wittgenstein's thought about rule-following, and whose resolution purportedly generates the argument against private language. Kripke's book concentrates almost exclusively on the Sceptical Paradox and the accommodation with it—the Sceptical Solution—which, in Kripke's view, underlies Wittgenstein's ideas about privacy and the self-ascription of sensation and other psychological states. But he anticipates (Kripke, 1982, 3–5) a perfectly direct application of his interpretation of the ideas about rules to the philosophy of mathematics, and does not hesitate to suggest that both the philosophy of mind of the *Investigations* and the philosophy of logic and mathematics expounded in the *Remarks on the Foundations of Mathematics* should be seen as driven by them.[3]

[3] For the record let me say that Kripke's ideas about these issues and mine seem to have developed in complete isolation from each other. Kripke's interpretation originated, as he recounts, in graduate seminars given in Princeton as early as the spring of 1965 and was subsequently developed through a series of conferences and colloquia from 1976 onwards. I first proposed such an interpretation of aspects of Wittgenstein's later thought on mathematics in my (1968); and the material that constitutes the first six chapters of *Wittgenstein on the Foundations of Mathematics* (Wright, 1980) was first written up for graduate seminars given in All Souls College, Oxford in the summer of 1974. Kripke and I were, indeed, colleagues for several months at All Souls in the academic year 1977–8, when he held a Visiting Fellowship there. But we never discussed the interpretation of Wittgenstein.

This is a natural thought which it is worth filling out briefly. Kripke's Wittgenstein holds, crudely, that there are no facts of the matter about what an expression means, how it is generally understood, what accords or fails to accord with a particular rule, what behaviour constitutes implementation of a particular intention, and so on. This is the Sceptical Paradox. We habitually talk as if there were normative realities, constituted by the contents of our sentences, rules, thoughts, intentions, and so on, but the truth is that there are none such. The whole conception of facts to do with meaning and its cognates is mythology.

This wild and absurd-seeming thesis is backed by an impressive argument. In the first instance, Kripke's Wittgenstein constructs a debate about a token claim concerning any past meaning of mine—say, the claim that by '+' I formerly meant addition. I am to defend the claim and the sceptic is to contest it. You might think that even if I were to lose the debate, no conclusions about the *reality* of meanings, rules, etc. would be in prospect—the only conclusion licensed would be that the *epistemology* of claims about meaning was no more straightforward than, under sceptical pressure, the epistemology of *the past* or *the material world* has turned out to be. But that would be wrong. Traditional forms of scepticism make much issue of what are taken to be intrinsic cognitive predicaments of ours—it is contended that we are, necessarily, screened from direct knowledge of others' mental states, the past, and the characteristics of matter, and are therefore restricted to inferences from behaviour, the present and our own experience. By contrast, the debate with Kripke's Wittgenstein's Sceptic proceeds under conditions of *cognitive idealization*: in my attempt to justify my claim that by '+' I formerly meant addition, I am presumed to have perfect recall of all aspects of my former behaviour and mental life. And the governing strategic thought is precisely that, *were* there a fact about what I formerly meant by '+', it would have somehow to be constituted in aspects of my former behaviour and mental life; and would therefore, under the idealization, be salient to me. Accordingly, if I still lose the debate with the Sceptic, even so idealized, it follows that there can indeed be no such fact. This conclusion is then easily developed to generate, successively, that there are no facts about what I presently mean, no facts about what anyone else presently means, nor, therefore, any facts about what any expression means or, correlatively, about what uses comply with it.

Thus, in briefest outline, the overriding strategy of the argument for the Sceptical Paradox. And now it might seem quite straightforward how these ideas, if sustained, would dislodge the realist conception of pure mathematics and support the opposed Wittgensteinian ideas which we rehearsed. The basic conclusion is that there are, necessarily, no facts about meaning. It follows that there can be no such thing as a reflective exploration within the domain of meanings, no such thing as creating a concept and then, by an analysis and proof, verifying characteristics of it which, unwittingly, we have put into our creation. There simply is no coherent conception to be had, if the Sceptical Paradox is accepted, of the subject matter to which such an investigation would be responsive. So pure mathematical proofs cannot be instruments of discovery concerning such a subject matter—there are no such discoveries to be made. *A fortiori*, they cannot be a source of a special, *cognitively earned* certainty; and any sense of constraint, or compulsion, which they inspire in us cannot properly be conceived as a by-product of recognition of our obligations, so to speak, to conceptual structures which we ourselves have erected.

On further reflection, however, the ability of the meaning-scepticism, developed by Kripke's Wittgenstein, to motivate the philosophy of mathematics propounded by the actual Wittgenstein comes to seem less clear. Wittgenstein, as the passages above quoted illustrate, did not merely repudiate the intuitive realist conception of mathematical proof and objectivity; he proposed, in addition, a suggestive alternative conception—the conception of the mathematician as the developer of 'new measures' of reality, the architect of 'new roads for traffic', new tracks for the use of language to follow. The proper exegesis of this positive direction in his thought would be a matter of detail which we cannot undertake here. But this much seems to be clear: the general drift of the proposal has to be *conservative* of our intuitive understanding of rules, and rule-governed practices. If the pure mathematician is to be seen, broadly, not as the explorer of a special domain but the inventor of new forms of description, new rules linking together concepts which we are already accustomed to apply in non-pure mathematical contexts, then there has to be such a thing as *changing and extending* the way a discourse is properly practised. And that is a notion of which we can make sense only under the aegis of the distinction between practices which conform with the rules as they were before, and practices which reflect a modification in those rules generated by some pure mathematical development. Unless, then, there is such a thing as practice which is in line with a rule, contrasting with practice which is not, there is simply no chance of a competitive construal of Wittgenstein's positive proposals. But that distinction, it would seem, is precisely what we have lost if what is driving the negative proposals is the meaning-scepticism propounded by Kripke's Wittgenstein.

Someone familiar with Kripke's text may want to protest that this is to ignore the role of the so-called Sceptical Solution. The Sceptical Solution attempts an accommodation with the Sceptical Paradox. A proponent of the Sceptical Solution grants that there are indeed no substantial facts about meaning, understanding, or any of the other cognate notions; but disputes that the propriety of ordinary discourse in which such notions are implicated has to be a casualty of that concession. The casualty is rather a certain conception of the kind of content which such discourse has—the conception, precisely, that it is a kind of content which may be explicated in terms of the idea of correspondence to fact. The role of a statement like

The rules of addition dictate that $29+13$ is 42

is not to report a state of affairs, but, for instance, to express a condition compliance with which we treat as a criterion for competence in adding.[4] According to the Sceptical Solution, then, our right to continue with our ordinary talk of rules, and of what complies with them and breaches them, is not jeopardized by the Sceptical Paradox. What we lose is only a certain philosophical picture of what, when we engage in such discourse, underwrites the distinction between correct and incorrect assertions within it.

But it is doubtful whether this helps. Let us describe as *content-committed* all discourse which, in one way or another, deals with meaning or any of its cognate notions—in general, all discourse which falls within the scope of the Sceptical Solution if the Sceptical Paradox is accepted; and as *robustly truth-conditional* all putatively factual discourse whose status as such can survive the Paradox. It is a matter of controversy whether a proponent of the Sceptical Solution can provide in plausible detail the sort of semantic proposals for content-committed discourse which he owes. One, as it seems to me, very impressive reason for doubting so is that the scope of content-committed discourse threatens, given three natural assumptions, to become universal.

The first assumption is the platitude that the truth-value of a statement, as used on a particular occasion, is a function of its content, so used, and the then obtaining state of the world in relevant respects. The second is that it is an *a priori* truth, for anyone who understands English, that the result of substituting any truth-apt sentence in English for 'P' in the following schema will generate a truth:

'P' is true if and only if P.

The third is that no true biconditional can have as its constituents a fact-stating sentence—one about whose content a robust, truth-conditional conception is appropriate—and a sentence which is not apt for truth

---

[4] It might be said, similarly, by an opponent of moral realism that the role of the sentence

'Lying is wrong'

is not to describe a moral fact, but to express a condition compliance with which is a necessary condition for avoiding moral disapprobation.

and falsity at all, since it is not in the business of depiction of states of affairs but has a quite different role.

With these premises in place, we may reason as follows. Since, by the first, platitudinous assumption, truth-value on an occasion is always a function, in part, of content, and since—by the Sceptical Paradox—what it is correct to think about the content of a sentence, as used on a particular occasion, is not a substantial question, it follows that the truth-value of the sentence, as used on that occasion, is not a substantial question either. So no matter *what* English sentence we substitute for 'P'. '"P" is true' is never a robustly truth-conditional claim. And since, by our second assumption, it is co-acceptable with the claim that P, it follows—by the third assumption—that the claim that P is not robustly truth-conditional either. So nothing is robustly truth-conditional (cf. Wright, 1984, 769).

This reasoning may, perhaps, be resisted. In his (1989) Paul Boghossian independently develops a somewhat different argument to similar effect. Reacting to this argument, Simon Blackburn believes himself to find in it a confusion between use and mention; that is, he believes it illicitly jumps a gap between establishing a result, in point of robust truth-conditionality, about the *metalinguistic* assertion that 'P' is true, and justifying a conclusion in that respect about the object-language assertion that P.[5]

Which, precisely, of the two assumptions—the second and third—which just now enabled us to argue for the validity of that transition, Blackburn would want to deny, is a matter of speculation. But prescinding from the details of that argument, and of Boghossian's, it is hard to see in general terms how the result about the metalinguistic assertion could fail to be transferable. How could the claim that P escape the fate of its metalinguistic counterpart if the latter's fate is sealed merely by the involvement of content? Language is not a mere clothing for thought. We have no wordless contact with the thought that P: if we are to assess it, it has to be given to us *linguistically*. And our assessment will then be a function of the content which we find in its linguistic mode of presentation and of what we take to be the state of the world in relevant respects. Knowing what claim a particular use of a sentence makes is not and could not be a matter of pairing the sentence with an item that was somehow identified non-linguistically. If your and my sole language is English, then, in order to assess my claim that the cat is on the mat, it will be no less necessary for you to form a judgment about the content of 'The cat is on the mat' than if I had said that 'The cat is on the mat' is true. We have no grip on the question of

---

[5] Simon Blackburn, 'Wittgenstein's Irrealism' (forthcoming).

the truth-status of a claim that does not make it into the question whether a tokening of a sentence is true.

If all claims are content-committed—depend, in this way, upon the facts about meaning—then a proponent of the Sceptical Solution faces the daunting task of providing not merely a reconstructive, non-robustly truth-conditional semantics for all our declarative discourse, but also of explaining—when there are, perforce, no examples now to draw upon—what exactly it is that is being repudiated; what exactly robust truth-conditionality should be supposed to come to. And there is in addition a specific concern about how the *cogency* of the argument to the Sceptical Paradox can survive a non-truth-conditional reconstruction of its premises, lemmas, and conclusion. These issues are all very discussable.[6] But at present there seems every reason to question whether Kripke's Wittgenstein has the materials for a coherent philosophy of language.

That the package of Sceptical Paradox and Sceptical Solution is, if it is, unstable, is not, of course, a conclusive reason for refusing to ascribe it to Wittgenstein or for denying that it could have provided a key motive for his distinctive ideas about mathematics. But prudence, and the urge to learn, would dictate that we look for something better. What, if not that there are no substantial facts about the content of rules and about what complies with or breaches them, should the principal conclusion of Wittgenstein's discussion to be taken to be? And is there any prospect of a spin-off which, as Kripke anticipated, makes a case for each of the key features of Wittgenstein's philosophy of mathematics?

Since, for reasons that may already be apparent, the answer to the second question must, I believe, be negative, there is no point in getting embroiled—on this occasion—in the first. But I cannot forbear to say a little. Wittgenstein's general point, as I read him, is that coming to understand a particular rule, and acquiring thereby the ability to follow it in new cases, is not a matter of learning to keep track of something whose direction is dictated, somehow or other, independently of the judgements on the matter of anyone who might be regarded as competent. Wittgenstein's discussion of rule-following is directed against the mythological sublimation of rules and content, crystallized in traditional platonism, which allows the course assumed by the proper application of a rule—for instance, the identity of the series generated by an arithmetical function—to be thought of as generated purely by the rule itself, and of our judgements, when we competently follow it, as responses to states of affairs which are constituted quite independently. Such a picture seems to provide simultaneously both a certain

---

[6] And are further discussed in Crispin Wright and Paul Boghossian, 'Meaning-irrealism and Global Irrealism', forthcoming.

cognitive dignity for our rule-governed practices and an explanation of *why* we are able, by and large, to agree about what constitutes proper performance within them. It is rather as if we all had hold of the same railings. But for Wittgenstein, on the contrary, the conception of the content of a rule, thus sublimated, is unintelligible, and the epistemology of rule-following for which it calls—the account demanded of how we are able to *recognize* the requirements of rules when they are so conceived—impossible. In consequence, no real explanation is provided of our ability to concur in our use of language and in other rule-governed practices. And it is, indeed, a philosophical error to think that such an explanation is needed. No ulterior cognitive accomplishment underwrites our disposition, on receipt of similar explanations, to proceed to follow rules in similar ways.[7]

A host of questions arise, of course. The position outlined can maintain its distinction from that of Kripke's Wittgenstein, for instance, only if there can be an *unsublimated* conception of the content of rules, which nevertheless conserves our right to think of the requirements of rules as somehow substantial, and questions about whether a particular move is in or out of line as factual. Moreover it is all very well to say that we should not think of the requirements of a rule on a particular occasion as constituted, as it were platonically, in all independence of our judgements, but must there not also be some positive story: some account of the precise form of the dependence which we are being urged to recognize? Wittgenstein, it seems, thought not. And if so, then that view too requires explanation.

Whatever the correct upshot of engaging these various questions would be, it is hard not to feel that Wittgenstein is in range, in his discussions of rule following, of a most profound insight, even if philosophers have yet to clinch it definitively. And I think it is right that the general direction of his remarks, as just briefly characterized and without further analysis, does suffice to explain *some* aspects of his philosophy of mathematics. If our ongoing judgements are somehow primitively involved in determining the content of the rules that compose the decimal expansion of Π, would that not suffice to explain remarks like:

> however queer it sounds, the further expansion of an irrational number is a further expansion of mathematics . . . I want to say, it looks as though the ground for a decision were already there, and it is yet to be invented. (RFM, IV, 9, quoted above)

It is *we* who compose the decimal expansion of Π by the judgements concerning its expansion which, step by step, we find, ultimately,

---

[7] For further discussion of these ideas, and of the perplexities they generate, see my (1989a, b).

agreeable; for in making these judgements we do not align ourselves with requirements that are somehow constituted independently of us, but apply concepts primitively, in the sense that the conformity of such applications to some externally constituted standard makes no sense.

The truth is that the ideas on rules can motivate much of what Wittgenstein says about platonism in the philosophy of mathematics, and about mathematical objectivity and logical compulsion—and, in general, can explain his opposition to ideas about mathematics that overlook what we might call the 'anthropological contribution'. What they cannot explain are his distinctive remarks about proof and the status, in point of certainty, of the conclusions of proof. And we have, in effect, already glimpsed the reason for saying so, in the train of thought, levelled against the Sceptical Solution, that led to the conclusion that all discourse is 'content committed'.

That train of thought was that, since the recognition of meaning is an inextricable ingredient in the appraisal of any statement whatever, any general thesis about the epistemology and objectivity of meaning will be liable to widen into a thesis about the epistemology and objectivity of discourse in general. If, as in Kripke's discussion, the thesis is taken to be that discourse concerning such matters is devoid of genuinely factual content, then as noted, we get the dubiously coherent conclusion that that is the situation of all declarative discourse. If on the other hand the claim is the, in intention at least, more modest one which we are now entertaining—not that meanings, rules, etc., have no reality but that the truth about them and their requirements is somehow constitutionally responsive to our ongoing judgements and reactions—then the conclusion will be that truth in general is constitutionally responsive in the same way. The argument appealed to the platitude that the truth-value of a sentence, as used on a particular occasion, will be a function of its content and the state of the world in relevant respects. If its content, as so used—or, what comes to the same thing, the condition on how the state of the world in relevant respects has to be in order for the sentence to express a truth—is, so to speak, unmade in advance of appropriate, primitive judgements from us, then so is the truth-value of the utterance of the sentence in question. And now it seems that, in whatever sense the ideas about rule following afford the consequence that the further expansion of Π is a mathematical novelty, *all* discoveries, in whatever area of inquiry, are likewise novelties. We cannot keep our thumbs out of the scales anywhere.

But it is unmistakable that Wittgenstein intended a *distinctive* thesis about proof. His claim was not that, in some hopelessly sublimated sense of 'discovery', exploded by the rule-following considerations, proofs are not instruments of discovery; it was that, even when the notion of discovery is viewed aright, and many ordinary things do stand as discoveries, mathematical proofs do not. If the foregoing thoughts are right, then the ideas about rules, whatever the best development of their general direction and detail, cannot substantiate this claim. So we should think again.[8]

III

How should the claim that something is, or is not, a technique of discovery be appraised? Well, whatever constitutes the *discovery* that a proposition is true had better be a process, or sequence of events, which leaves someone who fully understands that proposition with no justifiable option but to assent to it. But of course one may always justifiably refuse assent to the conclusion of a proof in mathematics if one may justifiably refuse assent to the claim that what is presented is indeed a proof.[9] It follows that proofs are properly regarded as instruments whereby we discover mathematical facts only if there is in general no justifiable way whereby the status of a proof may be disputed—at least a wide class of proofs must be such that one who fully understands the concepts involved and works through all the steps has no justifiable option but to assent to the claim that what is presented is indeed a proof.

If this is right, then an effective way of attacking the mathematical realist conception of proof is to argue that a proper understanding of each of the notions in play in a proof and a full empirical awareness of its detail never completely constrain our assent; that the status of something as a proof is left underdetermined by its strictly cognitive aspects. When we ratify a proof, we go beyond anything that is required of us purely by acknowledgment of features of the presented construction.

This is, as we have noted, consonant with the general direction of Wittgenstein's remarks. Proofs do indeed do less than compel our assent:

> Do not look at the proof as a procedure that *compels* you, but as one that *guides* you. (RFM, III, 30)

But what does Wittgenstein say to make it clear that this is a practical option? What would it be to *refuse* the 'guidance' offered by a particular (putative) proof? The whole point about good proofs is that they strike us as *cogent*. And Wittgenstein himself stresses that it is of the essence of proof that it produce complete conviction:

[8] This point was perhaps the most important factor determining the overall direction of the argument of my (1980).

[9] Provided, of course, that no other proof of the same conclusion is known to one.

A proof shows what *ought* to come out.—And since every reproduction of the proof must demonstrate the same thing, while on the one hand it must reproduce the result automatically, on the other hand it must also reproduce the *compulsion* to get it. (RFM, II, 55)

How can these remarks be made to cohere? How can it be of the essence of proof that it produce complete conviction and, at the same time, of the nature of proof that it merely guides towards the conception of things embodied in its conclusion?

Take a simple example: suppose I calculate that $26 \times 23 = 598$. The calculation constitutes a proof only so long as it secures my conviction that no other outcome than 598 is possible if I correctly multiply 26 by 23. For if I have any doubt about that, I will not consider that I have a proof. Yet—according to Wittgenstein—I am simultaneously supposed to be able to see the proof as providing guidance, rather than compulsion, as constituting merely, as it were, an advocate of the complex set of convictions involved in accepting its conclusion—the conviction, for instance, that if 598 two-inch square tiles do not suffice to cover a rectangular surface, which I have measured as 46 inches by 52, then I must have mismeasured. So I am simultaneously *both* to see no alternative to accepting the proof which the calculation accomplishes, and the ways of looking at things dictated by its conclusion—otherwise I will not be persuaded that I have a proof at all—*and*, following Wittgenstein's advice, to view the proof not as *teaching* that its conclusion is correct, but merely as guiding me towards a decision, as it were, to count it so. How is this schizophrenic feat to be carried off?

The tension is resolved when we take the remarks about compulsion to pertain to the *phenomenology* of proof, and the talk of guidance to relate to its *cognitive status*. Consider an analogy. No-one but a theoretically committed philosopher would think that the sense of humour is, literally, a cognitive sense—something which enables us to detect real comic values, out there in the world. Finding a situation funny involves, no doubt, cognition of many features of it; but the comic response itself is contributed by the affective, rather than cognitive, side of our nature. Nevertheless, we should not count as finding a situation funny if our reaction to it were somehow a matter of choice. It is of the essence of comic responses that they seem to the responder to be elicited from without—you can simulate finding something funny, but you cannot bring it about by will that you do.

So also, in Wittgenstein's view, with the intellectual response—the conviction—generated by a proof. If a calculation is to impress us as proving its result, it has to convince us that no other outcome is possible if the sequence of operations which it contains are performed correctly. But it is one thing to say that we register that conviction in judging something to be a proof; another to say that the conviction is a purely cognitive accomplishment.

The question remains: given that the phenomenology of proof is essentially compulsive, wherein consists the cognitive freedom which Wittgenstein thinks we nevertheless possess? To get a sense of the kind of thought which leads him here, we need to look at his repeated discussions of the relations between proof, especially calculation, and experiment.[10]

Typical proofs, and all calculations, involve a *process* we start at a particular point, run through a series of prescribed operations—correctly, to the best of our ability—and get a certain result. So too with, say, a laboratory experiment: we set up an apparatus in a certain initial state, carry out certain operations upon it, and a certain result ensues. And both a proof and an experiment which, when repeated, consistently gives the same result, may prompt our assent to a conditional statement along the following lines:

> If, starting on such-and-such a basis, such-and-such procedures are properly carried out, then such-and-such results.[11]

This statement need not, in the case of proofs in general, be that which we regard the proof as primarily proving—though it always is precisely that in the case of a calculation. But one thing is clear: our willingness to acknowledge a proof as a proof—what marks it off for us from an experiment—depends upon our willingness to accept that this conditional statement holds of *necessity*: our willingness to accept that there is, in the case of the process in question, an *internal* connection between basis, steps and outcome.[12]

You can begin to get a sense of Wittgenstein's concern if, bearing in mind the very analogy between proof and an experiment, you now ask: what is it about a calculation, say—about the routine of carefully running through a calculation—which puts us in position to make a *necessitated* assertion? What do we recognize about the calculation that

---

[10] A selection of relevant passages from RFM (second edition) would include part I, sections 36–57, 75–103 and 156–64; part II, sections 55 and 65–76; part III, sections 46–53; and part V, sections 6, 14–15, 17 and 40. Germane material published for the first time in the third, revised, edition includes Appendix II, part VI, sections 1–10, 15–16 and 36; and part VII, sections 25–6. Cora Diamond's edition of the (1939) *Lectures on the Foundations of Mathematics* (LFM) touches on the issues in lectures iii (36–9), vii (71 and following), x and xi *passim,* and xiii (128–30).

[11] What I have elsewhere called the *corresponding descriptive conditional.* See my (1980), p. 452; also (1986c), pp. 203–4; and (1989c), pp. 231–2.

[12] This is what Wittgenstein means when he says—RFM, III, 41—that *causality* must play no part in a proof.

justifies the claim that the particular result *must* result from that particular process on that particular starting point? Why is our entitlement not exhausted by the claim, merely, that this is what resulted when, so far as we can tell, the calculation was done correctly—and probably always will result when we are so convinced?

The point to be explained is not that we are supremely certain of the truth of the corresponding conditional in the case of a calculation and merely, say, highly confident in the case of an experiment. I may well be more confident about the repeatability of an experiment than about the conclusion of a complex calculation, but still prepared to assert both the relevant conditionals. The crux is rather that, in the case of a calculation, we make a claim of a quite different kind. The 'must' is an expression, not of certainty, but of the conviction that the conditional, if true, is sustained by factors quite other than those which sustain its experimental counterpart. Yet the confirmatory processes seem similar; in each case we have, surely, only ordinary empirical grounds for identifying the starting point and conclusion, and only ordinary empirical certainty that appropriate controls have been properly applied on the intervening steps.

This is the problem that runs through much of Wittgenstein's discussion. A common thought, which will see no problem here, will want to credit us with a special intuitive faculty—a necessity-detector, as it were—which is summoned into action in 'reading' a proof. At the purely empirical level there is, it will be granted, no material difference between a proof and an experiment. And that just shows that, in order to detect the difference—to distinguish processes in which basis, steps and outcome are all internally related from processes in which they are not—more than merely empirical faculties are demanded.

But this response is at once obscure and *ad hoc*. And now we may feel the attraction of a simple opposing strategy of response: make out that the contrast between the two kinds of process, so far from needing explanation in terms of special cognitive faculties, is not properly speaking, a *cognitive* contrast at all. Consider a favourite example of Wittgenstein's: a rule of conversion between units of measurement in distinct systems—say, 'One inch equals 2.54 centimetres'. If we were at a point in history when there had been no interaction between users of the Imperial and Metric systems respectively, we would have to set about appraising that statement empirically: measuring objects using instruments calibrated in each unit, and determining statistically the limit of the ratios in which the results stood. Yet the proposition, if true, is surely *no contingency*—it expresses an internal relation between the concepts of correctly measuring in centimetres and correctly measuring in inches. So a similar problem arises: how could we possibly verify that an internal relation obtained by (broadly) statistical empirical methods?

The answer is that we do not. Rather, we *already* have the idea that there must be an internal relation here, and what we identify empirically is the *best candidate* for what the internal relation is. And so too, in Wittgenstein's view, with a calculation: the calculation excites no special intuitive faculty—rather we are already 'in the market' for an internal relation between basis, process and outcome, and doing the calculation, perhaps with repeated checks, makes an ordinary empirical case for what the internal relation in question is.

The crucial issue accordingly becomes: what puts us 'in the market'? Do we *recognize*, by dint of who knows what cognitive faculties, that the rules of multiplication *can* only ever generate one result when correctly applied to a particular set of factors? Or is it rather that here 'correctness' precludes variation in the outcome as a matter of (something akin to) *convention*?

The contrast, thus expressed, is crudely drawn. But many commentators have found in Wittgenstein a view of the second broad sort—albeit one in which the notion of convention is softened by considerations concerning our natures and unreflective practices. We do not, as it were, explicitly lay it down that the rules of multiplication do not count as correctly applied in cases where variation in output is unaccompanied by variation in input. It is merely that

> *We do not accept* e.g. a multiplication's not yielding the same result every time. (RFM, III, 52)

—our *practice* is not to tolerate such variation. And whereas, for the cognitivist, this practice is backed by a *perception*—an insight into what the rules of multiplication make possible—for Wittgenstein it may be accepted simply as primitive and groundless:

> This is use and custom among us, or a fact of our natural history. (RFM, I, 63)

What are the options if our inclination is to try to underwrite the 'must' which we incorporate into the conclusion of a calculation, with a substantial epistemology? Only the two canvassed, it might seem: *either* the details of a specific calculation somehow excite an intuitional recognition that what results must result, *or* there is only an empirical routine, but a routine which is informed by the general *a priori* insight that proper implementation of these rules cannot generate variable outcome. But either line precariously offers hostages for redemption by the theory of knowledge.

Wittgenstein's alternative, in contrast, promises what may seem the clear advantage of handling the mathematical 'must' within an empiricist epistemology. In Wittgenstein's view, the internal relations which articulate the interconnections within a proof are acknowledged by way of institution or custom, following on empirical findings. And this background of unreflective custom is not something in which our participation is imposed by purely cognitive considerations. So a faultless understanding of each of the notions in play in a proof and a full empirical awareness of its detail underdetermine assent to it; one needs, in addition, to be party to the relevant practices. And if that is right, then—by the criterion I offered at the start of this section—proofs are not instruments of discovery.

It remains to record the advertised cause for dissatisfaction. This is that the two alternatives we canvassed for the cognitivist—construction-triggered intuitions, or background *a priori* insights—do not exhaust the field. The reason is that the simplest ingredient steps in a calculation, or in formal proofs in general, are typically certified by operations which are primitively given as *functions*: operations which are *identified*, in part, by the characteristic that only variation in input can generate variation in output.[13] Wittgenstein's view has it that a culture might deploy the same arithmetical concepts as we do, but without the institutional setting that leads us to dignify the products of calculation as necessary. That requires that there be fully adequate modes of explanation of arithmetical operations that are, so to speak, neutral on the question whether their output may vary for fixed input. And that is most implausible. There is no hiatus between an understanding of arithmetical addition, for instance, and the knowledge that it is a function. Rather, it has to be an explicit part of any adequate explanation of the concept of addition that no pair of numbers has more than one sum. Not to know that is not to know what adding is. There is no stripped-down concept which is somehow neutral on the matter.

The crucial Wittgensteinian claim is that participation in the 'institutional setting' is no part of the conditions for *understanding* arithmetical operations. If that is wrong, then someone who fully understands those operations and properly assesses the empirical features of a correct calculation will have no rational option but to assent to its finding. And that will restore a scaled-down cognitivism, independent of intuitions and *a priori* insights: recognizing the 'must' that underlies a calculation will simply be a matter of applying concepts as one was taught them to an empirically given construction. These matters need much fuller discussion beyond the scope of this paper. But perhaps the preceding will convey at least something of the geography of the issues raised by Wittgenstein's mature thought about mathematical proof.[14]

[13] I am here by-passing complications to do with rules of inference, like vel-intro., which permit more than one conclusion from given premises. For further discussion, see my (1989c), pp. 234–5.

[14] For a somewhat fuller account see my (1989c), section IV.

Language and Conversation: Wittgenstein's Builders

RAIMOND GAITA

I

We may reflect on language in different ways. There is the way familiar to analytical philosophers. That may take different forms, but most of them are strikingly different from the way of someone like Elias Canetti or F. R. Leavis, whose thought is shaped by their concern with literature. In the latter case language appears as an essentially human phenomenon, not because it is limited to the species Homo sapiens, but because it is essentially connected with the culture and histories of *peoples*, whose plurality is underdetermined by any elaboration on the nature and environmental conditions of Homo sapiens. It is rare to find analytical philosophers of language for whom that is important or who have tried even to sketch the kind of importance it may have. That is because they assume that it is not important to language as such (to what makes something language) but only to the sophisticated use of language in poetry or literature. They have tended to misunderstand the sense in which a language such as English is a *natural* language.

Wittgenstein may be read as an important exception. Rush Rhees does so when, in a recognizably Wittgensteinian critique of Wittgenstein, he connects the kind of sense and nonsense in language with the dances, songs and literature of a people.[1] He does not elaborate the thought and I can go only a small distance on the way to its elaboration. But he goes far enough to invite us to rethink the relations between those parts of *Philosophical Investigations* (PI) which are naturally thought to belong to the philosophy of language and those which are thought to belong to the philosophy of mind. The place of rule following, the remarks on a 'private language' and their connection, then look quite different. I shall try to sketch the salient features of that perspective.

Wittgenstein invites us to imagine a language which 'is meant to serve for communication between a builder A and an assistant B':

A is building with building stones: there are blocks, pillars, slabs and beams. B has to pass the stones, and that in the order which A needs

[1] 'Wittgenstein's Builders' (Rhees, 1970).

them. For this purpose they use a language consisting of the words 'block', 'pillar', 'slab', 'beam'. A calls them out;—B brings the stone which he has learnt to bring at such-and-such a call.—Conceive this as a complete primitive language. (PI, I, 2)

Later he says: 'We could imagine that the language of #2 was the *whole* language of A and B; even the whole language of a tribe' (PI, I, 6). Few people would deny that Wittgenstein meant what he said but few will be untroubled by it—in itself and by the fact that he said it.

There is a natural temptation, but one which is profoundly against the spirit of Wittgenstein's philosophy, to say that something which is like what the builders do *must* have been the origins of all natural languages—that in their beginnings, natural languages must have consisted of a few names which were devised and used to further a common enterprise, and that the features of natural languages which are essentially connected with peoples, their histories and cultures, are sophisticated developments from such primitive languages. Therefore (the thought continues) whatever qualitative discontinuities there may be between language as we have it and what the builders do, they are not of a kind which mark the difference between language and a mere semblance of it.

The kind of language with which Wittgenstein is mostly concerned in *Investigations*—the kind which philosophers called 'ordinary language'—is evidently a natural language and, it would seem, non-accidentally so. If we ask why we are reluctant to call what the builders have a natural language, then, I think, we capture an important part of any answer when we remember that a natural language is not and could not be invented.[2] Anything whose nature is as unrelievedly and transparently purposive as the vocal activities of the builders is likely to be an invention. It would be absurd to say that the builders speak their mother tongue or that they have a living language in the sense in which English is a living language and Latin is a dead one. That does not prove that Wittgenstein should not think that the builders speak a 'primitive language', but it reveals that the difference between what the builders do and what we do when we speak to one another, is of a kind to justify scepticism about whether what they do could be thought to be even a primitive version of what we do—even if something like it was the primitive beginnings of what we do.

Rhees says that he finds it difficult to conceive that the builders speak a language, but not because they have such a small vocabulary. It is

---

[2] Wittgenstein writes (1946) 'Esperanto. The feeling of disgust we get if we utter an *invented* word with invented derivative syllables. The word is cold, lacking in associations, and yet it plays at being "language". A system of purely written signs would not disgust us so much' (CV, 52).

because he finds it hard to see that they have a vocabulary at all, that their shouts are words used in speech, because, *ex*, *hypothesi*, they do not speak them, or any other 'words' elsewhere. They do not seem to do more than signal to one another for the purpose of getting on with the job, in which case they may as well have whistled, as workmen often do. Language, even the most primitive, requires the distinction between sense and nonsense whereas signalling does not. Or—so that it is clear that this is not merely a verbal issue—something which does not permit the distinction between sense and nonsense is so far removed from what we do when we speak with one another, that the point of calling it a language, albeit a primitive one, will have been lost.

The reason Rhees thinks it is important whether or not the putative words of the builders are used elsewhere—that they be part of a way of living which is more than an association for the sake of a common enterprise—is that otherwise their vocal acts will not have the kind of relation to one another which they must have if they are to be sufficiently like the relation which our remarks have to one another in a conversation, or even sufficiently like the relation of our responses to requests or commands, for us to count them as speech. Wittgenstein speaks as though we might look upon what the builders do as like our language game of giving orders and obeying them (PI, I, 18, 19). But our language-game of giving orders—what within it counts as succeeding and failing, understanding and misunderstanding—has the character it has because our lives are penetrated by speech. To paraphrase Wallace Stevens: speech passes through our lives like a thread through a needle; everything we do is stitched with its colour. The same can be said of all language-games which is why it is a mistake to think of language as built up from language-games.

It is now commonplace to emphasize the dependence of meaning on the holistic nature of language. It is sometimes expressed in the claim that language forms a system, which encourages the idea that language is something which God might have bequeathed to us intact, and also the thought that language must be logically prior to speech. In order to speak we must have a language: speaking is something we do with language. That is the assumption. Rhees, however, emphasizes the *interdependence* of speech and language. He argues that the connectedness of language is the connectedness of what we say to one another, and that the kind of connectedness which what we say to one another must have in order for it to be speech, is a function of the fact that some speech is conversation. That is why he believes that in order for the builders' shouts to have *sense* they must have a use elsewhere, and it shows what kind of use he thinks it must be: they must be part of a life in which there is conversation and whose 'form' is conditioned by a common understanding.

In learning to speak [the learner] learns what can be said; he learns, however fumblingly, what it makes sense to say. He comes to have some sense of how different remarks have something to do with one another. That is why he can answer you and ask you things and why he begins to follow a conversation or to carry on a conversation himself. Or, rather, it is misleading to say this is *why* he does that, as though what we had were a condition and what results from it. For in beginning to carry on a conversation, in trying to tell you something and trying to understand your answer, he *is* getting a sense of how different remarks have a bearing upon one another . . . Not all speech is conversation, of course, but I do not think there would be speech or language without it (Rhees, 1970, 80–81).

That introduces a different perspective on the public character of language—the kinds of public-ness it may have—than we will have been used to if we were interested only in the conditions under which a sign (be it mathematical or linguistic) could be correctly used.

Wittgenstein used to speak of teaching a child to multiply by going through examples of multiplication with him, then getting him to go through these and other exercises while you corrected his mistakes, and then saying 'Go on by yourself now'. But if you said something similar about teaching a child to speak you would have left out the most important thing. If he can speak he has got something to tell you (Rhees, 1970, 80).

The implications for most traditional readings of the relation between language and rule following are radical. Rhees emphasizes speech, conversation, the bearing which one remark may have upon another, in order to reveal what *kind* of rule a rule of language is, what it is to keep such a rule and how different it is from rules in mathematics or in a game and the way they are kept. He warns that we will misunderstand the role which our agreements in reaction play in determining what a rule of language is and what it is to keep it, if we do not supplement the idea of agreement in reactions with that of a common understanding.

This does not mean that the remarks made in a language form a system and that they get their sense from that. But it does suggest something like a common understanding. To think of language as a system, or as a kind of method (cf. 'a method of representation', 'method of projection'), almost as a kind of theory, is wrong if only because language is something people speak with one another. In this way it is not at all like mathematics. And it would be confusing to think that 'the language' is related to what is said in it as pure mathematics is related to applied mathematics. At the same time, the comparison suggests something. And when I speak of a common understanding I do not mean simply what Wittgenstein used to call an 'agreement in reaction' which makes it possible to talk about using the word in the same way or using it correctly. It has rather to do with what is taken to make sense, or with what can be understood: with what it is possible to say to people: with what anyone who speaks the language might try to say (Rhees, 1970, 84).

There are two points of emphasis in Rhees' thought here which, although they are interrelated, need independent development. The first is forcefully developed by Cora Diamond. When commenting on Rhees' remark that 'grammatical rules are rules of the lives in which there are language' (Rhees, 1970, 45), she says that 'saying belongs to a life with words, rules of grammar belong to, are part of, having their identity in such a life' (Diamond, 1989, 16). She argues powerfully, through a range of examples, that concepts and rules are public in different ways and that we can form no clear conception of the way a concept or rule is public in isolation from the place of that concept or rule in the life people share (ibid., 25). She asks those who, like Baker and Hacker (1985), deny that Wittgenstein held what they call a 'community conception' of rule following: 'So what is the idea of a language in which the words have some determinate public character, independently of any practices in which who speaks is given this weight or that or none?'

The second point of emphasis is on the place of conversation in our understanding of language and on what that might teach us about the kind of intelligence or understanding which goes with it. Rhees thinks there could not be language without conversation. The interest in that remark lies in the inclination to think that it gets things precisely the wrong way round. In this paper I will focus on this second emphasis and try to diminish that inclination.

II

We may get clearer about the issues I have raised if we see what is wrong with a fine discussion of Rhees' paper by Norman Malcolm. He agrees that there cannot be language without sense and nonsense, but he thinks that there can be sense and nonsense in what the builders say and that it is not dependent on 'full blown conversation'. He writes

Let us suppose that a worker is building a wall. Only slabs are used in this wall: beams are used only in roofs. We may even suppose that beams physically *cannot* be used in walls because of their shape. Now this builder, at work on a wall, calls out to his helper "Beam". The helper looks at him in astonishment—then bursts into laughter.

The startled builder looks at the helper, then at the wall, then back at the helper with a grin of embarrassment, he slaps himself on the head, and then calls out "Slab". The chuckling helper brings him a slab.

Cannot we say that the builder's original call, 'Beam', was, in that situation, *nonsense*; and that first the helper and then the builder perceived that it was nonsense. The utterance 'Beam' was 'incompatible' with the situation. When the builder realized this he made his correction.

It is true that these people do not have conversation. But this exchange was similar to a conversation. The astonishment and laughter of the helper was a 'criticism' of the builder's utterance. The latter's response was an acceptance of the criticism. Rudimentary thinking occurred on both sides—thinking that was exhibited in the rudimentary behaviour. I do no see that full-blown conversation is essential for speech and language, or for the distinction between sense and nonsense (Malcolm, 1989a, 42–43).

Malcolm says that 'The utterance "Beam" was incompatible with the situation.' There is no doubt about that. But the *mere* realization of its incompatibility by both the builder and his helper together with the builder's correction of himself, do not take us beyond their recognition that the builder had made a mistake. It will not take us to the thought that he spoke nonsense as distinct from doing something 'nonsensical' in the sense which means that he did something very silly. If we do get there, then it will be because of the further details of Malcolm's example—the look of astonishment, the laughter and so on. Such behaviour raises the question whether the builders are speaking to one another, whether what they do expresses the kind of understanding and misunderstanding which would incline us to say that Malcolm's builder spoke a kind of nonsense. But Malcolm fails to reveal why that should be so and how it is so.

Suppose that instead of shouting an order the builder on the wall fetched a beam and brought it to the wall. His helper, who had been resting, looks on in astonishment and then bursts out laughing. The builder looks at the beam, looks at the wall and then at the helper with a grin of embarrassment. He slaps himself on the head and then accepts the slab that his chuckling helper had brought him. We can say that he tried to do something nonsensical: beams cannot be used here. But again, this is evidently not the kind of 'nonsense' which is necessary to language. The builder realizes that he cannot do anything with the beam on the wall; but if we discover that we cannot say anything with the words we have used, then that is a different kind of 'cannot'. Malcolm's example is richer than Wittgenstein's, but it does not show that the shouting of 'Slab' and 'Beam' is anything more than a means of achieving something and that our ways of failing to match means to ends may be silly, amusing and so on.

Malcolm says, that 'thinking occurred on both sides'. The nuanced reactions of the builders shows that it is thinking of quite a *subtle* kind even if it is 'rudimentary'. His builder slaps himself on the head as an expression of the recognition of his foolishness or absent-mindedness. He does not slap himself on the head because he tried to say something that could not be said, as happens when someone fails to mean anything with his words. He slaps himself on the head wondering what he is up to. His helper looks on in astonishment and also wonders what the builder is up to. But all this applies to the example I gave when nothing was shouted, and in which we need not attribute to them understanding of anything whose character is determined by that distinctive kind of sense and nonsense which goes with language. Adding their shouts of 'Slab' and 'Beam' to my example does not change the matter: these are merely vocal actions of the same kind, and of the same kind as when the builder points to a spot for his helper to place the beam or the slab. He may keep pointing to the wrong spot and his helper may be astonished, etc. None of this amounts to saying something and we do not get closer to speech just by making the actions vocal.

Immediately after what I have already quoted, Malcolm says;

> The vocabulary of this people consists of only four words. But the *uttering* of those words could have different functions in different circumstances. If a builder says "Block" when a helper expected "Slab", the helper might say "Block?" with an expression of uncertainty. And the builder might repeat "Block!" with emphasis. Here would be something resembling question and reply. The helper would be asking the builder whether he *meant* "Block", and the builder would be saying that he did mean that (Malcolm, 1989, 43).

Malcolm says this in response to the following remarks by Rhees:

> If I know that you can speak, then it makes sense for me to ask you what you mean, to try to get you to say more clearly what you want, and to ask you questions about it: just as truly as it makes sense for me to answer you. The example of the builder does not allow for any of these (Rhees, 1970, 81).

The builder emphatically repeats 'Block'. This is a response to his helper's uncertainty. But what is *unclear* about what the builder did in the first place? If the builder has often been getting things wrong, his helper will be bemused and, perhaps, anxious. Thus, when the helper says 'Block' with an expression of uncertainty we can take him to be expressing the desire to know what the builder wants. He wants to know whether he intended to shout 'Block', or if you like, whether he meant 'Block'. But that means only that either he wanted to know whether he meant to utter that sound, or whether he wanted a block. This is not the same as asking him *what he meant by what he said* in a sense which will give us reason to think that the builders have a language. When I ask you what you mean when you say something, I am not asking you whether this was the sentence that you intended to come out, even when I focus attention on some of the words you used; for if you say that they are exactly the words you intended to come out with, then the question of what you meant is not settled. Nor is it settled by further knowledge of your intentions, or by matching those intentions with features of the situation which are analogous to the fact that only slabs are used on the wall. The distinction between *uttering a sound* for some purpose against the background of an agreed function for that sound in a common enterprise, and saying something, may be obscure, but it is sufficiently serviceable to reveal that Malcolm's builders do not go beyond the former.

We often say things to achieve something, to realize some purpose; but Rhees argues that it is *speech* that we use to achieve our purposes only if there are times when the question of what we are trying to achieve drops out. His point is not merely that he would count what the builders do as speech only if their shouts were used elsewhere. It is that their use elsewhere must be different in kind from their use to achieve something. They must have uses such that questions about why a person said this rather than that, or whether he intended to say this rather than that, do not arise because of a failure on the route between intention, means and ends. When Wittgenstein directed our attention to the use of words or phrases he was not asking us to try to discover the purposes which their use was intended to achieve. We *do* things with words—we have *words* to do things with—only because we do more with them than achieve our purposes.

The builder does not slap himself on the head in order to achieve anything. Nor does his helper chuckle to himself in order to achieve anything. Not all the activity on the building site, as Malcolm describes it, is directed to some end. That is why his example seemed to have the making of a counter-example to Rhees' claims. Malcolm is quite right to say that we need not think that their behaviour on the building site is mechanical. He gives some eloquent examples of their humanity, but he fails to connect their humanity to their speech: it remains external to it. Everything that displays their humanity fails to enter their supposed speech and vice versa. The chuckling, the head slapping and so on in Malcolm's example, do not alter the unrelievedly purposive character of the builders' utterances of 'Slab', 'Beam', etc. That is the deep lesson of Malcolm's failure.

Language and Conversation: Wittgenstein's Builders

At the end of his paper Malcolm suggests why we need not find it implausible that the builders have words only for building stones 'but none for food and danger, day or night, sleeping or walking, illness or death, or changes in the weather' (Malcolm, 1989, 43). He offers a sketch of their lives. As I understand it, the point of the sketch is to reveal that they have no need of such words: they are 'simple people leading a simple life'. He asks 'Why is the activity of building so important for them that their only words are the names of building stones. And what is the purpose of the buildings?' He answers by inviting us to imagine that 'the adults of the tribe are like our small children, who delight in creating structures out of sand, or from little building blocks of wood—but for no purpose other than the activity itself. The people of the tribe do not use the buildings but sometimes they like to look at them' (ibid., 44). Building is a kind of game for them and Malcolm shows why their 'language' remains contained within the game. But that is exactly what troubled Rhees:

> The point of the various moves and counter-moves is within the game, whereas we may learn from a conversation and what is said in it. Generally each of us brings something to a conversation . . . not as he may bring skill to a game, but in having something to say . . . The pieces of chess are furnished to you—you do not have to find them or decide what they will be. (Rhees, 1970, 81).

The questions which emerge from Malcolm's elaboration of language game 2 are: how is the humanity of the builders relevant to whether or not they speak? And how does it connect with the kind of understanding which must be attributed to anyone who speaks?

III

Rhees writes:

> If I doubt whether you know the language, or if I doubt whether you ever know what you are saying, then in many ways I must regard you more as a regard [a machine]. *This is not because you do not do anything that other people do. It is because you do not take part in what they do.* [My emphasis.] And speaking the language they speak is not just uttering the words; any more than understanding the language is just 'recognizing' the words. It is carrying on a conversation, for instance; or it may be writing reports, or listening to a play in the theatre. It is being someone to whom the rest of us can speak and get an answer; to whom we can tell something and with whom we can make a joke and whom we can deceive. All this, and of course immeasurably more, belongs to speaking the language. And it

belongs to being able to follow words. You can follow words because you can know how to speak. And for the same reason a machine cannot follow words. This has nothing to do with what physics and engineering may achieve. It is just that it makes no sense to say that a machine might follow words. (Rhees, 1970, 67)

His point is that we misunderstand the difficulty we may have in believing that a machine might speak with us if we think it is over the question whether we could build a machine which would 'realize' those psychological states which are necessary for the capacity to speak. It is natural to think that the answer to the question whether machines could speak will depend upon what kind of machine we are (in principle) able to build. From one perspective it looks to be obvious. That is because it appears to be obvious that we are able to speak because of how we are psychologically; and many philosophers believe that how we are psychologically is a function of how we are physically in ways which will eventually be made perspicuous by one of the varieties of materialism. But it remains problematic for them what the relation is between psychological and physical states—could the psychological states be 'realized' in something other than flesh and blood (plastic perhaps)? Some also wonder whether interaction with other 'entities' of similar psychological and physical kinds is necessary for the actualization of the capacity for speech.

One way of characterizing the problem is to ask what would make us remove the inverted commas from the description of what machines do when they are also descriptions of things we do. Machines do not play chess they 'play' chess. The natural reply is that we could remove the inverted commas if we built into a machine the functional equivalent of whatever we have which enables us, or which, at any rate, gives us the unactualized capacity, to play rather than 'play' chess. However, that might merely extend the repertoire of things which machines can do in inverted commas. Is there an inverted commas capacity, or a cluster of them such that its justified attribution to a machine should convince us to remove the inverted commas from it and from others—understanding perhaps? If a machine could understand what it does then it would converse with us rather than 'converse' with us, play with us rather than 'play' with us and so on. But what would make us believe that a machine could understand what it does? Would we believe it if the machine could respond in ways which were both rational and unpredictable to its creators; or something of that *kind*?

Rhees' answer, and I am sure that it is also Wittgenstein's, is that the machine would have to live a life such as ours. Living a life and speaking out of it, is what is necessary for the attribution of the kind of intelligence, the kind of understanding, expressed by someone to whom it is even intelligible to respond as to someone who may bring something to a conversation, who may have 'something to say'.

Could we not, in principle, build a machine which leads a human life—give or take a little? We are inclined to say that then it would not be a machine. Is there a way of expressing that which avoids both begging the important questions and triviality? I think there is and that we get to it if we ask whether the acknowledgment of the need to build a machine which lives (more or less) a human life is compatible with the sense of 'capacity' which informed the original question whether machines might have, like us, a capacity for speech? It seems to be a sense of capacity which makes it *accidental* to our capacity to speak that we live the kind of life in time which we do, and accidental that our lives are the lives of creatures of flesh and blood.

Wittgenstein says that 'only of a human being and what resembles (behaves like) a living human being can one say: it has sensations; it sees; is blind; hears; is deaf; is conscious or unconscious' (PI, I, 281). Should we add: 'it speaks'? I think the answer is, yes. But the reason is not because only human beings and what behaves like them have what is psychologically necessary to speak. That is the thought Rhees was opposing when he said that whether or not a machine can 'follow words . . . has nothing to do with what physics and engineering may achieve'. But then why should we say that only human beings and what behaves like them can speak; and what should we count as 'behaving like' a human being?

In part two of *Investigations* Wittgenstein says: 'My attitude towards him is an attitude towards a soul. I am not of the *opinion* that he has a soul' (PI, II, IV). Peter Winch said that we should understand 'an attitude towards a soul' to be a condition rather than a consequence of the ascription of mental predicates.[3] This turns on its head the almost irresistibly natural thought that we react to one another as to persons—as to 'other minds'—because we know, believe, or conjecture that others have psychological states more or less as we do. The point here is not merely epistemological. We have two different conceptions of subjectivity and of what it is for another to be someone with whom we can speak. Wittgenstein seems to believe that our interactions with one another which are of the kind he calls 'an attitude towards a soul', are constitutive of (rather than based upon) our sense of being of a common kind, and of that humanly centred sense of what we find it *intelligible* to say of creatures who are in some respects like, but in others quite unlike, ourselves. He did not mean Homo sapiens when he spoke of human beings, nor did he think the extension of those terms would

³ Peter Winch, 'Eine Einstellung zur Seele', *Proceedings of the Aristotelian Society* (1980). Reprinted in Winch, 1987.

necessarily be the same. The main reason why he spoke as he did of human beings is not because the expression 'human beings' has, as we sometimes use it, moral connotations, but because the scientific definition of Homo sapiens, which determines its extension, treats as *superficial* properties of the species, those things which are fundamental to the kinds of reactions which are attitudes 'to a soul'. That is the first part of an answer to why the plurality of natural languages is not to be explained by elaboration on the nature and environmental conditions of Homo sapiens.

Wittgenstein says: 'If someone has a pain in his hand, then the hand does not say so (unless it writes it) and one does not comfort the hand, but the sufferer: one looks into his face' (PI, I, 286). Immediately afterwards (in the next paragraph) he asks 'How am I filled with pity *for this man*? How does it come out what the object of my pity is?' Binding a person's wounds and looking into his face is an example of an attitude towards a soul: that it is, in general, natural for us to do such things conditions the concepts through which we understand the object of our pity—of what it is to be one-who-suffers-in-that-way. I intend, by this lapse into such unsightly nominalization, to signal the interdependence of our concept of pain, the kind of suffering which it is to be in pain (the sort of thing philosophers call the 'phenomenological qualities' of pain, or its 'qualia'), the kind of subject to whom we may intelligibly attribute such suffering, and those interacting responses which are 'attitudes towards a soul'. It is fundamental to Wittgenstein's thought on this subject that we cannot affect a radical detachment of the forms of our sympathy from our understanding of the object of our sympathies. Or, to put the point more generally: *we cannot extract our reactions from the bodily forms which constitute their expressiveness, without threatening the concepts with which they are interdependent*. If we think our attitudes towards a soul are paradigmatically directed to members of the species Homo sapiens and to other creatures through sympathetic extension, for reasons which, at their deepest, will be revealed by those sciences which study Homo sapiens, then we will misunderstand the kind of subjectivity—and thus the kind of intersubjectivity—which goes with speech. This leads to a distortion of the kind of understanding which is internal to speech, as being a kind of brain power. It is the sort of thing which Colin McGinn seems to have in mind when he imagines that 'Romulus [of Romulus and Remus] upon reaching the age of reason, hits upon the idea of distributing signposts around his island as an aide memoire' (McGinn, 1984, 196).

Winch (following Wittgenstein) called the reactions which are attitudes towards a soul 'primitive'. That has many connotations—that they are pre-linguistic, that they are without justification, but it also suggests that they are *natural* reactions (I called them that myself), and one might wonder, in the light of what I have been saying, in what sense are they 'natural'? Are they not animal reactions and does not Wittgenstein himself speak this way?[4] Are we not animals of the species Homo sapiens and will not our understanding of our reactions and capacities be deepened by science? And have we not now uncovered the route to the kind of materialism which goes with that sense of 'capacity' which makes it plausible that we could construct a machine which might converse with us?

The answer is yes and no, but mainly no. It is common to contrast our animality with what has been shaped by culture, to contrast nature with nurture, in ways which assume that science will deepen our understanding of those aspects of ourselves we attribute to nature. But there is much which has to do with our animality—the characteristic demeanours and inflections of the human form and face, the modes of their expressiveness—whose place in the constitution of our concepts will not be made clearer to us by the sciences of nature. There is, to be sure, a sense of 'capacity' according to which we have a capacity to speak which may be investigated by different sciences—by neurophysiology, for example, or by biology. It is the sense we express when we say that a person's capacity for speech was impaired by an accident. Nothing I have said is at odds with that or with our hopes for the most detailed knowledge of such a capacity. However, our responses to one another as to another perspective on the world, as to one who has the kind of inner life from which he may speak as someone who has something to say, or something to learn—something to bring to a conversation—brings with it a certain sense of individuality, which continental philosophers have sometimes tried to express when they speak of the *otherness* of the other, or sometimes simply of the Other. That may be obscurantist, but it need not be. David Wiggins tried to capture something, which he presumably believed we miss in our tired ways of speaking of intersubjectivity, when he said 'the moral view especially involves . . . the recognition of the *alterity*, the otherness of the subjectivity of others' (Wiggins, 1987, 70). And Peter Winch (1987) bring out what is involved (and why it is more basic than the moral view) when he quotes, as an example of the way an attitude towards a soul is a primitive reaction, the following passage from Simone Weil:

> The human beings around us exert just by their presence a power which belongs uniquely to themselves to stop, to diminish, or modify, each movement which our bodies design. A person who crosses our path does not turn aside our steps in the same manner as a street

[4] For example, in *On Certainty*.

sign, no one stands up, or moves about, or sits down in quite the same fashion when he is alone in a room as when he has a visitor.[5]

I have not the space to spell out, even if I were capable of it, the details of a convincing development of these themes, but it should be clear that they are part of an importantly different philosophy of mind than the one which treats the human subject as essentially an observer who responds to things in nature, including other human beings, on the basis of his epistemic appropriation of those properties which are relevant to his desires and interests.[6] It has become common to reject the passivity implied in such a picture, as inadequate both to epistemology and to a proper understanding of concept formation, but the thoroughgoingness of Wittgenstein's break from it has not been sufficiently appreciated. It is likely to have implications for the kind of publicness, the kind of intersubjective agreement, which he believed belonged to language.

It is certainly plausible that an appreciation of the deep and pervasive inadequacy of such a picture must alter our sense of the intersubjectivity of conversation. Martin Buber who wrote a lot, for better and for worse on this subject, said:

> Every attempt to understand monologue as fully valid conversation, which leaves unclear whether it, or dialogue, is the more original, must run aground on the fact that the ontologically basic presupposition of conversation is missing from it, the otherness, or more concretely, the moment of surprise. The human person is not in his own mind unpredictable to himself as he is to anyone of his partners; therefore he cannot be a genuine partner to himself, he can be no real questioner and no real answerer. (Buber, 1965)

The interest in whether we can build a machine which would be both rational and unpredictable to its makers is, I believe, the shadow cast by the more substantial conception of the surprise, which is both promised and threatened by conversation and which is internal to our sense of how other than, *and other to*, oneself another human being can be. It has little to do with novelty and is not conditional upon routine or ignorance. Buber and Rhees are close on this.

We may now see why Malcolm's humanization of the builders was important. And it may be clearer why I said that it remained external to their speaking. Malcolm's builders slap their heads and chuckle over their mistakes. This creates the illusion that they 'have something to say' or that 'they could bring something to a conversation' if only they

[5] The quotation is from, Simone Weil, 'The Iliad: A poem of Might' in *Intimations of Christianity Amongst the Ancient Greeks* (Weil, 28).

[6] For some further development see Gaita (1990), Ch. 10.

had a larger vocabulary. I call this an illusion because they lack a focused subjectivity, an inner collectedness, of the kind which comes when partners in a conversation call each other to a kind of sobriety— come now do you mean that? are you serious? can I take *you* seriously? *think* about what you are saying!, and so on. It is difficult to imagine that we could credit the kind of understanding which goes with speech unless it were in a subject to whom we may intelligibly respond in such ways. As things stand with us, it is equally difficult to imagine the mutually constitutive sense of self and other without conversation, and it is certainly impossible to conceive of conversation without it. That is the kind of interdependence which Rhees emphasized.

Can we imagine calling a machine to sobriety in the ways I sketched above? I think that we cannot and that our difficulty in seriously conceiving it is the basis of our reluctance to remove the inverted commas from what they do. Our reluctance (if we have it) is not diminished by proliferation and sophistication of their inverted commas capacities. It diminishes only when we are asked to imagine machines which look so like us that we begin to respond to them as to 'one of us'. But that is contrary to what inclines people to speculate about whether machines might speak—for in the light of that inclination such things must be superficial and, at best, psychological aids to the acknowledgement that it is time to remove the inverted commas. That is why Wittgenstein's remarks on an attitude towards a soul seem to them to beg the question and to be willfully perverse. However, if we appreciate the importance of the conversational attitudes which I have described, to our conception of the kind of understanding which is necessary for speech, then we may see the kinds of connections between speech, conversation and our humanity, which Rhees emphasized. Only to a human being and what resembles a human being does it make sense to respond as to one who may converse with us; and that is a condition, rather than consequence of, the attribution of the kind of understanding which is necessary for there to be speech.

'I heard a plaintive melody': (*Philosophical Investigations*, p. 209)

OSWALD HANFLING

Asked about Wittgenstein's contribution to aesthetics, one might think first of all of his discussion of 'family resemblance' concepts, in which he argued that the various instances of games, for example, need not have any feature or set of features in common, in virtue of which they are all called games; the concept of a game can function perfectly well without any such set of conditions. This insight was soon applied to the much debated quest for a definition of the word 'art', and it was claimed that here too the various instances of art were related by way of family resemblance, so that it was futile to look for a condition or set of conditions, which works of art, and only works of art, had in common. Wittgenstein himself did not extend his argument to the concept of art. Although he was deeply interested in the arts, especially music, he wrote very little on aesthetics, his most sustained treatment of the topic being available for us only in the form of notes taken of a set of his lectures on aesthetics (LC).

In this paper, however, I wish to take up certain other remarks which appear rather briefly in various parts of his writings, but which seem to me of importance for an understanding both of aesthetics and of other areas of philosophy. One such remark is that which I have chosen for my title: 'I heard a plaintive melody'. Having imagined someone making this remark, W asks: 'Does he *hear* the complaint?' (PI, p. 209).[1] Here he touches briefly on a well known aesthetic theory, the 'expression theory', according to which works of art are expressions of feeling. In the case of music especially, this theory seems to gain support from what are described as 'expressive qualities'—such as 'plaintive' in the present example. This term certainly suggests that the melody is the expression of a complaint.

> Perhaps the plaintive numbers flow
> For old, unhappy, far-off things,

---

[1] I have preferred 'complaint' to 'plaint', as printed in the published translation. The latter has the advantage of using the same word in both sentences, as does the German original (*klagend, Klage*), but whereas the English 'plaint' is a rather unusual word, the German *Klage* is the straightforward word for complaint (as well as for *plaint* in the legal sense).

And battles long ago;
Or is it some more humble lay,
Familiar matter of today?
Some natural sorrow, loss or pain,
That has been, and may be again?

But critics of the expression theory have argued that music is not, except in special circumstances, an expression of its author's feelings. A person who writes a sad piece of music may do so, not to express his feelings, but because he wants to create a beautiful work of art or in order to fulfil a commission.

Another, related theory is that the function of music is to arouse such feelings in the listener. But against this it is objected that one may enjoy the music as a beautiful work of art without thereby being made to feel sad, or indeed having any desire to feel sad. Sadness is connected with sorrow, grief and unhappiness, but listening to music, sad or otherwise, that we love, makes us happy. Music certainly arouses our feelings, but they are feelings which are peculiar to the hearing of music, and to particular pieces of music. Again, even if it were true that sad music makes us feel sad, this would not explain why it is called sad. A drug which makes us sad would not on that account be described as sad. It is the music itself we are describing when we say it is sad, and not its causal powers.

Similarly, a person who listens to a plaintive melody does not do so with the desire of hearing a complaint. And if he had such a desire, then a piece of music would not be a suitable vehicle for satisfying it. For it is essential to a complaint that it be *about* something, and what this is is communicated when we make a complaint in words. But a piece of music, whether plaintive or otherwise, is not a suitable medium for such communication. It is, to be sure, possible to say that one has a complaint without yet saying what that complaint is; but then one must be prepared to say what it is on being questioned (to answer the questions posed in Wordsworth's poem, for example). But the composer who has written a plaintive melody is not accountable in this way. He may indeed be astonished, or regard it as some kind of joke, if he were asked what his complaint was (or had been when he wrote the music). And similarly the listener who had heard the melody would not wish to answer 'yes' to Wittgenstein's question 'Does he hear the complaint?', since he would not be able to say what the complaint was.

The error of postulating a correspondence between a composer's state of mind and the description of his music as sad or plaintive, cheerful or majestic, may be compared with a similar mistake in the case of animals. An example of this occurs in the writings of Hume. 'The very port and gait of a swan, or turkey, or peacock', writes Hume, 'show the high idea that he has entertained of himself, and his contempt of all others' (Hume, 1888, Bk. II, Part 1, Sect. xii, 326). We do describe the bearing of such animals as 'proud', etc. and this usage may seem inexplicable unless we postulate a corresponding mental life on the part of the animal. But what can it mean to speak of a swan 'entertaining ideas of himself' and holding other creatures in contempt? In any case, we do not *need* to make inferences about an animal's mental life in order to describe its appearance as proud, sad etc.[2] And similarly, we do not need to make inferences about a composer's mental life in order to describe his music in these and similar terms.

But how, in that case, are our descriptions of music as sad, plaintive, cheerful, profound, etc. to be explained? How are the so-called 'expressive qualities' to be accounted for? Perhaps it will be said that a plaintive melody is so called, not because it expresses a complaint, but because it resembles a plaintive voice; and the latter is so called because it is the kind of voice that is typically used for making complaints. But is there a kind of voice that is typically used for making complaints? And if so, does it resemble a plaintive melody? On the first question, we must bear in mind the great variety of complaints. If there are typical kinds of voices here, they are more likely to be for certain kinds of complaints, made by certain people in certain circumstances, etc., than for complaints in general. Again, we must not assume that what we call a plaintive voice is so called because of an experienced correspondence between that kind of voice and the making of complaints. Our description of it as 'plaintive' may be no more based on such a correspondence than our description of a peacock as proud or a St. Bernard dog as sad. John Hospers has written that when we call a work of music sad, we mean that 'it may contain some of the features which characterize people when they are sad; it is soft, seldom loud; it is slow, seldom fast; it is hushed, never strident' (Stolnitz, 1965, 54). But this is to overlook the role of weeping and wailing as expressions of sadness.

Turning to the second question, is it true that a plaintive voice resembles a plaintive melody? There is obviously much difference between the sound of a melody and the sound of a speaking voice; we would be unlikely to mistake one for the other. As Urmson has pointed out, 'sad music does not much resemble the sounds that people make to express their sadness, which are typically disagreeable and even raucous' (Vesey, 1973, 111).

According to another view, the resemblance is between the music and the appearance of sad people (as distinct from their voice). Peter

---

[2] The example of sadness is used by Peter Kivy in his interesting discussion of the present topic, and a picture of a 'sad' Saint Bernard dog appears as the frontispiece of his book *The Corded Shell* (Kivy, 1980).

Oswald Hanfling

Kivy has claimed that we hear a given piece of music as 'expressive of sadness, because we hear it as a musical resemblance of the gesture and carriage appropriate to the expression of our sadness' (Kivy, 1980, 53). In support of this he refers to an example from Bach: 'Don't we hear the melodic line droop in the oboe solo of the first Brandenburg?' He appears to think that 'drooping' is a typical expression of sadness among human beings, and that this drooping resembles that of a melody. Perhaps the drooping behaviour he had in mind was that of people standing with bowed heads at a funeral, or something of that kind. This is of course a rather special kind of case, and it is unlikely that any such behaviour can be generalized for all or most cases of sadness. But turning to the claim about resemblance, how can a melody be said to resemble a drooping person? A piece of music does not stand on the ground and does not have spatial parts such as are involved when we describe a person (or other physical object) as drooping.

These and similar explanations of why we apply such descriptions to music are inadequate and this usage of words remain puzzling. Now the answer to this puzzle is not to be found in Wittgenstein's writings, but what he wrote does, at least, throw a new light on it. Wittgenstein once remarked that 'in philosophy it is always good to put a *question* instead of an answer to a question' (RFM, 147). Doing this will not, of course, give the same kind of satisfaction as providing an answer, but it may put the question into a different perspective, removing or reducing the sense of puzzlement and the temptation to put forward explanations which do not really work.

The relevant 'other question' in the present case are questions about uses of language in areas other than aesthetics, which are puzzling in the same kind of way. By generalizing the problem in this way we discover, at least, that the case of 'expressive qualities' is not *especially* puzzling. Moreover, this approach will take us to one of the central concerns of Wittgenstein's later philosophy, which was to investigate the extent to which our uses of language can be explained. This is a general question about language, though it applies differently to different areas and aspects of language.

Family Resemblance and Other Relations

Fundamental to the nature of language is the fact, as we might put it, that not all words are proper names: a given word can be used for a number of different things. This is so in two ways. Firstly, a word, such as 'red' or 'chair', is not confined to *one* object (one red object, one chair). Secondly, the objects to which it is applied may (and usually do) differ in a *qualitative* sense—the word 'red' is applied to objects which differ in colour, and the word 'chair' to a great variety of chairs.

It is natural to suppose that there must be a unity underlying the diversity—that all chairs must have something in common in virtue of which they are called chairs, and similarly with the word 'red'. Otherwise, we might think, language would be reduced to anarchy. There would be no justification for using these and other words as we do, no rules to hold the different occurrences of a given word together; and communication by means of language would be impossible.

This assumption was challenged by Wittgenstein in his famous discussion of the word 'game', in which he argued that there is no need to postulate an underlying unity of this kind. Even if there is no set of features that games and only games have in common, the concept may be held together by an informal 'network of similarities overlapping and criss-crossing' (PI, I, 66), rather as a thread may hold together, not because 'one fibre runs through its whole length, but (through) the overlapping of many fibres' (PI, I, 67). This looseness in the organization of language is tolerable because of a general agreement among users of language as to what is an acceptable usage and what is not—an agreement that shows itself in practice but is not based on any formal rules or definitions.

Wittgenstein's discussion of games and family resemblances is well known and will not be further expounded here. What is not so well recognized, and is indeed less prominent in his writings, is that the question 'What do they have in common?' is also applicable to other uses of language, where the analogy of family resemblance is not appropriate. In some passages of the *Brown Book*, for example, Wittgenstein asks this question in connection with colour words such as 'red' and 'blue'. 'What do light blue and dark blue have in common? (BB, 134). The family resemblance and fibre-to-fibre analogies would not be appropriate here, since colour words are not based on features as is the case with the word 'game'. There is no counterpart in the case of 'blue' to such features as amusement, competition, and winning and losing, which Wittgenstein mentions in his review of games. Now these features are available as *reasons* for calling something a game, but no such reasons are available for describing an object as blue. If you were asked "Why do you call this 'blue' also?", you would say "Because this *is* blue, too"' (BB, 133–134). There is, according to Wittgenstein, nothing behind the use of such words which would serve as a justification for it.

> To say that we use the word 'blue' to mean 'what all these shades have in common' by itself says nothing more than that we use the word 'blue' in all these cases. (BB, 135)

We could, he says, 'easily imagine a language . . . in which there existed no common expression for light blue and dark blue', in which the former, say, was called 'Cambridge', and the latter 'Oxford'. If you ask a man of this tribe what Cambridge and Oxford have in common, he'd be inclined to say 'Nothing'. (BB, 134–135)

It might be thought that what holds our word 'blue' together is the continuity of shades between light and dark blue. We might think of this in terms of a colour chart on which the intermediate shades, each differing only slightly from its neighbour, are displayed. But such explanations will not take us very far. For the same continuity would extend, at both ends, *beyond* what we, in our language, call 'blue'. 'But when two colours are similar', says Wittgenstein's imaginary partner, 'the experience of similarity should surely consist in noticing the similarity which there *is* between them' (BB, 133). But, replies Wittgenstein, 'is a bluish green similar to a yellowish green or not? In certain cases we should say they are similar and in others that they are most dissimilar.'

These rejections of explanation are profoundly disturbing to many readers of Wittgenstein, for they may seem to leave our use of language without any rational foundation. What is at issue is not just the validity of this or that justification, but the very idea of justification. In the end, if Wittgenstein is right, it is just a fact of our nature—part of 'the natural history of man' (PI, I, 415)—that we use words in these and these ways. However, the examples mentioned so far—family resemblance, and the range of colour words—are only part of the story. There are other areas of language where the need for justification may be felt even more acutely; where, in the absence of some justification, our use of language may seem altogether bizarre.

In a passage in the *Investigations* Wittgenstein speaks of an inclination to describe certain days of the week as 'fat' and 'lean' (PI, p. 216; also BB, 137); and in the *Brown Book* he imagines someone describing the five vowels as 'darker' and 'lighter' and arranging them in that order (BB, 136). Here the question arises 'What made you use the word "darker" in this case at all?' In this case, of course, it is not just a matter of explaining what two qualities on the same spectrum—such as light blue and dark blue—have in common, but of how the words 'darker' and 'lighter', 'fat' and 'lean', can be transferred out of what we may regard as their normal categories, into altogether different ones. We are familiar with the idea that a given predicate is suitable for a certain category of objects; that we cannot ascribe a given property to any object whatever without falling into nonsense. Thus 'lighter' and 'darker' are applicable to objects of sight, and 'fat' and 'lean' to animals and parts of animals; and if they are extended to other kinds of objects (by way of metaphor perhaps), then we would expect some explanation to be available.

Now when we first read these examples in the text, we may be inclined to dismiss them as fanciful, belonging to the margins of language and of little importance for a philosophical understanding of language. It would be quite reasonable, after all, to comment that they are nonsense. As Wittgenstein himself remarks:

> if such a person was asked whether u was '*really*' darker than e, he would almost certainly answer some such thing as 'it isn't really darker, but somehow it gives me a darker impression' (BB, 136).

Such uses of language are idiosyncratic and do not belong to that consensus of usage which, according to Wittgenstein, is an essential feature of language.

Wittgenstein's examples may also make us think of a kind of playful use of words in which we sometimes indulge. Thus we may be asked (perhaps by way of a party game) to write down how we would apply the words 'fat' and 'lean' to days of the week, etc., and most people would 'have à go' by way of amusement. It might also be fun to compare what different people have written down. Such choices might be influenced by more or less unconscious associations of a personal kind; or they might be due to more or less superficial resemblances between words. (Perhaps Wittgenstein chose 'lean' for Tuesday because of a resemblance between the German *dünn* and *Dienstag*.)

It is clear, however, that Wittgenstein wanted to make a more radical point by means of these examples, and that he introduced them in order to throw light on the question of justifying our *normal* uses of words (such as light blue and dark blue). In another passage he imagined someone who 'has been taught a use of the words 'lighter' and 'darker' by means of ordinary 'objects of various colours'.

> Now he is given the order to put down a series of objects, arranging them in order of their darkness. He does this by laying out a row of books, writing down a series of names of animals, and by writing down the five vowels in the order u, o, a, e, i . . . Perhaps we shall say: 'But look, surely e isn't lighter than o in the way this book is lighter than that'. But he may shrug his shoulders and say 'I don't know, but e *is* lighter than o, isn't it?' (BB, 138–139).

This use of words is not one of idle amusement, but one in which the learner regards it as obvious that 'e *is* lighter than o'—though he can only shrug his shoulders when asked for a justification. Similarly, returning to the example of light blue and dark blue, 'if you were asked "Why do you call this 'blue' also?", you would say "Because this *is* blue, too"' (BB, 133–134).

'But surely', resumes Wittgenstein's imaginary partner in the discussion about the person who had been taught the words 'lighter' and 'darker', 'he used "lighter" in a different sense when he said e was lighter than u' (BB, 139). But may not the same be said in the case of light blue and dark blue?

> What if somebody said, pointing to two patches which I had called red, 'Surely you are using the word "red" in two different ways'?—I should say 'This is light red and the other dark red,—but why should I have to talk of two different usages?' (BB, 139); the switch from 'blue' to 'red' is irrelevant)

No doubt, as Wittgenstein points out, 'we may be inclined to treat [the case of vowels] as some kind of abnormality' (BB, 139), but as far as justification is concerned, this is no more available in the normal that in the abnormal cases.

More Examples

The examples of fat and lean and lighter and darker vowels are disorienting because these words are being used out of what we may regard as their normal categories of objects. But the same phenomenon may be found, and is readily accepted, in many areas of language. A striking example is given by Wittgenstein (PI, I, 377) where he points out that 'high' may be an object of hearing as well as of sight. In this discussion he questions the power of *sameness* to account for our uses of words.

It is true, and fundamental to our idea of language, that we apply the same word to things that are *the same*, in some sense, as one another. (In the limiting case of proper names the sameness is that of numerical identity.) But according to Wittgenstein, such ideas as 'the same' (and 'similar', and 'what they have in common') can only explain our use of language up to a point. (Are light red and dark red *the same* colour?) Having quoted an imaginary 'logician' who declares that 'the same is the same—how identity is established is a psychological question', he replies: 'High is high—it is a matter of psychology that one sometimes *sees*, and sometimes *hears* it.' (PI, I, 377)

What does the Eiffel Tower have in common with the sound of a whistle? In what way are they the same? The question seems absurd, and the justification for applying the same word, 'high', to both of them, cannot be that they are 'the same'. Yet there is no sense of awkwardness or disorientation when we apply this word to a non-spatial entity.

Perhaps it will be pointed out that high and low sounds correspond to high and low numbers of frequencies of sound waves, and that this explains our usage. This might have been so if the usage had come about through knowledge of the scientific facts about frequencies, but of course this is not so. The correspondence with frequencies is no more than a coincidence, and there may well be languages in which the words for high and low sounds are reversed, or in which sounds are not described in these terms at all, but, let us suppose, in terms of darker and lighter—or, to take another example, degrees of sharpness.

'Sharp' is of course a word that is actually used, in English, to describe notes, and its use here is puzzling in just the same kind of way as the use of 'high'. How, we may ask, can a note be described in the same way as a knife? What do they have in common? A sharp knife is one that cuts well, but such ideas make no sense in the case of notes. And similar puzzles arise in other languages, for example the German *dur* and *moll* (for major and minor), derived from words meaning 'hard' and 'soft'.

Speaking of 'sharp', we may notice a number of other uses of this word. We speak of a sharp pain and a sharp frost. Is this because of some connection with being cut by a sharp knife? A sharp knife is probably less likely to produce a sharp pain than some other cause or object. Similarly, Gilbert Ryle's explanation of 'a stabbing, a grinding or a burning pain' as being the sort that would be produced, respectively, by 'a stiletto, a drill or an ember' was motivated by a craving for explanation rather than by an observation of facts (Ryle, 1949, 203). Again, we speak of 'sharp words', but they are not related to blunt words as sharp knives are related to blunt ones.

The word 'sweet', to take another example, is used to describe children, but such children are not sweet to the tongue: and neither is what Shakespeare called the 'concord of sweet sounds'. It might be said that 'what they have in common' is that sweet foods, sweet children and sweet sounds are all nice. But sweet foods are not always nice. On the other hand, what we mean in describing a child as sweet is not just nice, but nice in a particular way. And whereas in the case of food 'sweet' is related to such words as 'tasty' and 'savoury', these words are not applicable to children.[3] Here again it is interesting to compare English with other languages. In French, for example, 'sweetly' and 'high' *doucement* and *haut*, are used for soft and loud speech, but children are not describable as *douce*.

Another example, introduced by Wittgenstein, is that of 'a *deep* sorrow, a *deep* sound, and a *deep* well' (which he compared with the example of darker and lighter). What do a sorrow, a sound and a well have in common, in virtue of which we describe them all as deep? Perhaps it will be said that a deep sound is such as would emanate from a deep well or a deep hole; but no such justification is available for 'a

---

[3] A similar example, mentioned in the *Remarks on the Philosophy of Psychology*, is that of a bitter food and a bitter sorrow (RPP, I, 68).

deep sorrow'. A deep sorrow, it may be said, is one that penetrates deeply into the soul. But this would only raise further questions of the same kind. For the soul is not a spatial entity, and there is no process of penetrating into it, starting at the surface and so on, as when we speak of penetrating in the physical sense.

Such examples can be multiplied at length, as the reader will find. There are various intriguing differences and relations among them, such as we saw in the case of 'sharp'; and some of them seem to be shared by different languages to a greater extent than others. In each case the urge to say 'There *must* be something common, or they would not be called . . .' is very strong—more so, perhaps, than in the case of games, where the words just quoted were put by Wittgenstein in the mouth of the imaginary opponent. But, if Wittgenstein is right, there is no 'must' about it; the language-game may proceed perfectly well without any such justification.

Wittgenstein on 'Secondary Sense'

Having introduced the example of fat and lean days of the week in the *Investigations*, Wittgenstein comments that this use of words is in a certain sense 'secondary'; if he wanted to explain the meanings of 'fat' and 'lean', he could not do it by 'pointing to the example of Tuesday and Wednesday'. 'Here', he continues:

> one might speak of a 'primary' and 'secondary' sense of a word. It is only if the word has the primary sense for you that you use it in the secondary one (PI, p. 216).

The first point is about explaining the meaning, the second about *using* the words in question: their use in the secondary sense is parasitic on one's knowledge of the primary sense. It is because of the latter that they seem, somehow, appropriate in the secondary use, and not replaceable by other words chosen, say, at random.

> Now have 'fat' and 'lean' some different meaning here from their usual one?—They have a different use.—so ought I really to have used different words? Certainly not.—I want to use *these* words (with their familiar meanings) *here*. (PI, p. 216)

In another part of the work the idea of secondary sense is introduced in a different context. Here the question is raised whether inanimate objects can be said to feel pain. Such ascriptions, he points out, do occur in fairy tales and 'when playing with dolls' (PI, I, 282). But, he comments,

> this use of the concept of pain is a secondary one. Imagine a case in which people ascribed pain *only* to inanimate things; pitied *only* dolls!

He compared this with an example of 'children of a tribe unacquainted with trains' who nevertheless play at trains; they have learned this game from other children, but 'without knowing that it was copied from anything'. 'One might say', he concludes, 'that the game did not make the same *sense* to them as to us.'

If we consider these examples, we can find two different relations between primary and secondary, a stronger and a weaker. In the case of fat and lean the secondary use could not exist without the primary. In the case of playing at trains, however, the dependence of secondary on primary meaning is a weaker one. For it is clearly possible (as supposed in the example itself) that the children of a tribe play this game in the secondary sense even though they have no concept of trains in the primary sense. The point here is that 'game does not make the same *sense* to them as to us'.

Another way in which this kind of language is characterized by Wittgenstein is by distinguishing it from metaphor.

> The secondary sense is not a 'metaphorical' sense. If I say 'For me the vowel *e* is yellow' I do not mean 'yellow' in a metaphorical sense,— for I could not express what I want to say in any other way than by means of the idea 'yellow'. (PI, p. 216)

Strictly speaking, this is not a valid reason against describing a usage as metaphorical. For this word means no more than 'transferred' (the German is *übertragen*—'carried over'), and it may be said that the words under consideration are being used metaphorically in just this sense.

However, another difference between secondary sense and many familiar metaphors concerns the question of rational explanation. This difference is not, as far as I know, stated by Wittgenstein, but is of importance in the context of his general position and his insistence that 'explanations come to an end'. Familiar metaphors such as 'sift the evidence' and 'head of the organization' can be accounted for by reference to analogies: and the same is true in the case of many new metaphors, such as David Lodge's description of someone driving through a congested city: 'She feels as if she is negotiating the entrails of the city in the slow peristaltic procession' (Lodge, 1988). It is necessary to understand the rational basis of this metaphor (or simile) in order to understand and appreciate the description. But this is not so in the case of secondary sense, where there is no such rational basis.

I have heard it suggested that the reason for describing notes as high is that in the case of the human voice more effort is needed to produce high notes. Against this it may be said that very low notes are also hard to produce (though the effort feels different). But in any case, there is a fundamental difference between these attempted explanations and those that exist in the case of straightforward metaphors. The former are no more than *theories* or *suggestions* as to what may lie behind the relevant uses of language. By contrast, we know perfectly well why we speak of 'the head of the company' (in spite of the fact that a company is not an animal) and this knowledge is essential to a proper understanding of this expression.

Secondary Sense and Feelings

Among the various examples of secondary sense, some are more dispensable than others. The description of days as fat and lean is obviously one that we could do without, and the same is true of other idiosyncratic examples. The example of ascribing pain to dolls is not so easily dispensed with. Although it is 'only a game', it is one that matters a good deal, at least to children. But no doubt life could easily go on without it. But in certain other areas the use of secondary sense is more important to us: we need to use the descriptions in question, and there is no other (non-secondary) way of making them. This is so especially in three areas that are of interest to philosophers—mental processes, feelings and aesthetics.

According to Wittgenstein, our descriptions of mental processes are 'secondary'. Having introduced this term by reference to 'fat' and 'lean', he immediately introduces another example.

> Only if you have learnt to calculate—on paper or out loud—can you be made to grasp, by means of this concept, what calculating in the head is. (PI, p. 216)

In a passage in the *Brown Book* he introduced the example of 'looking for a word in your memory', and asked: what similarity is there between this and 'looking for my friend in the park'? It might be replied that in both cases 'we experience tension and relaxation', etc. But what, asks Wittgenstein, do these cases 'have in common that makes us say they are cases of strain and relaxation'? Similar questions may be asked about another concept which has been important in the history of philosophy—that of mental images. Our mental life, it appears, is largely described in terms which are, according to Wittgenstein, secondary; but there is no other way of describing it. This leads to the false assimilation of mental to physical processes, with disastrous consequences for the philosophy of mind, as discussed at length by Wittgenstein in various passages (e.g. PI, I, 368ff).

Another area in which secondary sense is important is that of sensations. In the case of certain sensations, of which pain is probably the best example, there is a strong and well defined behaviour by means of

which the feeling is identified. For this reason we can speak of *seeing* that someone is in pain and not merely (as some sceptical philosophers would have it) *inferring* that this is so, from his behaviour. It is because of this close connection between pain and pain-behaviour that the language-game of pain can get established in the case of a pre-verbal infant, as described in *Philosophical Investigations*, I, 244. Two other examples of this kind are giddiness and nausea, where, again, there is a strong and well defined behaviour. But this is not so in the case of most sensations, which are more dependent, for their identification, on verbal means, that on any particular kind of behaviour; and here again we need to help ourselves in many cases to secondary uses of words. Thus we speak of 'pins and needles', 'butterflies in the stomach', and 'stabbing' pains. These descriptions are only vaguely related to behavioural manifestations, and it would make no sense to ascribe them to a pre-verbal infant. On the other hand, they cannot be explained by way of analogy either. It would be absurd to think that 'pins and needles' is a kind of feeling that results, or would result, from an application of (real) pins and needles; or that if one had real butterflies in one's stomach, the result would be 'butterflies in the stomach'. And the same applies to Ryle's claims about 'a stabbing, a grinding or a burning pain', as noted on page 125 above. It is sometimes assumed that Wittgenstein's account of pain and pain-behaviour can be generalized, and that he had a general theory about feelings, involving 'criteria'. The slogan 'An "inner process" stands in need of outward criteria' (from PI, I, 580) is often quoted in support of this. This view is mistaken in various ways, as I have tried to show elsewhere (Hanfling, 1989, 121ff). But one thing that is wrong with it is that it overlooks the logic of feelings of the kind just described.

Now Wittgenstein did not say much about feelings of this kind, but one example that he discussed in RPP was a 'feeling of unreality' which he had experienced at some time (RPP, I, 125). 'Everything seems somehow not *real*': but this description, again, was to be understood in a secondary sense. It was not 'as if one *saw* things unclear or blurred; everything looks quite as usual'. If this feeling were ascribed to another person, it would not be done on the basis of behaviour. 'How do I know that another has felt what I have? Because he uses the same words as I find appropriate.' He went on to ask himself why the words seem appropriate.

But why do I choose precisely the word 'unreality' to express [this feeling]? Surely not because of its sound. (A word of very like sound but different meaning would not do.) I choose it because of its meaning. But surely I did not learn to use the word to mean: a *feeling*. No; but I learned to use it with a particular meaning and now I use it spontaneously like *this*.

There is no rational explanation for using it 'like this'. We may be tempted to explain it as some kind of simile; but, says Wittgenstein, 'what is in question here is not a simile, not a comparison of the feeling with something else' (RPP, I, 125).

Secondary Sense and Aesthetics

The secondary uses of language arise in response to certain needs, such as the needs to describe mental processes and the need to describe feelings of the kind that are not tied to a particular kind of behaviour or causal condition. Such a need also arises in the case of aesthetics, and especially in the description of music, where, as Arnold Isenberg has put it, 'the needs of discussion will force us to grope for metaphors and analogies' (Isenberg, 1973, 9), a groping which may result in secondary sense rather than in analogy. A nice example of the operation of secondary sense both outside and inside aesthetics, was given by Isenberg: 'It seems rather silly to ask how music can be *light-hearted*, as if you already knew how a *heart* can be *light*.'

The false assimilation of secondary to primary sense may lead to confusion in the case of aesthetics, no less than in the case of mental processes and feelings. We have already seen how descriptions like 'a plaintive melody' may lend a spurious support to the 'expression theory', whereby art is regarded as essentially an expression of feeling. But there are various other descriptions of music where similar problems arise. Bach's music is sometimes described as 'mathematical', and some people say they don't like it because it is 'too mathematical'. It seems almost incredible that the music is describable in this way unless some rational connection can be made with 'mathematical' in the primary sense. Hence people who dislike Bach's music may be misled into thinking that their dislike is really of the same kind as a dislike for maths, or that the music may be *criticized* for having a quality ('mathematical') that is not appropriate for works of art (rather as one might criticize a work of art for being too much like a technical exercise).

Another example, discussed by Peter Kivy, is the description of music as 'profound' (Kivy, 1990). How is this to be justified? In the case of literature, as Kivy points out, a work may be praised for its profundity if it deals with important human concerns, and deals with them in a suitable way. But what can it mean to describe, say, the late quartets of Beethoven as profound? Are they 'about' human concerns? Do they contain questions, statements and discussions about the human condition? After various attempts to account for the use of

'profound' in the case of music, Kivy confesses that he has 'failed to find any rational justification' for it.

It has indeed been claimed that music is essentially a kind of language, differing from spoken language only in its medium of expression, with musical notes and phrases doing the same kind of work as the words and phrases of spoken languages; and we sometimes find descriptions of music which seem to bear this out.

> [Beethoven's] sonata in G major, Opus 31, No. 1 . . . opens with a startling statement, a running gesture, and then the assertion of a theme whose dogma is beyond all doubt . . . [The player] emphasized that dogma with the vehemence of a Savonarola castigating the pleasure-loving Florentines . . . Then, after violent assertions running to and fro . . . (Church, 1955, 89)

Wittgenstein, using a rather less dramatic description, makes the point that this kind of language is, again, parasitic on primary meaning:

> If I say for example: Here it's as if a conclusion were being drawn, here as if something were confirmed, *this* is like an answer to what went before—then my understanding presupposes a familiarity with inferences, with confirmations, with answers (Z, 175).

These uses of language cannot be understood in a primary sense, because the logical surroundings of the relevant language-game are lacking; the concepts of question, answer, and assertion cannot have the logical relations by which they are understood in their primary sense. Wittgenstein speaks of 'a strange illusion [that] possesses us'

> if repeating a tune to ourselves and letting it make its full impression on us, we say 'This tune says *something*', and it is as though I had to find out *what* it says. And yet I know that it doesn't say anything such that I might express in words or pictures what it says (BB, 166).

We may also be led into false ideas about what it means to *understand* a piece of music, if we fail to notice the logical disparities between music and language. In the case of language, understanding is correlated with meaning. We understand a word or sentence if we know what it means; and the meaning can be *explained* to us, by means of other words or by ostension. But these ideas make no sense in the case of music. 'Understanding' a piece of music cannot be understood in its primary sense.

What I have said may seem to go against certain passages in which Wittgenstein sees a similarity between understanding language and understanding music. 'Understanding a sentence', he writes, 'is much more akin to understanding a theme in music than one may think' (PI, I, 527). His point here, however, is not to assimilate music to language, but the other way round. There is a sense of 'understand' in which understanding a sentence is akin to understanding music; it is so in a *secondary* sense of 'understand'.

> We speak of understanding a sentence in the sense in which it can be replaced by another which says the same; but also in the sense in which it cannot be replaced by any other. (Any more than a musical theme can be replaced by another.)

The second (and secondary) sense of 'understand' is connected with what Wittgenstein called 'experiencing the meaning of a word'. This is the kind of meaning 'you would be missing . . . if you did not feel that a word lost its meaning and became a mere sound if it was repeated ten times over' (PI, p. 214).

This kind of meaning is important in poetry. When one reads a poem 'with feeling', says Wittgenstein, 'the sentences have a different *ring*'; and a particular word in the poem may be 'completely filled with meaning' (PI, pp. 214–215). There might be a language, he supposes, 'in whose use the "soul" of the words plays no part. In which, for example, we had no objection to replacing one word by another arbitrary one of our own invention' (PI, I, 530). In one of the remarks collected under the title *Culture and Value* he expressed his contempt for Esperanto for being 'soulless' in this way.

> The feeling of disgust we get if we utter an *invented* word with invented derivative syllables. The word is cold, lacking in associations, and yet it plays at being 'language'. (CV, 52).

These ideas of meaning and understanding are very different from those which are involved when we say that the meaning of a word is its use, or that the criterion of understanding a sentence is acting in accordance with it. Hence, having made his remark about a word that is 'completely filled with meaning', Wittgenstein asks: 'How can this be, if meaning is the use of the word?' (It would hardly make sense to say that the word is completely filled with use.) And having made his distinction between the two senses of 'understanding a sentence' (PI, I, 531), he asks: 'Then has "understanding" two different meanings here?' (PI, I, 532). If it has, they are not like the two meanings of the word 'bank'. The latter strikes us as a mere coincidence, and we would not care if two different words were used. (This is not to deny the historical connection between the two senses of 'bank'; but what matters in the present context is how we 'experience the meaning' when the words are used today.) But this is not so in the case of 'understand': for, as Wittgenstein writes, 'I *want* to apply the word "understanding" to all this'. It is the same reply as that which he gave to a similar question about 'fat' and 'lean'. 'So ought I really to have used different words (to describe days of the week)?' No, he replies: 'I want to use *these* words (with their familiar meanings) *here* (PI, p. 216).

The primary sense of 'understand' is that in which we can get someone to understand a sentence by explaining its meaning, and this may be done by means of another sentence which 'says the same' (PI, I, 531). But this is not so with the other sense of 'understand', where it is more appropriate to speak of 'leading' someone to understand.

> But in the second case how can one explain the expression, transmit one's understanding? Ask yourself: How does one *lead* a person to the understanding of a poem or a musical theme? (PI, I, 533)

Understanding in the second sense is important in the case of music and poetry. But it also plays a role in the use of language in general, in so far as 'understanding a sentence is much more akin to understanding a theme in music that one may think'—and, we may add, akin to understanding a piece of poetry. In this way the language of poetry has a counterpart in the poetry of language.

Religion in Wittgenstein's Mirror

D. Z. PHILLIPS

There is a well-known remark in Wittgenstein's *Philosophical Investigations* which even some philosophers sympathetic to his work have found very hard to accept. It reads:

> Philosophy may in no way interfere with the actual use of language;
> it can in the end only describe it.
> For it cannot give it any foundation either.
> It leaves everything as it is. (PI, I, 24)

Surely, it is said, that is carrying matters too far. Wittgenstein's hyperbole should be excused as a harmless stylistic flourish.

That reaction does a great disservice to Wittgenstein's work, whether one is sympathetic to that work or not. It obscures, or even ignores, what a philosophical problem was for him. When we are puzzled philosophically, Wittgenstein argued, what we stand in need of is not additional information, but a clearer view of what lies before us. We need to appreciate how we have become confused concerning the diverse areas of discourse in which we are engaged. This is why Wittgenstein says that he is not trying to get us to believe something we do not believe, but to do something we will not do.[1] In striving for clarity, it is difficult for us to leave everything as it is. Wittgenstein expressed his philosophical ideal as follows in 1931: 'I ought to be no more than a mirror in which my reader can see his own thinking with all its deformities so that helped in this way, he can put it right' (CV, 18).

This ideal remained Wittgenstein's to the end of his life. He strove after it in every area of philosophical inquiry he engaged in. In 1950, the year before his death, he wrote of religious belief:

> Actually I should like to say that in this case too the *words* you utter or what you think as you utter them are not what matters, as much as the difference they make at various points of your life. How do I know that two people mean the same when each says he believes in God? And just the same goes for belief in the Trinity. A theology which insists on the use of *certain particular* words and phrases, and outlaws others, does not make anything clearer (Karl Barth). It

[1] Quoted in Rush Rhees, 'The Philosophy of Wittgenstein' (Rhees, 1970, 43).

gesticulates with words, as one might say, because it wants to say something and does not know how to express it. *Practice* gives the words their sense. (CV, 85)

Wittgenstein's appeal to practice has been badly misunderstood in contemporary philosophy of religion. No single account can be given of it, since different things need to be said in different contexts. What does it mean to give practice its due, by being no more, as a philosopher, than a critical mirror? In this paper I shall consider five contexts in which this question needs to be answered.

I

The first context to consider is that in which we may be tempted to think that all forms of religious belief are confused. We fail to give religious practice its due because we bring to it preconceptions concerning what words *must* mean. For example, we may assume that all words operate as names and refer to objects. Thus, when we come across the word 'God', we start looking for the object it stands for. We may even think that we can come across pictures, such as Michelangelo's painting of God creating Adam, or the Last Judgement, in which we actually have depictions of the reference of the names 'man' and 'God'. But, of course, it will be said, this old man in Michelangelo's *Creation of Adam* no more exists than the man in the moon.

Wittgenstein is too optimistic when he says of Michelangelo's painting, 'we certainly wouldn't think this the Deity. The picture has to be used in an entirely different way if we are to call the man in that queer blanket "God" and so on' (LC, 63). The philosopher J. L. Mackie used the picture precisely in the way Wittgenstein thought to be obviously mistaken. He thought that while a believer need not commit himself to every detail in the painting of the Last Judgement, *some* details of this kind must be an approximation to a description of an empirical event, if the notion of a Last Judgement is to mean anything. Mackie says: 'I am saying only that talk about a last judgement *can* be understood literally' (Mackie, 1982, 3). But if by 'literal' use we mean 'standard' use, why should we assume that the literal is always the empirical or the factual? When we speak of creation or the last judgement, we are not talking metaphorically, or in some non-literal sense. For Mackie, Michelangelo's painting is taken to be an attempted approximation to empirical accuracy; a case of Michelangelo 'doing his best', as Wittgenstein comically remarks (LC, 63). We might then say, 'Of course, I can't show you the real thing, only the picture'. Wittgenstein retorts: 'The absurdity is, I've never taught him the technique of using this picture' (LC), a technique which applies to pictures of aunts and plants. Wittgenstein says, 'I could show Moore the picture of a tropical plant. There is a technique of comparison between picture and plant' (LC). But this use cannot be invoked where our use of the word 'God' is concerned: 'The word "God" is amongst the earliest learnt—pictures and catechisms, etc. But not the same consequences as with pictures of aunts. I wasn't shown [that which the picture pictured]' (LC, 59).

Even if we are sympathetic to religion, we may interpret Wittgenstein's remarks in a disastrous way. We may take him to be pointing out a shortcoming in religious pictures, as though they *try* to refer to God, but fail to do so because God is transcendent. This interpretation ignores the fact that Wittgenstein is endeavouring to clarify *the kind* of picture concerning God this picture is. This is shown in the use made of it; a use which will fix the meaning of 'divine transcendence'. The meaning of 'transcendent', like the meaning of any other word, does not transcend its use. If it made sense to claim otherwise, which it does not, the meaning of religious concepts would be said to be beyond our practices; that is, beyond what we do with them. In thinking this, we would be turning away from the practices that we need to be clear about. Wittgenstein emphasizes the point as follows:

> Religion teaches that the soul can exist when the body has disintegrated. Now do I understand this teaching?—Of course I understand it—I can imagine plenty of things in connection with it. And haven't pictures of these things been painted? And why should such a picture be only an imperfect rendering of the spoken doctrine? Why should it not do the *same* service as the words? And it is the service which is the point. (PI, I, 178)

If we wanted to understand what Michelangelo's painting shows about creation, we should have to pay attention to the nakedness of the figures in it: 'Naked came I from my mother's womb, and naked shall I return thither'. In Socrates' account of divine judgment in the *Gorgias*, both the judged and the judges are naked. Naked at birth, what comes our way comes from God. Naked at death, it is the state of one's soul which reveals purity or shame. Clothing, worldly status, is what is said to obscure these spiritual realities.

If we look at religious pictures as Mackie looked at them, it is not surprising to find description giving way to explanation. This is exactly what happened in post-Enlightenment thought. How *could* people possibly believe such things? Anthropologists, sociologists and psychoanalysts suggested that the belief was the superstitious product of a primitive mentality, unavoidable at that stage of human development. Wittgenstein showed that such thinkers are themselves in the grip of a primitive superstition: 'In other words it's just false to say: Of course, these primitive peoples couldn't help wondering at everything. Though perhaps it is true that these people *did* wonder at all the things around them—To suppose they couldn't help wondering at them is a primitive superstition' (CV, 5). The appeal to necessity, which seeks to be explanatory, is idle. We need to concentrate on what the wonder amounted to in people's lives; to concentrate on practice.

In the same way, it is idle to claim that people in a scientific culture *cannot* entertain religious hopes and fears. Wittgenstein insists: 'we cannot exclude the possibility that *highly* civilized peoples will become liable to this very same fear once again; neither their civilization nor scientific knowledge can protect them against this' (CV, 5). This does not mean that science cannot threaten religion. Wittgenstein acknowledges in 1930: 'All the same it's true enough that the *spirit* in which science is carried on nowadays is not compatible with fear of this kind' (CV, 5). But this incompatibility cannot be said, in general, to be between a sophisticated mode of understanding and primitive superstition. Rather, it is an incompatibility between the values, interests and spirit of two very different modes of thought.

If we say that religious belief is *necessarily* confused, we have failed, philosophically, to mirror its practices. In emphasizing this, Wittgenstein calls into question the intellectualist assumption that religion is an outmoded way of thinking. He combats prejudice which asserts that 'the science of culture is essentially a reformer's science' (Tylor, 1920, 453).

II

Even if we do not think religious belief is necessarily confused, we may still fail to mirror its practice in our philosophical accounts. We may be participants in religious practices and still give conceptually confused accounts of them. This is the second context we need to take into account. In 1950 Wittgenstein wrote:

> If someone who believes in God looks round and asks: 'Where does everything I see come from?', he is *not* craving for a (causal) explanation, and his question gets its sense from being the expression of a certain craving. He is, namely, expressing an attitude to all explanations—But how is this manifested in his life?

That is the crucial question for Wittgenstein. He continues:

> The attitude that's in question is that of taking a certain matter seriously and then, beyond a certain point, no longer regarding it as serious, but maintaining that something else is even more important. Someone may for instance say it's a very grave matter that such and such a man should have died before he could complete a certain piece

of work; and yet, in another sense, this is not what matters. At this point one uses the words 'in a deeper sense'. (CV, 85)

Someone whose intellectual powers are failing in old age may regret, as a grave matter, some work he has not completed. But he may come to look at old age and its infirmities as something that comes from God. This acceptance influences how he regards his earlier powers. He comes to see them as gifts of grace which the Lord gives, but also takes away.

The question, 'Where did everything come from?' may lead to this religious reflection. Yet, when someone philosophizes about this reflection, he may do so in terms of a super-explanation. He may feel that he cannot do justice to his religious belief unless he does this. Dominant philosophical trends may influence him. That is why Wittgenstein wrote in 1947: 'God grant the philosopher insight into what lies in front of everyone's eyes' (CV, 63). In making this insight explicit, the philosopher neither adds nor takes anything away from what is there to be appreciated. He does not replace practice with his own theories. Wittgenstein warns: 'Don't concern yourself with what, presumably, no one but you grasps' (CV, 63). Instead, he insists: 'Anything your reader can do for himself leave to him' (CV, 77).

Wittgenstein's appeal to practice has been greeted with a chorus of impatience. In philosophy, disputes will arise about whether certain philosophical accounts of religion distort or do justice to religious practices. Agreement may not be forthcoming. As a result, many come to feel that these philosophical discussions are pointless. For example, Stewart Sutherland writes:

> Much stimulus to the philosophical discussion of religious belief is to be found in the writings of D. Z. Phillips, but equally much sterile debate has resulted because both Phillips and his opponents have at times argued as if one appropriate criterion of the acceptability of his account of, say, petitionary prayer or the belief in eternal life, is whether or not this is what Christians *really* believe. Phillips has given weight to this by his interpretation and application of Wittgenstein's dictum that 'philosophy leaves everything as it is'. This is not the place for a full discussion of Phillips' views. It suffices to define my own enterprise over against his (and his opponents') by pointing out that I welcome his accounts of petitionary prayer and belief in eternal life; *but* I welcome them as interesting constructions upon or revisions of the Christian tradition rather than as they are apparently offered, descriptions of the most essential or continuing elements of that tradition. It is not clear that Phillips would accept my emphasis on the terms 'construction' or 'revision' (Sutherland, 1984, 7).

D. Z. Phillips

It should be clear that I would not accept this emphasis, but not because I want to show that my account of these beliefs is right and that the account offered by my opponents is wrong. I reject Sutherland's emphasis because it misses what Wittgenstein meant by a philosophical problem.

Sutherland describes himself as a theological reformer. He wants myself, and others, to admit that we, too, are prescribers rather than describers. I have nothing against theological reform, but it is different from the philosophical reflection I am concerned with. The language we use in religious practices may confuse us. We have seen already how we may be tempted to look for the object which the word 'God' stands for. To rid ourselves of these confusions we must unearth the tendencies which lead to them. This is no easy matter. Part of the work involves trying to give perspicuous representations of the practice we are tempted to distort. Wittgenstein explicitly contrasts this kind of discussion with desires to reform practice. He writes as early as 1931: 'I might say: if the place I want to get to could only be reached by way of a ladder, I would give up trying to get there. For the place I really have to get to is a place I must already be at now. Anything that I might reach by climbing a ladder does not interest me' (CV, 7). What we need in order to dissolve our philosophical puzzlement is not more facts or reforms which tell us how we *ought* to think but, rather, clarity about the ways in which we *do* think. Wittgenstein writes: 'One movement links thoughts with one another in a series, the other keeps aiming at the same spot. One is constructive and picks up one stone after another, the other keeps taking hold of the same thing' (CV, 7). Sutherland may want to reform practices. Wittgenstein wants to mirror their grammar.[2]

Sutherland's theological impatience is matched by a philosophical impatience in others. Whereas he wants to reform religious practice, they want some method by which its character can be settled once and for all. In response to my work, they have said that if believers reject the accounts of their belief I offer, their rejection is the last word on the matter. The believers' account is final. Wittgenstein certainly does not agree. He writes:

> Christianity is not a doctrine, not, I mean, a theory about what has happened and will happen to the human soul, but a description of something that actually takes place in human life. For 'consciousness of sine' is a real event, and so are despair and salvation through faith. Those who speak of such things (Bunyan for instance) are simply

[2] For a further discussion of this distinction see my paper, 'Grammarians and Guardians' (Phillips, 1988b). The paper is placed in a wider context in my *Faith After Foundationalism* (Phillips, 1988a).

describing what has happened to them, *whatever gloss anyone may want to put on it*. (CV, 28, my italics)

According to the impatient philosophers, we must accept the believers' gloss. The suggestion is baffling. These philosophers would not dream of advocating this procedure elsewhere in philosophy. I can be told any day of the week in my local pub that thinking is a state of consciousness. Does that settle the matter? I can also be told that thinking is a brain-state. Does that settle it too? No philosopher is going to accept these procedures. Why advocate them, then, in the philosophy of religion? On this view, no philosopher could capture deformities of thought in his philosophical mirror since, if every gloss is to be accepted, there are no deformities to mirror.

As an example of a misleading theological gloss, Wittgenstein referred to the historical status of the Gospel narratives. He writes:

God has *four* people account the life of his incarnate Son, in each case differently and with inconsistencies—but might we not say: It is important that this narrative should be no more than quite averagely historically plausible *just so that* this should not be taken as the essential decisive thing? So that the *letter* should not be believed more strongly than is proper and the *spirit* may receive its due. (CV, 31)

Some theologians see the variations and inconsistencies as indications of what is essential in the Gospels, whereas Wittgenstein sees them as indications of what is inessential: 'the historical proof (the historical proof-game) is irrelevant to belief. This message (the Gospels) is seized on by men believingly (i.e. lovingly). *That* is the certainty characterizing this particular-acceptance-as true, not something *else*' (CV, 32). We do not believe on the basis of a second-best account. What is essential for belief is not hidden: 'The Spirit puts what is essential, essential for your life, into these words. The point is precisely that you are only SUPPOSED to see clearly what appears clearly even in *this* representation' (CV, 32).

In disputing the gloss on religious beliefs which theologians, believers or philosophers may give, Wittgenstein does not take himself to have tampered with these beliefs in any way. His touchstone is what is shown in practice. He says of the believer: 'If I say he used a picture, I don't want to say anything he himself wouldn't say. I want to say that he draws these conclusions' (LC, 71). These conclusions are found in a believer's practice, not in his philosophizings about them. Wittgenstein acknowledges that a philosopher would have to revise his account if he found a believer drawing conclusions he did not expect him to draw: 'I want to draw attention to a particular technique of usage. We should disagree, if he was using a technique I didn't expect' (LC, 71). Once the

D. Z. Phillips

unexpected technique comes to light, its practice has the last say: 'All I wished to characterize was the conventions he wished to draw. If I wished to say anything more I was merely being philosophically arrogant' (LC, 72). Philosophy mirrors practice; it does not change it.

III

As a result of our conclusions so far, it may be thought that we cannot be critical of any religious practice. An absurd conservatism has been attributed to Wittgenstein.[3] In the third context I want to consider, however, philosophical reflection reveals confusions *in* religious practices. It may be asked how this is possible if Wittgenstein's final appeal is to practice. Difficulties arise only if we think of practice in too formal or restricted a way. If we think 'practice' must refer to something as formal as a ritual, and say that appeal to practice is final, we come to the unhappy conclusion that no ritual can be confused. But Wittgenstein's use of 'practice' is not confined to these formal senses. He means no more by 'practice' than 'what we do'. If some things we do are confused, how is this to be pointed out except by reference to other things we do? What does not make sense is the suggestion that all our practices might be confused. Wittgenstein says: 'It is true that we can compare a picture that is firmly rooted in us to a superstition; but it is equally true that we *always* eventually have to reach some firm ground, either a picture or something else, so that a picture which is at the root of all our thinking is to be respected and not treated as a superstition' (CV, 83). These remarks were written in 1949, but as early as 1930 Wittgenstein recognized the possibility of confused rituals and practices: 'Of course a kiss is a ritual too and it isn't rotten, but the ritual is permissible only to the extent that it is as genuine as a kiss' (CV, 8). Whether a ritual is superstitious is shown in its practice. Philosophy, in making this explicit, is not prescriptive.

Wittgenstein certainly thought it important to distinguish between religion and superstition: 'Religious faith and superstition are quite different. One of them results from fear and is a sort of false science. The other is a trusting' (CV, 72). For example, it is superstitious to think that there is some kind of queer causal connection between sin

---

[3] This accusation with others, equally unfounded, constitutes what has been called 'Wittgensteinian Fideism'. I challenged the accusation, with textual evidence, in *Belief, Change and Forms of Life* (Phillips, 1986). As far as I know, the challenge has not been answered by the critics who indulged in such accusations for twenty years. Some try to forget that the criticisms were ever made!

and worldly punishment. Being distanced from God is not a causal consequence of sin. Sin, pride and envy, for example, create the distance in simply being what they are. Praying to avoid God's anger is thus not a praying to avoid consequences, but a praying to avoid becoming a certain kind of person. Wittgenstein writes: 'God may say to me: "I am judging you out of your own mouth. Your own actions have made you shudder with disgust when you have seen other people do them"' (CV, 87). If we are only afraid of sin's consequences, there is no disgust.

A person may see a natural disaster which befalls him as punishment. There are two different ways he may think about it. 'If he is ill, he may think: "What have I done to deserve this?" This is one way of thinking about retribution. Another way is, he thinks in a general way whenever he is ashamed of himself, "This will be punished"' (LC, 54–55). Wittgenstein thinks that the first way of thinking is superstitious. The belief that at some future event, final punishments of this kind will be meted out, he takes to be a confused version of belief in a Last Judgement. He comments: 'Queerly enough, even if there were such a thing, and even if it were more convincing than I have described but, belief in this happening wouldn't be at all a religious belief' (LC, 56). He can make little of the way certain forms of predestination seek to explain the outcome of divine judgment so conceived. In them, man 'was created so that the interplay of forces would make him either conquer or succumb. And that is not a religious idea at all, but more like a scientific hypothesis' (CV, 86). The proposed explanation makes nonsense of ethical ideas: '"Out of his goodness he has chosen them and he will punish you" makes no sense. The two halves of the proposition belong to different ways of looking at things. The second half is ethical, the first not. And taken together with the first, the second is absurd' (CV, 81).

Sometimes, Wittgenstein equates the distinction between religion and superstition with a distinction between what he calls a higher and lower level of expression. In 1937 Wittgenstein wrote:

> In religion every level of devoutness must have its appropriate form of expression which has no sense at a lower level. The doctrine, which means something at a higher level, is null and void for someone who is still at the lower level; he *can* only understand it *wrongly* and so these words are not valild for such a person. (CV, 32)

Taking predestination as his example, Wittgenstein says:

> at my level the Pauline doctrine of predestination is ugly nonsense, irreligiousness. Hence it is not suitable for me, since the only use I could make of the picture I am offered would be a wrong one. If it is a good and godly picture, then it is so for someone at a quite different

level, who must use it in his life in a way completely different from anything that would be possible for me. (CV, 32)

How do we know the level to which particular religious pictures belong according to Wittgenstein? Peter Winch writes:

> His attitude towards the acceptance of pictures involved in religious belief was not a settled one; and this is one reason for not regarding what he says as constituting a theory. He treats different cases differently and his reactions to particular cases are avowedly very personal sometimes. (I am reminded of the remark in his *Lecture on Ethics*, that on certain matters he has 'to speak for himself').[4]

In what sense could the distinction between religion and superstition be said to be a personal one? The answer is that the same religious picture, the same form of words, may be superstitious in one practical context, but not in another. So if we ask whether a given religious picture is confused then, as Winch says, 'it is a question the force of which will only be apparent within the life of the believer; it is not one to which the philosopher can give any general theoretical answer' (1987, 74). On the other hand, *whether* a religious belief *is* superstitious is not up to the individual concerned to decide. Someone else may recognize that his belief is superstitious when he does not. Later, the person who was superstitious may come to recognize this; it is 'possible for someone who once did apply the picture without qualm later to think this had been possible only because he had failed to think about certain matters vigorously enough' (1987, 73). For these reasons, I do not think it is to the distinction between religion and superstition that we must turn to appreciate those reactions to religious beliefs where every person *must* 'speak for himself'.

IV

We must turn to our fourth context if we want to appreciate the sense in which reactions to religious beliefs *must* be personal. Here, too, we may speak of higher and lower levels of expression, but in this fourth context, this distinction will *not* correspond to that between religion and superstition. For example, we have seen already that whereas the Pauline picture of predestination, for Wittgenstein, would be 'ugly nonsense', he acknowledges that it may have a higher expression in someone else's life, where it might be 'a good and godly picture'. The

---

[4] Peter Winch, 'Wittgenstein, Picture and Representation' (Winch, 1987, 71–72).

further question to be raised now is this: are there *lower* expressions of belief, for Wittgenstein, which he does not regard as nonsense or superstitious? Clearly, there are. He may regard such beliefs as banal, vulgar, shabby or uninteresting. In so regarding them he is, of necessity, speaking for himself. We need to look at examples to illustrate this point.

Consider Wittgenstein's reactions to miracles. Sometimes, he simply disbelieves the reports he has heard. 'It would be an instance if, when a saint has spoken, the trees around him bowed as if in reverence.—Now, do I believe that this happens? I don't' (CV, 45). On the other hand, he might respond to the movement of the trees in this way, after the saint had spoken, without believing there to be any queer causal connection between the saint's words and the movement of the trees: 'The only way for me to believe in a miracle in this sense would be to be *impressed* by an occurrence in this particular way' (CV, 45). But there is a third possibility: 'And I can imagine that the mere report of the *words* and life of a saint can make someone believe the reports that the trees bowed' (CV, 45). The belief is vague, not one which invokes any causal connection. It seems to be an extension of the impression the saint's words made on the person. Speaking for himself, however, Wittgenstein adds, 'But I am not so impressed' (CV, 45).

Consider a different kind of example. I recall an elderly widow asking me why God had called her two sons home before her. She proceeded to provide her own answer. She said that if she went into a garden to pick flowers, she would not choose weeds, but the best blooms. In taking her sons to himself, God had picked the best blooms. Does this picture imply that the longer one lives, the less one counts in the eyes of God? Obviously not. She does not push the picture in that direction. She is saluting her sons, that is all. Her practice is decisive. It need not be confused or superstitious. On the other hand, I do not find the picture very helpful. It sustained her, but it would not sustain me. Here, she and I have to speak for ourselves.

In other examples, it may be hard to determine whether the practice of belief is superstitious or not. Wittgenstein asks:

What would it feel like not to have heard of Christ?
Should we feel alone in the dark?
Do we escape such a feeling simply in the way a child escapes it when he knows there is someone in the room with him. (CV, 45)

When I look at what the presence of Christ means to a certain person, I may be inclined to call the belief superstitious: 'No great harm can befall me. He's always there, unseen and unheard. But if the worst comes to the worst, he'll intervene to stay the blow.'[5] How little that has

[5] I like the story of the mountain climber who, seeing his rope begin to fray

in common with, 'The Lord gave, the Lord hath taken away. Blessed be the name of the Lord.' On the other hand, religious belief may be far removed from the Book of Job without being superstitious. A person may go through a life which has not been overtaxed, comforted by the thought of the cosy, Constant Companion. I am reminded of the lady who was comforted by the thought that she could always cuddle up to God. Even when tribulations occur, they are perceived in terms of a religious romanticism. Such words at funerals are often thought to be wonderful. We may find these reactions banal and shabby, but they are fixed, regulative paradigms in the lives of those they sustain. These pictures, the Mills and Boon products of religion, are 'laid up in heaven', occupying a grammatical position which others reserve for a God of a very different kind. It is pictures such as these that led the dramatist Dennis Potter to say: 'the human dream for *some* concept of "perfection", some Zion or Eden or Golden City, will surface and take hold of whatever circumstances are at hand—no matter how ludicrous. Even in a future land of Muzak, monosodium glutamate and melamined encounters, the old resilient dreams will insist on making metaphors and finding illumination in the midst of the surrounding dross. There is, then, no place where "God" cannot reach' (Potter, 1983, Introduction, p. 3). What god emerges and our reactions to him are another matter. Here, everyone has to speak for himself.

Underlying the treatment of all these examples is Wittgenstein's question, 'How should we compare beliefs with each other? What would it mean to compare them . . . The strength of a belief is not comparable with the intensity of a pain' (LC, 54). The strength of a belief is measured, partly, by what a person is prepared to risk for it, by the way it governs his life. For Wittgenstein, these considerations affect what he wants to say about the character of the belief.

This is illustrated in Wittgenstein's hints about spiritualism: 'Cf Flowers at seance with label. People said: "Yes, flowers are materialized with label." What kind of circumstances must there be to make this kind of story not ridiculous? (LC, 61). What if explanations carry no weight with the participants? What if they regard attempts at explanation as blasphemous? For Wittgenstein, that they do so affects the character of their practice. He does not insist that we *must* assume that these spiritualists are playing the game of offering explanations. Wittgenstein's attitude even extends to cases where duplicity is involved: 'I have a statue which bleeds on such and such a day in the

---

on a steep climb, called out to the heavens in desperation, 'Is there anyone there?' A voice replied: 'I am here my son. I am always with you. Let go the rope. Underneath are the everlasting arms.' The climber paused, then shouted: 'Is there anyone else there?'

year. I have red ink etc. You are a cheat, but nevertheless the Deity uses you. Red ink in a sense, but not red ink in a sense' (LC, 61). We may or may not be impressed by the fact that a phenomenon which depends on cheating leads to a devotion such cheating could never have anticipated. Some may speak of gullibility, while others say, 'Look, God even used the cheat.' I have been in churches where the statue 'bleeds'. For some, the availability of an explanation destroys its impressiveness, while for others it does not. At other times, reactions depend on the statue in question.

Wittgenstein does not call the beliefs in the examples we have considered superstitious or confused, but he does not call them impressive either. I suspect he would call most of them lower expressions of belief. Whether he or we find particular expressions of belief high or low, however, is a matter of personal reaction; reactions in which we all speak for ourselves. This is something the philosopher of religion ought to point out. It means that in considering reactions to religious beliefs, we cannot divide them neatly into reactions to beliefs we find spiritually impressive, and reactions to beliefs we find superstitious or confused. Philosophers must find room for the ugly, the banal and the vulgar for these, too, may be forms of religious belief.

V

In the fifth and final context I want to consider, philosophers' relations to practices are seen to be far more pragmatic than they often suppose. Mention of a pragmatic attitude will increase misgivings many philosophers will have felt already about the conclusions reached in this paper. They fear that talk of pragmatism is simply an excuse for intellectual sloppiness or even dishonesty. Its result, they would argue, is to let people get away, without criticism, with all sorts of confused, and possibly dangerous practices. I want to show that such misgivings are without foundation.

Of course, the misgivings I have mentioned are bound to be felt by those who think that *all* forms of religious belief are necessarily confused. But then, as indicated in the first context we considered, Wittgenstein finds this general thesis philosophically suspect.

Taking a pragmatic attitude to religious practice, as we saw in the second context we considered, does not mean that Wittgenstein lets anyone, participants included, whether they happen to be philosophers or not, get away with confused accounts of religious practice. Consider, for example, a religious belief Wittgenstein says he understands: 'Suppose someone before going to China, when he might never see me again, said to me, "We might see one another after death"—would I necessarily say that I don't understand him? I might say [want to say] simply, "Yes, I *understand* him entirely."' When Lewy suggests that Wittgenstein might mean only that he expressed a certain attitude, Wittgenstein replies, 'I would say "No, it isn't the same as saying I'm very fond of you"—and it may not be the same as saying anything else. It says what it says. Why should you be able to substitute anything else?' (LC). But he does not hesitate to criticize certain philosophical accounts of such meetings: 'Philosophers who say: "after death a time-less state will begin" or: "at death a timeless state begins", and do not notice that they have used the words "after" and "at" and "begins" in a temporal sense and that temporality is embedded in their grammar' (CV, 22).

In the third context we considered, it is clear that taking a pragmatic attitude to religious practice does not condone superstition. Whenever reflection shows superstition to be present in practices, Wittgenstein does not hesitate to point it out. Although Wittgenstein distinguishes between religion and superstition, one cannot save religion from criticism by calling anything open to such criticism 'superstition'. The reason why is obvious: superstition sometimes takes a religious form. Religion is capable of making a distinctive contribution to superstitious practices.

It is the fourth context which will probably cause most concern if we speak of a pragmatic attitude to what might be regarded as lower expressions of religious belief. It may seem that where such religious beliefs are concerned, their adherents can say what they like. But is this true?

What if a believer said that the meeting he longed for after death was like a meeting between human beings on earth. A myriad objections would occur to one. How could one meet one's father or wife after death despite the cessation of the circumstances which give such relationships their sense? How can one meet a friend again when the friend was drowned when ten years old and one is dying aged ninety-one? And so on for a hundred other questions. Suppose someone responded: 'I know what I mean even if these practical contexts are absent', what then? A humorous incident related by Norman Malcolm, concerning Wittgenstein, illustrates what our reply should be. Malcolm writes: 'On one walk he "gave" to me each tree we passed, with the reservation that I was not to cut it down or do anything to it, or prevent the previous owners from doing anything to it: with those reservations it was hence-forth *mine*' (Malcolm, 1958). Without the appropriate practice, such a 'gift' is no gift at all. Similarly, it may be said, without the appropriate practice, the 'hope of a meeting' is no hope of a meeting at all. As A. G. N. Flew once said, the 'hope' 'dies a death by a thousand qualifications' (Flew, 1955, 96). It is no good saying that it is an ordinary hope, but that one is unaware of the details, since it is the details which make the hope an ordinary one.

If a believer were making claims such as these, Wittgenstein would agree with the philosophical objections made against them. But why should we assume that believers are making such claims? Their practice may show that they are not. The hope of meeting a loved one after death may dominate a life without the person who entertains the hope bothering himself about the kind of details we have discussed. In that sense, the hope is a vague one. Someone says he will see his dead friend again. Wittgenstein comments: 'He always says it, but he doesn't make any search. He puts on a queer smile. "His story has that dreamlike quality." My answer would be in this case "Yes", and a particular explanation' (LC, 63). For Flew, the vagueness which surrounds this story *disqualifies* it. For Wittgenstein, the vagueness *qualifies* the story; it shows us the kind of story it is. It is a story 'laid up in heaven'; a fixed paradigm which governs a person's life.

In such a story images of 'sleep' and 'waking' may be used. *Must* we say they are confused? Must we say that death is being confused with a sleep of long duration? But when a person speaks of waking from the sleep of death 'it does not keep him from the terrible recognition that his brother is not asleep but dead: he does not try to wake the corpse, and he knows it would make no sense to speak of waking it. There is no need to ask him, "Don't you know what death is? Don't you know what it is when someone's dead?" He would not bury or cremate his brother when he was asleep. And yet he may go on using this imagery.'[6] As we have seen, this does not mean that the user of the imagery cannot become confused:

> We may speak of people who have died as 'the departed' because they are not *here*; they are no longer among us. When my brother had died it is obvious—too obvious—that he is not among us. But if I thought it must have sense to speak of 'where he is' or to say 'he must be somewhere', this would show a confusion of grammar. And this may be because the grammar of personal names and personal pronouns is not clear to me. (Ibid.)

Believers may talk of meeting loved ones again at the end of time, or of the meeting 'happening outside time'. Rhees comments:

> Here there are images which must be left as images. We might call some of them deep and others tawdry, that is all. But this does not mean that the distinction between what there is and what will be is unimportant; or that we can give an *equivalent* expression of the

[6] Quoted from a letter by Rush Rhees (4 August 1970) in response to my book, *Death and Immortality* (Phillips, 1970).

belief in which the difference of 'now' and 'then' has vanished. (Ibid.)

At one point in *Lectures and Conversations*, Wittgenstein is reported as saying that he himself does not speak of seeing friends after death (LC, 63). But he does not always take himself to be denying or contradicting what is said by those who do. He is taking a far more pragmatic attitude than many philosophers think appropriate. By all means point out confusion and superstition when practice reveals it. Yet, there will be times when, confronted by beliefs which are obviously important in people's lives we, as philosophers, may feel that there is little we can say about them or even make of them. In that case, is it not philosophically arrogant to want to say more? Religious allegories may cause confusion or they may not. Even when they do not, some will be able to appropriate them while others will fail to do so. Wittgenstein said as much of Bunyan's *The Pilgrim's Progress*: 'If anyone gets upset by this allegory, one might say to him: Apply it differently, or else leave it alone! (But there are *some* whom it will confuse far more than it can help)' (CV, 77).

Philosophers are reluctant to leave things alone. They are tempted to make matters tidier than they are. But as we have seen in the five contexts we have considered, the relation of philosophy to religious practice cannot be summed up in any once-and-for-all fashion. Neither can the practices themselves be summed up in this way. These are the things Wittgenstein shows in his philosophical mirror. If we appreciate how he does this, we see that while Wittgenstein describes actual uses of language, he does not interfere with them. He does not try to give them foundations either in terms of preconceived paradigms of rationality. In fact, he shows how searching for such foundations is confused. Wittgenstein's mirror shows that he is striving constantly after that end which is extremely difficult to achieve—to leave everything where it is. In *Culture and Value* the whole task is summed up thus 'My ideal is a certain coolness. A temple providing a setting for the passions without meddling with them' (CV, 2).[7]

[7] An earlier version of the paper was read at a colloquium on Wittgenstein and the Philosophy of Culture at the Inter-University Centre, Dubrovnik, in May 1989, and to the Philosophical Society of the University College of Swansea. I benefited from the discussions on those occasions.

Psychoanalysis: A Form of Life?[1]

MICHAEL BREARLEY

Introduction

My aim in this paper is to consider the suggestion, made in an unpublished paper by Peter Hobson, a psychoanalytic colleague, that psychoanalysis is a form of life. Hobson is impressed by the peculiarity of psychoanalytic thinking, by its specialness, by the fact that its concepts are embedded in a system of practices and beliefs such that an outsider to all this may be unable to understand what the analyst says, whether to his patient or to another analyst. Hobson uses Wittgenstein's notion of a form of life to refer to this system of practices and beliefs, but he does not criticize or examine the notion itself.

I shall attempt to do this, partly for its own sake, but mainly to throw light on the nature of psychoanalysis and its relations to ordinary, non-psychoanalytic understanding. I shall argue that it is closer to the facts and to Wittgenstein's notion of forms of life to say that psychoanalysis, though an extension of ordinary understanding, is rooted in it; that it is part of *the* form of life which characterizes human beings; that the verification of a psychoanalytic framework lies, in the long run, in our ordinary stock of understanding about people and their inner worlds; that the sense in which we may be inclined to say that psychoanalysis is a separate form of life is epistemologically innocuous, that is, that it implies no logical gap between those who practise it or explicitly use its ideas and those who do not.

I. The Example

But first to Hobson. I will start with the example from clinical practice which he offers as illustration of his claims; he offers it, that is, in order to persuade us of the 'dimension of psychoanalytic knowledge concerning people which is of a different order from *all other ways* of knowing people' (my italics).

---

[1]An earlier version of this paper was given as the J. R. Jones Memorial Lecture at the University College of Swansea in October 1986.

Hobson's patient had been adopted early in life. On the Friday of the first week of analysis, he telephoned the clinic under whose auspices the treatment was happening to leave a message that he would be unable to attend his session that evening. He said he did not know the name of his analyst, it might be Hobbs, but he could give the number of his own file so that the analyst's name might be traced. On Monday, he asked as he came through the door whether the analyst had received the message. The analyst gave a brief nod. The patient said 'Good—I am afraid I was unable to remember your name.' After one or two further remarks, the analyst asked if his name was not on the letter he had received from the Clinic; the man said he had lost it under a file. The analyst then said 'The name is Hobson'. The patient replied that he thought it was, that was what he had said: it had been silly of him, he had forgotten that on Friday he had something important to go to.

Hobson's comments on this series of events include the following: he resented having been manoeuvred into a premature response; he felt increasing dismay at the patient's story and his own discomfort. He felt churned up bodily as well as in thought and feeling when he made his 'peculiarly disembodied protest: "The name is Hobson."'

Only when he tried to make sense of his discomfort did he reach a new understanding of the patient and of the interaction. Recognizing something alien to himself in the churned-up state, he came to realize that the patient had orphaned *him* that Friday, turned *him* into a number, into Hobbs—no-one's son, not Hobson. To the patient it mattered not a jot, as he had had something important to go to.

Hobson shows us an example of what analysts call projective identification. The patient got rid of an acutely painful part of his own experience by inflicting it on the analyst, who was aware of his discomfort as something alien that tempted him to abandon his customary analytic stance and insist in this way that 'the name is Hobson'. Such an enactment by the patient could also have been intended, unconsciously, as a communication, in the only way the patient could, at this stage, communicate, of the painful experience of being orphaned. Even if it was not so intended, the analyst could use the interaction in the service of understanding, once he himself had been able to understand it.

Hobson's example would, I think, be recognized by analysts as typical of the processes of discomfort, struggle and (sometimes) understanding that are intrinsic to our work. We would also recognize the need we all have had, and continue to have, for initiation into, and improvement on, this peculiarly analytic frame or set of mind, an initiation and training which more resembles an apprenticeship than the application of book-learned concepts.

II. Hobson's Argument

However, Hobson uses it to exemplify a stronger claim. For he believes that the initiated (the analyst) relates to the uninitiated as an ordinary adult relates to an autistic youth called 'Stephen', a patient in a mental hospital, who was 'unable to work out what a "friend" was'. Stephen would 'pester the staff with endlessly repetitive questions, returning again and again to ask: "What are friends?"' Stephen, Hobson suggests, could not understand the meaning of the word 'friend' because 'he does not share in that form of life in which friends, and the language of friendship, find their existence . . . In order to share in *our* understanding of friendship, Stephen would need to become involved in personal relationships of the kinds that are fitting between friends'.

Hobson goes on to connect the question 'what is a friend?' with the question 'What is psychoanalysis?' He claims that 'there is a dimension of psychoanalytic knowledge concerning people which is of a different order from all other ways of knowing people, and that to be a party to such knowledge an individual must participate in experiences of a special kind, in special kinds of way . . .'. It is only through the discovery that there is an understanding which is uniquely psychoanalytic that he can know what psychoanalysis is. 'I suggest', Hobson continues, 'that an individual without psychoanalytic knowledge understands our psychoanalytic discourse about as well as my patient Stephen understands talk about friends.'

Hobson goes on to give the example quoted above of experience of his own in relation to an analytic patient, experiences of discomfort which he needed to reflect on in 'a peculiarly psychoanalytic way' before he could come to understand something about the patient. As a result of this process—the patient's actions and remarks, his own discomfort and reaction, and his reflection on his discomfort—Hobson himself came to understand more deeply an area of analytic discourse as well as the particular exchange with his patient.

Now I would sugest that in Hobson's paper there are to be found two claims, one strong, one weaker. The strong claim is that the relationship between psychoanalytic discussion and ordinary discourse about the emotional life of people is like that between ordinary discourse about friendship and Stephen's discourse—or lack of it—about friendship; to repeat the quotation from Hobson's paper: 'to be a party to such knowledge' (that is 'psychoanalytic knowledge of people', which 'has a dimension which is of a different order from all other ways of knowing people') 'an individual must participate in experiences of a special kind'. It is hard not to read this as saying that only psychoanalysts, and perhaps analysands, can be parties to such knowledge, that the 'experiences of a special kind' are available only to those who have first-hand acquaintance with the extra 'dimension which is of a different order from all other ways of knowing people.' According to this view, the position of non-analysts (with the possible exception, as I say, of analysands) is like that of a person born blind in relation to colour-language. 'In order to achieve pyschoanalytical ways of understanding, people need to have the wish . . . to enter a new form of life,' Hobson writes, 'one that will involve them in specifically psychoanalytic struggles.' 'Entering a new form of life' seems to imply a conversion to new ways of living, specifically, entering into psychoanalytic relationship with someone who can help in the 'specifically psychoanalytic struggles'. The non-participant can, on this view, offer only distantly analogical remarks about psychoanalytic discourse, rather like the man born blind, referred to by Dr Johnson, who, 'after long inquiry into the nature of this scarlet colour, found that it represented nothing so much as the clangour of a trumpet'. The blind man cannot experience scarlet, cannot enjoy it, recognize it, compare it with other colours; and therefore he is shut off from much of our ordinary discourse about colours.

The second, weaker, claim implicit in Hobson's paper appears in footnote and qualifications, as if the author jibbed at the more extreme implications of his thesis. One such qualification is that psychoanalysis is not *'fully'* independent as a form of life; and, this being so, there *is* much about it that may be communicated to those who have never experienced psychoanalysis.

On this view, when Hobson says that psychoanalytic discourse 'cannot be understood without psychoanalytic knowledge', he is making a modest conceptual claim (which may be important and illuminating when fleshed out with detail and example) not a bold conceptual/psychological claim about the necessity for first-hand knowledge of the analytic process. Similarly, when he talks of 'the specifically psychoanalytic struggles' that entry into the new form of life entails, he may not be talking necessarily of struggles that can *only occur within* an analysis. He may be saying that specifically psychoanalytic struggles may take place within a person's mind or within a relationship, struggles that are of the same species as the ones that typically go on within the psychoanalytic consulting-room.

On this view, having an analysis, or becoming an analyst, are not the only routes to that sort of sensitivity to the dimensions of thought and feeling that characterize the best sort of analysis. It is, of course, a corollary of this version that psychoanalytic experience and training are no guarantee of a truly psychoanalytic understanding of mental processes. Put another way, psychoanalytic discourse may be used without the spirit of psychoanalysis.

Returning to Hobson and the more moderate view to be found in his paper: the language of psychoanalysis is a part of and ramifies into a wider language of the emotional life. Hobson may be seen as arguing that some people are unable to enter into the sort of exploration of the dimensions of their inner life that is the quintessence of the psychoanalytic struggle. Such limitations are of course a matter of degree; but in an extreme form, in which what is immediately and crudely available to consciousness is taken to be the whole of mental life, the limitation *is* like Stephen's in relation to those who in ordinary ways talk about friendship.

The contrast, then, should not be between the psychoanalytic community and the rest, but between those, including psychoanalysts, who give credence to the dimensions of the mind, and those who do not; or, in the words of the analyst John Rickman, between 'those who actively accept the notion of the unconscious and those who actively refuse to acknowledge it'.

Hobson's stronger claim, I will argue, is false as it stands, but true when modified to the less strong form which is also to be found in his article.

III. Forms of Life: One or Many?

In fact the question whether or not psychoanalysis is *a* form of life (or a *fully independent* form of life) is not a question to which unequivocal meaning has been given. We do not yet have criteria for specifying and differentiating forms of life. To make this clearer, think of a large extended family living in a single house. The house has been divided into flats, some more separate from the central dining and living areas than others. Ramshackle extensions have been tacked on. If someone now asks 'But how many families live in the house, is it one or many?' the answer may be that no-one has yet decided whether or not the word 'family' is to be used in a wide or a narrow sense here. Which answer one is inclined to offer will depend on whether one is concerned to stress the interconnectedness of all the residents of the house or the separateness of each sub-set.

Hobson takes the latter course with psychoanalysis. For him the members of the psychoanalytic nuclear family, though not, as he says, entirely independent, 'co-exist within a matrix of commonly acknowledged experiences of a very special kind, and share a language which is correspondingly unique'. Psychoanalysis is like, say, Gujerati within the family of Indo-European languages.

I am inclined to stress the opposite point of view. I want to say that psychoanalysis is part of the wider family of personal interactions and its discourse part of the ordinary sophisticated discourse of emotional life. Psychoanalytic language is not, essentially, unique. Psychoanalysts speak the same language as the other members of the human family. Psychoanalysis is partly extension, partly original fabric. The main house looks different thanks to the light and spaces that the new extension provides.

This question, 'how many forms of life?' is, when applied to our topic, closely related to another, raised above: 'when Hobson refers to psychoanalysis as a form of life, with what is he implicitly contrasting it?' Let us call the person who 'partakes of the psychoanalytic form of life' A or 'Analytic Man'. We have some notion of what this says about A, Analytic Man, that when faced with certain sorts of emotional problem he or she would seriously consider consulting an analyst or having an analysis; A might advocate analysis for a friend and when considering disordered emotional behaviour would use analytic concepts to understand and explain it. And so on. But with whom is A to be contrasted? With B, Broad Man, perhaps, who supports dynamic psychotherapy but disagrees with some psychoanalytic beliefs and practices, so that he is inclined to recommend for himself or others therapists who are not analysts? Or C, Church Man, whose mind turns to religion and to religious pundits in times of trouble? Or what about D, Down to Earth Man, who questions all so-called expertise and training in the field of emotional life, and advocates talking to one's friends? Or does Hobson have in mind as one who does not share in the psychoanalytic form of life E, who believes that all emotional disturbance is caused by chemical imbalance and calls therefore for chemical or physical therapies? Perhaps we could call E Endocrine Man.

Before attending to this question in more detail let us pause to consider why these questions—the general question about identifying and enumerating forms of life and the specific one about where Hobson draws his lines in his use of the notion of a psychoanalytic form of life—matter. Is there any harm in a proliferation of forms of life, such that not only do B, C and D have different forms of life from A, but Kleinian analysts from Freudians? By the same slide, each one of us may be said to have our own form of life, and within that, split-off aspects of ourselves (which, indeed, it is one of the aims of analysis to bring into communication with each other) may also be categorized as forms of life.

According to Wittgenstein's use of the concept it does make a difference how broad it is. For he uses it to refer to the limits of justification. 'If I have exhausted the justifications,' he writes, 'I have reached bedrock, and my spade is turned. Then I am inclined to say: "This is simply what I do"' (PI, I, 217). And, later, 'What has to be accepted, the given is—so one could say—forms of life' (PI, 226).

A. C. Grayling writes:

> It follows for Wittgenstein that questions about the ultimate explanation or justification of the concepts embodied in our thought and talk very soon *come to an end*—what justifies our usage is the shared form of life underlying them, and that is that: no more either need be or indeed can be said . . . Explanation and justification neither need to nor can go beyond a gesture towards the form of life. (Grayling, 1988)

The problem arises: if there is more than one form of life, and if psychoanalysis is one, how can an exponent use reason to persuade an outsider (whether B, C, D or E) of the validity of his language-activity? Is he reduced to saying 'This is simply what I do'? Does the 'ultimate explanation of the concepts embodied in our (analytic) thought' . . . 'very soon come to an end' . . . with a 'gesture towards the form of life'?

In order to explore this question further, let us examine it in light of the contrast between Analytic Man and Endocrine Man. I choose this contrast since we would be on safe ground, I think, in assuming that Hobson would accept the idea that A and E, or at least the somewhat extreme versions of A and E that I will now describe, operate in different forms of life. Let us suppose that both are fanatical champions of their own theories and practices, A a fanatic for psychoanalysis, E for chemotherapy, so that about cases presented for discussion they propose radically different lines of treatment. The arguments that A adduces for analysis carry no weight for E, and *vice versa*. A sees potential patients as emotional beings whose qualities as persons have no relevant connection with their brain-states, whereas E sees them as bodies which have produced mental discomfort or as persons for whom a talking cure (such as B, C and D as well as A propose) is inappropriate. The nature of A's and E's consultations will differ; different questions will be asked and the answers differently responded to. So the data on which they will base their respective diagnoses, prognoses and prescriptions will differ.

When asked to defend their approaches, both A and E may, in the end, refer to assumptions which are not descriptions but, in Wittgenstein's words 'norms of description'. E at least would concur with the whole of this section, which reads:

> It is clear that our empirical propositions do not all have the same status, since one can lay down such and such a proposition and turn it from an empirical proposition to a norm of description.
>
> Think of chemical investigations. Lavoisier makes experiments with substances in his laboratory and now he concludes that this and that take place when there is burning. He does not say that it might happen otherwise at another time. He has got hold of a definite

world-picture—not of course one that he invented: he learned it as a child. I would say world-picture and not hypothesis, because it is the matter-of-course foundation for his research and as such also goes unmentioned.' (OC, 167)

E might add that a patient's state of mind is like the residue of burning: we know little about the brain's chemistry as yet, but as we know more we will be able to explain and control more. What we do not question is that people are part of nature and subject to natural laws. E, like Lavoisier, lives, we might say, a different form of life from that of a naive believer in miracles, who would say that 'it might happen otherwise at another time.'

A, in his/her approach, would insist on other categories of description. Like B, C and D, A might remind us of the role of reason and talk in affecting people's states of mind. A child who is frightened of a snake in the bedroom may have his fear removed by being shown that what it thought was a snake was the sleeve of a dress. Secondly, A might point to the role of unconscious, unarticulated fantasies whose articulation may gradually change states of mind; for example, a child who is frightened when told that the sun and stars are bigger than the earth may have his terror modified when someone understands with him that he has the idea that the sky is like the ceiling of a room whose floor is the earth, so that the stars and sun would be images painted on the ceiling, in which picture there is no room for a heavenly body bigger than the earth. Third, A could point to the role of mother-love is easing terrors in the child, a loving attention which includes the elements mentioned above, but which also has to do with tolerating the child's anxieties and detoxifying them. In short, A uses a different set of paradigms of personal change from those used by E; the forms of life which inform their approach are, we may be inclined to say, radically different.

Now it might seem that A and E can only each 'gesture to the form of life', each to his own, and that this is the end of the argument; that there is no possibility of their bringing to their discussions considerations capable of influencing the intellect of the other. But this is not so. For however wide the disagreement, both A and E accept each other's form of life. A could not deny that *some* states of mind are caused by physical changes in body and brain, for example by toxic drugs, and that in some cases he could imagine using antidotes against such effects. A could not deny that the symptoms of Alzheimer's disease or GPI are caused by chemical changes in the brain. A has no need to deny Lavoisier's 'norms of description'. Equally, E would accept that some changes in mental state have psychic causes, whether or not he believes in the reducibility, in principle, of such explanations to chemistry; for example, one's mind is changed by rational argument! I recall the story of a psychiatrist who prescribed ECT to a patient; when it was pointed out to him that the patient had had ECT before without beneficial effect, he replied 'But he has never had ECT given by *me*!' Such psychiatrists may well accept the impact of a social setting on the patient's well-being. Even Pavlov's dogs were, it turns out, affectionately treated by their experimenters, and this, though not of course considered relevant in the 'scientific' account, was not perhaps entirely irrelevant to the experiment. It is mere assumption to say that it must have been.

We may say that A and E have different forms of life; or we may prefer to describe the facts differently and say that the form of life which we understand as being human includes both sets of presumptions, both world-pictures. Being human involves accepting as explanatory paradigms examples both of the physical causation of mental states and of the practical effect of reason on emotional life. Differences between A and E which we are inclined to call differences in forms of life are explicable to A and E and amenable to reason if and only if agreement in basic forms of life or world-picture can be found. Similar arguments apply to other disagreements, for example, those between A and B, C or D.

A psychoanalyst might well explain his point to another analyst by a 'gesture' to their shared, analytic understanding (form of life, construed narrowly). But he is not neccessarily at a loss for words when questioned by an outsider. He has then to pitch his explanation at a different level, linking analytic uses of language with the wider everyday language of emotional life. Thus his 'ultimate' explanation calls for reference to the whole of our form of life concerning other people and ourselves, including, in some contexts, a discussion of people as physico-chemical organisms.

What cannot intelligibly be doubted is this whole form of life (concerning others and ourselves) all at once. Any bit of it can be doubted and challenged in respect of its validity in comparison to some part of life which is not then being challenged; bits of the whole can be re-aligned in relation to other bits.

The challenge may or may not be rationally upholdable. Two astronomers arguing about the relative size of sun, earth and stars expect to settle their argument by reference to shared paradigms of explanation. To an uninitiated person, the child mentioned above, perhaps, who expresses incomprehension at the idea that the sun and stars could be larger than the earth, the astronomers' paradigms are of no help, and for this child explanation and justification need to be pitched at a level more basic than that assumed by the astronomers. Moreover, the child's terror needs to be addressed. When someone finds out by listening, and then articulates with him, his world picture it becomes possible for him to understand how on the basis of this picture what the astronomers say could not be true. Once the child has come to see that his picture is not the only possible one, astronomers and child can begin to use ideas that both share, like 'this is bigger than that', 'this looks bigger than that', 'this object is further away from that than that is'; so that the idea that the sun is bigger than the earth becomes thinkable. Explanation and proof for the child require an expansion of his language-game and thus of his form of life (narrow sense) such that all that his old picture included is included in the new picture, plus more. The expansion is possible only given a form of life (broader sense) that he and the astronomers share.

If on the other hand two astrologers were discussing the influence of the position of the constellations on a person's life, though they, like the astronomers, might equally be able to settle their disagreement by reference to paradigms accepted within their system of ideas, within, we might say, their form of life, the child's challenge in this case might rationally be valid; for it may be that the astrologers' form of life is an example of pseudo-science cut off from the ordinary scientific understanding. If, for instance, it can be shown that the stars that form constellations have no connection with each other except in so far as from a geocentric point of view certain patterns can be made out, then, it seems to me, it is hard to maintain that the appearance of a particular pattern can make any difference, objectively, to events.

So, if form of life is construed in a narrow way 'bedrock' of justification and explanation is not reached only by reference to it, and Grayling is not right when he says that 'explanation and justification neither need to nor can go beyond a gesture to the form of life.' When on the other hand the concept is used broadly it is not true that explanation cannot go beyond a *gesture* to it, or that explanations 'very soon come to an end'.

In the narrower sense, one may say that philosophers (people doing philosophy) share in a form of life. When Wittgenstein argues that when we do philosophy a picture holds us captive (PI, I, 115), he asks us to look at our narrow form of life (how we tend to talk when doing philosophy) in the light of our broader form of life (how we tend to talk when not doing philosophy, how our concepts actually work in their natural habitat). His later philosophy may be described as just such an enterprise; it is hardly a 'gesture towards a form of life'; his explanations do not '*very soon come to an end*'. Nor does Wittgenstein think that the (narrow-sense) philosophical form of life is self-justifying. It is only by contrast with non-philosophical, down-to-earth usage that (some of) our philosophizing is shown to be 'language idling' (PI, I, 132), a 'bewitchment by language' (PI, I, 109).

To sum up this section: talk of separate forms of life may wrongly encourage the idea that there is no room for rationality in evaluating the frameworks and the claims in what may too readily be thought of as *one* form of life. Whereas, I maintain, there are no settled criteria for 'the same' or 'different' forms of life. My claim is that comprehension of the meaning of statements in what we are inclined to call another form of life is possible because of forms of life shared or shareable between the two, and that therefore there are criteria for rationally assessing the claims made within, and the conceptual frameworks of, a (narrowly construed) form of life.

The more closely we link form of life with ultimate justification and explanation the stronger the case for the idea that human life is *the* form of life. The more we are inclined to describe the variegated practices and beliefs of people as differences in form of life the more need we have to sever the link between form of life on one hand and ultimate justification and explanation on the other, and the more we need to stress in other terms the assumptions and beliefs shared between those whose forms of life vary.

IV. Forms of Life and Theoretical Ethology

When Wittgenstein writes about the incomprehensibility, to us, of talking lions (PI, 225), I do not think he means that we could never, in principle, understand them; for he has just written that 'one human being can be a complete enigma to another' and has reminded us of strange countries with strange traditions. 'We do not understand the people' . . . 'even given a mastery of a country's language'—but none of this implies that we, the stranger, cannot come to understand the people. Here he writes as a theoretical ethologist. It is *only* by knowledge of cultural diversity that we can understand strangers, including the strangeness of those close to us, and our own strangeness. Talking of different forms of life, as Wittgenstein at times does, and as Peter Hobson does, reminds us of at least two things. (i) Where conceptual perplexity is pervasive or radical the elucidation of the meaning of an area of language calls for attention to its whole natural habitat. And the habitat includes the non-verbal practices of the language community. So it is natural that when Hobson introduces the notion in connection with Stephen and friendship he should talk about participating in forms of life, about the having of certain experiences.

(ii) From either side of the divide the problem may appear insuperable. The initiated may feel that they cannot find sufficient agreement and openness in the uninitiated for a dialogue to begin, and the uninitiated may feel that the initiates speak in mysteries and obscurities which cannot be got through. In such impasses there may be feelings of incomprehension and inscrutability. Hobson's use of forms of life to mark the differences between insiders and outsiders may be salutary in stressing the actual and possible impasses, in underlying the fact that we cannot omnipotently assume that we can convert everyone to our point of view, to our way of life.

To return to psychoanalysis. Certain of its practices and certain of the analysts' formulations strike outsiders as esoteric and, until their place in the whole practice is understood, encourage scepticism on one side and a sense of futility in explaining oneself on the other. One such practice is the peculiar physical arrangement of the analytic pair. Not only is the setting, unlike other settings in which scientific data are presented, private; but also the patient characteristically lies on the couch while the analyst sits behind him or her. As to the analyst's formulations, they often interpret the patient's words and behaviour in ways that suggest there is more reference to the analyst than would on the surface appear justified. Now, both these apparently bizarre phe-nomena need to be seen in the whole context of analytic therapy. For patients come to an analyst with the idea that they might be understood, and with the idea that they have certain troubles for which they hope to find understanding or help. The patients also come with fears or anxieties about not getting helpful understanding, which, on top of their own repressions and distortions, further muddies the communica-tion. The combination—a hope for understanding and a fear both of being understood and of not being understood—makes explicable the analyst's assumption that he or she is being told something by the patient about his or her inner state; thus Hobson's patient's belittling of the analyst (he had something important to do, more important, of course, than coming to see 'Dr Hobbs') may be a way of opening up with him the whole area of his pain and anger at being orphaned. Moreover, although in all our interactions with others are to be found traces of our childhood relationships with significant people, especially parents or parent-figures, in analysis these traces are encouraged, focused on, and experienced anew. Thus Hobson comes to see the sequence as an enactment with him of one of the patient's ways of coping with the early traumas and as an enactment of his early patterns of feelings, defences against feelings, and fantasies. And the whole setting of analysis, much of that which to sceptics and outsiders appears arbitrary and precious, is designed to permit this re-occurrence of early feelings in a safe-enough situation. The analyst sits behind the patient partly at least so that the latter can more freely use him or her as a peg to hang projections on, as a relatively anonymous wax that can in the patient's mind be moulded to fit the patterns or templates that are carried around within, and, unthinkingly, applied, without awareness or examination, in everyday life. The analyst tends to focus on this aspect of the patient's communications for the good reason that here, in the safety of the analysis, with the mutual agreement that anything can be said and the mutual contract that the analytic pair will try to understand whatever occurs, the deep-seated neurotic and psychotic aspects of the character can be repeated in the relationship with the analyst, looked at, understood a little, and, in the end, transformed.

So the setting (couch, privacy, reliability, quiet) and the style and content of the analyst's formulations (especially this focus on the trans- ference, as we call this reliving of the child's feelings in the relationship with the analyst) hang together. Only by examining the whole form of life of analysis can the analyst's formulation ('the patient had orphaned me') be understood.

I have in this paper hinted at the stranger within; the form of life within each of us that is to some degree alien to that lived by our conscious selves. Such splits are most glaring in multiple personalities, cases such as one described by Samuel Taylor Coleridge:

> A young woman of four or five and twenty, who could neither read nor write, was seized with a nervous fever; during which she con- tinued incessantly talking Latin, Greek and Hebrew, in very pom- pous tones and with most distinct enunciation. (Coleridge, 1983)

(It turned out that the girl had been brought up by an old pastor, who used to read aloud to himself 'out of a collection of Rabbinical writings, together with several of the Greek and Latin fathers'.) These splits are also striking in the perversions, where people who for the most part lead rational and sober lives find themselves compelled to enact in some corner of their lives sexual fantasies which strike themselves as utterly bizarre and incomprehensible.

In less dramatic ways we all have such experiences, if only in dreams and daydreams, and it is a central part of the aim of analysis to make us more comprehensible to ourselves, more integrated or whole. A patient of mine presented her problem in a way which vividly portrayed her knowledge that valued but frightening parts of herself were foreign to her and the fear that I, like her mother, would throw them away as of no value, along with the hope that I might come to understand and help her to understand this language of her unconscious.

I will illustrate this with extracts from a session. The patient began by saying that words had no meaning for her. We explored this in the light of her feeling that I had failed to understand her the day before. This led to her saying that her hot Turkish pepper sauce had run out, her boyfriend had had some in his house but his mother had thrown it away. I said I thought she was talking about her hot strong feelings which came from the child-her (Turkish carried for her implications of the primitive), but she was afraid that the me whom she experienced as a mother might discard them. She replied with feeling that her mother would not allow them; after some silence I said that it was hard for her to allow them too. She then expressed a stream of ideas and thoughts connected with Turkey—of a sanctuary outside an old Hittite town, of the Turkish for 'is this hotel for women?'; she remarked that a friend called Mike was trying to learn Turkish, and that it is possible that brain lesions can cause bilingual people to lose one language altogether, while the other remains unimpaired. She also talked about a church on an island which contained beautiful mosaics. There was more, but I think this sufficiently exemplifies my points—that this patient at first sees me as a mother hostile to her Turkish hot sauce; but later, when this has been understood there is hope in the fact that I, like the other Mike, am trying to learn her primitive language. The sanctuary may represent analysis, like the island; but it may also be an area of herself which is dangerously close to ancient aggression (The Hittite town). She also questions my capacity to understand her as a woman ('Is this hotel for women?') and again expresses her fear of the ancient, primitive language being completely lost (due to 'brain lesion'). There was, however, a change in the mood of the session, for when she spoke of the 'lovely mosaics' which were of 'whales with ears like a dog and scales like a fish', *she* had become a grown-up with a loving affectionate attitude to this child-like art, she was no longer the mother who throws out the hot Turkish sauce.

I introduced the idea of a stranger within as a *reductio ad absurdum* of the notion that a form of life, narrowly conceived, is the bedrock of justification; that there are no rational means of intercommunication between such forms, no common ground. And now it is clearer that we analysts, in helping our patients to find the pictures that hold them captive, to understand why they have disowned, disavowed, denied, distorted, repressed areas of themselves and to reown them, are aiming to enable them to find common ground with these alien aspects of themselves, between their inner forms of life.

V. Psychoanalysis and Ordinary Understanding

So, there is no harm in talking of different forms of life provided that it is accepted that bridges between them may be rational, that bridging them calls for agreement in a wider form of life, and that there need be no more mystery in the initiation into a form of life than in the development of someone from his or her rudimentary beginnings as a musician or games-player into a skilled participant or critic in these fields.

Moreover, however peculiar its practices may appear, psycho-analysis is also *not* alien to our ordinary sensitive understanding of people, and the kind of interaction and understanding that Hobson describes is not peculiar to psychoanalysis.

When my daughter was about two years old, she naturally resented my leaving her to go downstairs to see my patients, and sometimes she would make it difficult for me to leave. But she had another ploy, which she would use in play. This was to switch roles. *She* would be the one to walk out of the living-room into the hall, on her way downstairs, while I was forced to stay behind. She delighted in repeating this game endlessly, laughing as she slammed the door shut on me. Do I need to be a psychoanalyst to understand that the pleasure my daughter found in this game derived from the fact that she was in the position of the one leaving while I could experience the feelings of the one left?

I heard of a child who had to stay in hospital for a week at the age of two and a half. When she came out she refused to look at her mother for months. No doubt she was punishing her mother for allowing her to be taken away; but perhaps she was also letting the mother know how it feels to get a cold shoulder. Once again, the mother does not need analysis to help her reflect on this painful rejection by the daughter and try to understand it. The reflection that Peter Hobson refers to is not peculiar to analysis.

When I worked as a nursing assistant in a clinic for disturbed adolescents I was struck by the fact that the patient who seemed most likely to be attacked, verbally and even physically, by other patients was one of the quietest of the group. At a staff seminar, we discussed this phenomenon in the light of *our* emotional responses to the victim. To our surprise, we all felt an annoyance and impatience with this girl that bordered on the aggressive and even the violent. What was it about her that so got to us, got under our skins, as we say? Could it be that there was expressed through her blank exterior a hidden violence and passive anger that other people picked up? This certainly made sense of the situation in a new way. It seemed plausible that it was her own anger that mingled with ours and turned back on herself. If we could under-stand this, by reflecting on our own emotional sensitivities, we would be less likely to act the anger out, in our case, by spiteful or sadistic remarks, in the case of some of the disturbed adolescents, by violent action.

Hobson is quite right to point out that as analysts we can often gain insight into our patients' problems by reflecting on the effect they have on us, reflecting on the parts of us that their pathology stirs up. Moreover, by such experience and reflection we as analysts may move to a fuller understanding of the concepts used in psychoanalytic discussion. But his own description of this process helps any reflective person to move to a fuller understanding not only of psychoanalytic discourse (or, rather, of psychoanalytic thought, feeling and levels of understanding), but also of the discourse of emotional life.

Having a psychoanalysis is one route to an enlargement and integration of one's inner world. Psychoanalysis is part of a wider form of life which acknowledges the unconscious dimensions of thought and feeling. It did not discover these wider dimensions, though it has made our awareness of them more stable, extensive and systematic. Poets and other intuitive, perceptive people have of course also been well aware of all this. But what is not always acknowledged is that we all have some access to such wider awareness; we all know that the mental is not co-extensive with the conscious.

If a husband forgets his wife's birthday, he knows and she knows that this was a slight. She will feel hurt, and he guilty. But why? He could not in the ordinary way be guilty of *mens rea*, that conscious intention to hurt or do wrong that in courts of law and elsewhere makes so crucial a difference to our moral responses and evaluations, as indeed it does here, for we—husband, wife, onlooker—would feel differently about him if he had not forgotten but had deliberately ignored her birthday. Still, why do we all acknowledge this wider responsibility? Is it not that some doubt is cast on the quality of his love? We know too little about the example to know what sort of doubt, or how serious a doubt is cast—it might be that he is regularly absorbed in himself and his worries, or that he is absorbed in some other woman, or that he has some unconscious resentment towards his wife such that when his reasons for the resentment are faced or fade he will not find himself hurting her without consciously meaning to—but some doubt there is, and all of us recognize it. So we all recognize that the answer to the question 'Do I love her?' is not one to which my conscious feelings necessarily give a complete or true answer; we accept the possibility of self-deception.

In a WEA class in Philosophy many years ago, we were discussing the notion of the unconscious. The class had been going for several weeks by now; a local sixth-form English teacher who sat in the front row contributed frequently to the discussion. He was sometimes impatient with and critical of some of the less articulate members of the class, amongst whom was a man whom I will call Mr Lulworth. On the evening in question the man in the front row felt unusually generous to Mr Lulworth, and turned round to him to agree with his recent point. What he said was, 'As Mr Littleworth so rightly says . . .' He remained serenely unaware of his slip, but Mr Lulworth and some others in the class were shocked, chagrined, or amused. Their reaction showed that they did not regard the slip as purely accidental.

So, in ordinary living we are aware of some remarkable facts; that we can mean something by our omissions, slips, etc., without intending to mean it and that we can deceive ourselves about our own present state of mind. When in an untutored way we talk about ourselves and others we naturally allow such ideas their expression. We are all potential psychoanalysts and analytic patients!

In a much more fundamental way, though, the role of psychoanalysts resembles part of the work done (or not done) by parents in relation to babies and small children, and also the inner work we all (better or worse) do on our own experiences. It would take another paper to make this point adequately—here I can only gesture towards the fact that we all in our growing through babyhood and childhood need help in handling instinctual excitements, fears and frustrations. For most of us, this help comes from our parents, and if all goes well they help us to sort out turbulent feelings, to control them without destroying spontaneity, and to make up with reparation for damage that we have done, actually or in fantasy, in our hate and anger. These helpful parents we gradually learn to identify with; we acquire such capacities in our own selves.

An adult patient who initially found it hard to sort out her bodily feelings (she would for instance wonder, and not know, if she wanted to go to the toilet) gradually was more able to sort out the muddle of discomfort. Moreover, though she still from time to time felt empty, she was no longer desperate about it: she said that in analysis she 'had become able to walk around her emptiness and look at it.' As the child grows it is not so much overwhelmed by bad feelings which seem to be all there is, without end or shape: it takes in the good-enough mother's capacity to observe and think while feeling. Something similar happens in analysis.

To conclude: we all in our growing towards maturity experience, and gradually internalize, parents who help us with unruly emotion. In quite unintellectual ways we learn to help ourselves. We are all psychoanalysts, that is helpfully reflective parent-figures, to ourselves. These fundamental interpersonal and intrapersonal interactions, which are central to psychoanalysis, are central in our upbringing. We are all, to however small a degree, psychoanalytic; we share in the form of life that is psychoanalysis.[2]

[2]The author wishes to thank those who contributed to the discussion at the meeting of the Newcastle branch of the Royal Institute of Philosophy in May 1989; also Peter Hobson, Renford Bambrough and Ilham Dilman for their help.

Wittgenstein on Freud's 'abominable mess'

FRANK CIOFFI

The 'abominable mess' of which Wittgenstein complains is that of confounding reasons and causes. What does Wittgenstein mean to call attention to by this contrast and why does he think himself entitled to hold that Freud confounded them? Sometimes by reasons he means just what someone says on being asked why he did what he did or reacted as he reacted, and sometimes what an experience meant to a subject on further reflection upon it—its 'further description'.

There is certainly a confusion, in Freud and about him, over the status of explanations invoking unconscious wishes, motives, thoughts, fantasies but calling it a confusion between reasons and causes is not felicitous and perhaps no brief characterization could be. Wittgenstein thinks that Freud sometimes falls into confusion (or summons it to his rescue) through denying patients their say on matters on which their say is authoritative and sometimes through according them a say to which they were not entitled. Freud is doing the first when he tells his patients what they really thought or dreamt since this is 'not a matter of discovery but of persuasion' (LC, 27) and the second when he treats his patients' acceptance of his empirical explanations as criteria of their validity 'What the patient agrees to can't be a hypothesis' (Moore, 1966, 310).

Wittgenstein's formula 'Freud confuses reasons and causes' masks a variety of related but distinct antitheses and this complicates the task of assessing its justice.[1] What Freud is accused of confounding are, vari-

---

[1] For example, in the following remarks a different antithesis is in view. '"Because" and "why" can refer to either a reason or a cause. If a traffic signal acts on you in a manner analogous to a drug, then your explanation of your action is giving a cause. If, on the other hand, you see the red light and act as if someone had said "The red light means stop" then your explanation would be giving a reason' (WLL, 783). Here the drug-cause of the stopping isn't even capable of being a reason. Furthermore it is not clear whether when Wittgenstein says 'Freud had genius and could therefore sometimes give someone the reason for his dream' (Moore, 1966, 310), the genius in question is the fertility in felicitious further descriptions kind, or of the kind which enabled Poe's Dupin to infer the location of the purloined letter.

ously, hypotheses with 'further descriptions'; the cause of an impression with 'getting clear about' it, e.g. getting clear about why you laughed; an empirical explanation of a mental state with an account of what was 'at the back of our minds'; science with 'sounding like science' or a 'good way or representing a fact' and 'discovery' with 'persuasion'. Even if I am right in thinking that there is one core antithesis inhabiting most of these expressions—that between that of which we can bethink ourselves and that which we can only learn through empirical inquiry—it is one so problematic that to confound them might seem beyond even Freud's obfuscatory powers. Nevertheless there are specimens which allow us to make the distinction with some confidence and which Freud does confound.

I

This is one of Wittgenstein's accounts of his 'further description' alternative to psychoanalytic dream interpretation construed as a scientific decoding of the dream: 'It's like searching for a word when you are writing and then saying, "That's it, that expresses what I intended!" Your acceptance certifies the word as having been found and hence as being the one you were looking for . . .' (CV, 68). We can recognize Wittgenstein's 'further descriptions' in these remarks of Carl Rogers (though Rogers calls them 'inner hypotheses'):

> Any datum of experiencing—any aspect of it—can be symbolized further and further on the basis of continuing inward attention to it. (Rogers, 1966, 127). Any one who has experienced psychotherapy will have lived through this way of contradicting or sharpening previously held inner hypotheses. Often an example of it in psychotherapy is the way in which the client searches and searches for a word that will more accurately describe what he is experiencing, feeling or perceiving. There is a sense of real relief when he discovers a term which 'matches' his experiencing, which provides a more sharply differentiated meaning for the vague knowing which had been present (Ibid., 111).

This is Wolfgang Koehler making the distinction (in a work that Wittgenstein had read by the time he gave the lectures on aesthetics and psychology):

> We ought to distinguish between two things: in some cases the Freudian may be right, while in others people merely fail to recognize their inner states. I am inclined to believe the many observations which the Freudians interpret in their fashion are actually instances in which recognition does not occur. (Koehler, 1947, 196).

This is Gustave Ichheiser describing the same phenomenon in a paper in which, like Koehler, he accuses Freud of misrepresenting it:

> Our feelings are often peculiarly vague and elusive (so) we have considerable difficulty in describing them correctly. . . We are aware of the innumerable symbolic meanings which permeate our perceptual experience . . . and we must react to them . . . in a peculiarly implicit way . . . What we call insight consists in the ability to make these implicit meanings explicit. (Ichheiser, 1970, 141–142).

On Freud's conception of the unconscious, when, for example, Dora spoke of Frau K's 'adorable white body', there was some substrate occurrence in a realm discovered by him which made it true that her remark expressed an homoerotic infatuation rather than an aesthetic appreciation; whereas on Wittgenstein's view there need only have been the manifest character of the utterance and the less manifest features which nevertheless made it the utterance it was and of which the subject was capable of coming to a more explicit cognition. This contrast can also be illustrated in the case of associations. The associations to a dream are epistemically heterogenous. Or, as Wittgenstein puts it, 'Interpretations are not all of one kind. Some still belong to the dream.' In the Wolf Man's nightmare the tree on which the immobile wolves sat was later identified by the dreamer himself as a Christmas tree (Freud, 1924, 505). It is natural to mark this distinction by saying that he was indicating a feature of his dream image that was internally related to it, that made the image, the image that it was rather than identifying a causal antecedent of it. But it is a distinction that Freud often confounds or ignores.

Here is an example of the confusion which also brings out its affinity to what Wittgenstein objects to in Russell's behaviouristic account of wishing and desiring. One of Freud's paradigms of a manifestly wish-fulfilling dream is his water-quaffing dream. He tells us that he has this dream on nights on which he has eaten anchovies and consequently wakes thirsty during the night, though only after the dream has enabled him to prolong his sleep by providing him with an hallucinatory gratification of his thirst. But it is not the concomitance of thirst-inducing circumstances and water-quaffing dreams that makes these dreams wish-fulfilling; their wish-fulfilling character is intrinsic to them however they came about and whatever their effects are. Freud goes on to say that his water-quaffing dream could not satisfy his need for water as his need for revenge against his friends and colleagues was satisfied by the Irma dream. But we have no more reason to say that Freud's thirst for revenge was assuaged by the Irma dream than his need for water by the water-quaffing dream. Otto's negligence and Dr M's glibness is internal to the manifest content of the dream of Irma's injection just as

Frank Cioffi

Freud's water-quaffing was and we have no more reason to think that Freud was any less prone to critical reflections on his two unappreciative colleagues after the Irma dream than that Freud was less thirsty after he dreamt of drinking water. Freud fails to see this because his vocabulary allows him to conflate desire and need, motive and function. The dream which provides him with an hallucinatory satisfaction is wish-fulfilling in quite a different sense from that in which the same dream permits him to prolong his sleep before attending to his wants. The sleeping was not hallucinated.

I will try to convey the feel of this contrast between hypotheses and 'further descriptions' by comparing some specimens of each.

Jung tells the following story to illustrate how the unconscious may influence perception. A poet on a Sunday country walk once expressed unaccountable irritation at some pealing church bells which, though famous for their beauty, he described as ugly and unpleasant. Jung's explanation was that the pastor from whose church the offending sounds came was also a poet but unlike the listener a successful and appreciated one; thus the sound of the bells had activated the listener's 'rivalry complex' and so caused him to perceive the bells as ugly. Contrast the epistemic status of Jung's explanation in terms of an unconscious 'rivalry complex' with the following case. Two English friends were trying to work out why the sound of some church bells at Winchester had so distinctive an effect on their spirits. One remarked that it was because 'their sound was unchanging from age to age' and Chaucer and Shakespeare and Dr Johnson had heard those very same peals. 'One's own tastes's take different forms from age to age but church bells are always the same.' His friend agreed and added, 'And so they recall the transitory expectations of the past and being unchanging themselves promise something that does not pass away.'

Of the plethora of hermeneutic issues that this exchange raises I want to confine myself as far as possible to one. Were the friends advancing causal conjectures? These are my reasons for saying that they were not but that Jung was. It is not just that Jung was entitled to insist on the correctness of his acccount irrespective of the endorsement of the irate poet, but that we can readily imagine other reasons why the same experience of disagreeableness might have been produced. The reason the bells sounded cacophanous might have been due to rivalry in love rather than poetry, or the displeasing impression might have been due to a complex other than rivalry. By contrast, in the case of the impression made on the two Englishmen the characterizations of the peals profferred were what made the impression the impression it was. We might even prefer to call their remarks elucidations or analyses rather than explanations. Wittgenstein marks this distinction by saying that further descriptions are internally related to the impression they explain whereas hypotheses are externally related to them.

There are instances which are more epistemically ambiguous and where we enjoy a considerable degree of discretion as to which epistemic direction discussion of such remarks is to be taken though we may be unaware of this until our account of an impression is challenged or our attention called to its ambiguity.

D. W. Harding once suggested that the striking impression made on us by atrocity stories was due to our harbouring, unconsciously, the same impulses, which led to their commission:

> People . . . feel what they can only describe—if they are honest with themselves—as the magnetic quality of atrocity stories . . . they find themselves in a state of horrified fascination. This quality of feeling is at its strongest when the atrocities have an admixture of the obscene or sexual. The conscious effect of the story is to arouse pity, indignation or disgust. Unconsciously, however, it has brought up the possibility of committing or suffering such an atrocity ourselves. Any submerged sadistic or masochistic impulses which we may harbour are immediately stimulated. It is this which give our feelings a special quality. We may find that other crimes—for instance—the conviction of Dreyfus by forged evidence—give rise to equally strong or stronger indignation or pity. But many people find that such crimes claim less compulsive attention than a story by torture and brutal flogging, and a view that is due to some unconscious fascination seems the most plausible that psychology can offer. (Harding, 1941, 143).

Harding presents his analysis as a conjecture and in his last sentences appeals to external, empirical considerations. But, though we may have no difficulty in imagining the issue being discussed in empirical terms, reflection also convinces us that as natural a direction for the discussion to take is one in which the linking of our state of 'horrified fascination' with morbid or perverse sexual feelings provokes us to recognize a quality of which we were already peripherially aware so that the case seems more felicitously described as a 'focusing utterance'—one which puts 'into unambiguous words something which has been vaguely "known", suspected or "felt" . . . just outside the focus range of consciousness' (Jones, 1968, 95), and so results in our recognizing, and not just in our inferring, the sexual quality of our experience.

Our ordinary discourse is often ambiguous with respect to this distinction. 'Meaning is mainly potential', as Frank Ramsey said a long time ago, and it is often for us to decide in which direction to take the discussion. And so, when presented with questions or conjectures as to our feelings or impressions, we may decide rather than determine their epistemic status. It is not possible to say whether, when Eliot's Prufock asks, 'Is it perfume from a dress which makes me so digress?', it is appropriate to proffer him an hypothesis rather than to help him to get clearer about the relation between the perfume and his digression. And one reason for this ambiguity might be the restriction on our ability to make in practice the distinction it obscures. Though it is clear enough when we are proceeding independently of the say-so of the subject, it is often far from clear, when we decide to consult him, what the epistemic character of his authority to resolve our perplexities with respect to his actions or reactions is. To take a familiar example, when Proust's Marcel asks on the famous occasion of his tasting the tisane-soaked madeleine, what it was about the experience that made him so happy, we are clear what it would be to give an account in a Pavlovian or Skinnerian spirit; but when we restrict ourselves to his own self-deliverances we are not clear at what points, and to what extent, these are based on evidence only adventitiously unavailable to us.

Nevertheless there are also cases where the distinction is clear, and in the lecture in which he accuses Freud of malpractice Wittgenstein presents what he takes to be some. How good are his grounds for saying that Freud confounds them?

II

In the third of the lectures on aesthetics Wittgenstein gives two examples of explanation in terms of unconscious thoughts and wishes, one in which someone is pushed into a river with unconscious intent, the other in which a woman who has a 'pretty dream', 'which expressed her joy at having succeeded in passing through life immaculately', is said to have 'quite lost her liking for this pretty dream after it had been interpreted'. This is what Wittgenstein says about it:

> Freud does something which seems to me immensely wrong. He gives what he calls an interpretation of dreams . . . A patient, after saying that she had had a beautiful dream, described a dream in which she descended from a height, saw flowers and shrubs, broke off the branch of a tree, etc. Freud shows what he calls the 'meaning' of the dream . . . The coarsest sexual stuff, bawdy of the worst kind . . . Freud says the dream is bawdy. Is it bawdy? He shows relations between dream images and certain objects of a sexual nature. The relation he established is roughly this. By a chain of associations which comes naturally under certain circumstances, this leads to that etc. Does this prove that the dream is what is called bawdy? Obviously not . . . Freud calls this dream 'beautiful' putting 'beautiful' in quotation marks. But wasn't the dream beautiful? I would

say to the patient: 'Do these associations make the dream not beautiful? It was beautiful. Why shouldn't it be?' I would say Freud cheated this patient. Cf. scents made of things having intolerable smells . . . You don't say that a person talks bawdy when his intention is innocent. (LC, 23–24).

This is from Freud's account of the flowering branch episode:

The dreamer saw herself climbing down over some palisades holding a blossoming branch in her hand. In connection with this image she thought of the angel holding a spray of lilies in pictures of the Annunciation—her own name was Maria—and of girls in white robes walking in Corpus Christi processions when the streets are decorated with green branches. Thus the blossoming branch in the dream without any doubt alluded to sexual innocence . . . However, the branch was covered with red flowers each of which was like a camellia . . . Accordingly the same branch which was carried like a lilly and as though by an innocent girl was at the same time an allusion to La Dame Aux Camelias who, as we know, usually wore a white camellia except during her periods when she wore a red one (Freud, 1954, 354).

What is it which Freud does which is 'immensely wrong'? Though Wittgenstein felt that it was wrong of Freud to imply the incompatibility of the dreamer's sense of the beauty of this episode with its unconscious meaning, this is unlikely to be all that he objected to, since not all dreams are beautiful and the objection would not have the generality which it obviously is intended to have. What does have generality is the assumption that the associative connections which explain the appearance of the dream image also constitute its meaning and thus undermine the dreamer's own account of this meaning.

David Pears takes Wittgenstein's thesis to be that though the 'path through the complicated maze of the dreamer's associations may lead him to an interpretation of his dream this does not prove that this is what his dream must have meant or even that it had any meaning at all' (Pears, 1970, 195). This formulation leaves open several possibilities (as do Wittgenstein's own remarks). I think the pertinent one is that dream images, utterances, episodes may have a sense which is not the sense that the psychoanalytic procedure, conceived as an objective method of inquiry, uncovers and that it is in failing to assist in the elucidation of this sense of the dream and even undermining it by persuading the dreamer that it was Freud's psychoanalytically inferred one that was its real meaning, that Freud cheated.

Wittgenstein holds that a causal connection between the flowering branch and repressed ideation involving the phallus, say, is not enough to make the phallus the meaning of the branch or what the branch 'really' stood for. What is 'immensely wrong' then is not that the connections uncovered by Freud's methods are 'fanciful pseudo-explanations', as Wittgenstein puts it elsewhere, but rather that Freud has adopted a convention according to which, when certain evidential conditions are fulfilled, it is to be said of the patient that in dreaming her dream she was having such and such thoughts; the patient is not informed of this convention, she is only informed as to what she was 'really' thinking, dreaming etc. (Freud did something similar with the term memory in the early expositions of the infantile aetiology of the neuroses. Only after repeated attempts at paraphrase does it become clear that when Freud says that his patients had such and such memories of remote infantile events, often he only means that he is convinced of the historicity of certain images which the patient 'produces' in the course of the analysis so that even when the patients deny any recall of the events in question they are to be described as having remembered them.)

Freud writes: 'The ugliest and most intimate details of sexual life may be thought and dreamt of in seemingly innocent allusions' (Freud, 1949a, 382). It is Wittgenstein's view that whatever the role of these ugly and intimate details in the production of the dream through which they were detected, it did not constitute either the thinking or the dreaming them. ("The dream is not bawdy; it is something else".) Hanly (1973, 93) says, 'Wittgenstein had to reject the idea that anything could be taking place in the mental life of the individual of which he was not aware at the time.' This is not Wittgenstein's view. What is correct to say is that Wittgenstein rejects the idea that anything 'taking place in the mental life of the individual of which he was not aware at the time' could be the meaning of that of which he was aware. Consider for example Freud's treatment of the theme of masturbation. Freud says of the flowery dreamer's request to 'take one too', of some branches which had been cut down and to which people were helping themselves, that she was asking whether she might masturbate. I think that Wittgenstein's objection here is that whatever the causal influence of the German idiomatic expresssion for masturbation on the wording of her request she cannot be described as asking for permission to masturbate. The dream narrator's sentences cannot be given a meaning other than the meaning she gives them.

Consider the sentence, 'Father I am burning', from the dream of the burning child. Freud invokes a rule according to which sentences heard in dreams must be based on sentences heard while waking and advances a plausible conjecture as to when this sentence was addressed by the child to its father. Now, the question what this sentence meant on such occasions and whether these were indeed a *sine qua non* of its occurrence in the dream are distinct from the question what it meant to the dreamer or dream narrator. We can imagine that the dream utterance has quite another significance for the dreaming, or dream-telling, father attempting to fathom his child's words. Reflection on this significance would take us in a different direction from that of Freud's conjectural causal origins.

But Wittgenstein's other example of the cause/reason distinction does not serve him as well as that of the flowery dream. He asks us to consider the following case. While walking along the river with his friend, Taylor, Taylor extends his arm and pushed Wittgenstein into the river. Taylor believes it to have been an accident, his intention in extending his arm was to point out a church spire. The psychoanalyst says it was due to unconscious hostility seizing on the occasion as a pretext for pushing Wittgenstein in the river. How are these two accounts related to each other and what would confusing them amount to? This is Wittgenstein's view: 'Both explanations may be correct. Here there are two motives—conscious and unconscious. The games played with the two motives are entirely different. The explanations could in a sense be entirely contradictory and yet both be correct' (LC, 23).

Though the expression 'in a sense' weakens Wittgenstein's compatibility thesis it does not weaken it sufficiently. The games played with the two motives are not 'entirely different' since both are used to answer the question why Wittgenstein was pushed into the river and one denies that he was. Though there may be occasions when Freud treats his explanations as undermining the correctness of the subject's own account of matters where he has not the authority to do so and so might be thought to confuse two 'games' this is not one of them. How can we distinguish between these occasions?

Unlike the image of the flowering branch, the experience of pushing Wittgenstein into the river had no interest such as invites further description—if Taylor had been asked not why he pushed Wittgenstein into the river but what his feelings toward Wittgenstein were, we would once again be addressing issues for which an eligible course might be reflection and its elaboration rather than hypothesis and empirical inquiry. Earlier in the lecture Wittgenstein had argued that if someone finds a facade displeasing and wonders why, then the statement 'if the height of the door were altered you would no longer find it displeasing' is an inappropriate answer because what the inquirer wants is to get clearer as to what was at the back of his mind when he found the facade (or the door) displeasing. Even if this is right, can we say anything analagous of the question why Taylor extended his arm, thus pushing Wittgenstein into the river? As it stands the pointing/pushing example is not suited to bringing out the rival interest that the non-causal 'further description' question might have. Taylor did not stand to it as the flowery dreamer to the image of the flowering branch. Suppose that Taylor stood to the pointing/pushing episode in an epistemic relation like that in which the flowery dreamer stood to the camelia sprouting branch—it seemed to be saying something and it was as if he had to discover what it was that it was saying and this finally precipitated out as a reminder of the precariousness of life, the abrupt transformation of an idyllic riverside walk with a church spire on the horizon into a companion's drenching with the risk of worse. Then we would have something of which we could say that 'an entirely different game' was being played.

Thus far I have argued that, though Wittgenstein was mistaken as to how the action of the pointer/pusher is to be described in the light of its psychoanalytic explanation, he has some ground for his objection to Freud's comments on the flowery dream. On the psychoanalytic view, Freud, in uncovering the nocturnal transactions between the unconscious ideas and images of phalluses, menstruation, courtesanship, masturbation and the dream image of the camellia-sprouting branch, is not confusedly bypassing the subject's question as to the meaning of her dream for one about its causal conditions—he is answering it: his knowledge of the mechanism of dream-formation permits him to explain the dream while simultaneously informing the dreamer what she 'really' had dreamt, what thoughts she was expressing, what states of affairs she was unconsciously entertaining, though this is not what we normally mean by expresssing thoughts or entertaining images.

In his 1933–1934 lectures Wittgenstein said that though Freud had really discovered 'phenomena and connections not previously known' he talked as if he had found 'unconscious hatreds, volitions, etc, and this is very misleading because we tend to think of the difference between a conscious and unconscious hatred as like that between a seen and unseen chair' (Moore 1966, 304). And in the 1938 lecture Wittgenstein says the flowery dreamer did not 'really' have the thoughts imputed to her by Freud though he got her to believe that she had. What, short of being aware of them, would constitute 'really' having them? Wittgenstein is more tolerant of such innovation in the Blue Book where he says of the statement that someone has unconscious toothache, when used to refer to the fact that he suffers from tooth decay without accompanying pain, that 'there is nothing wrong about it' but 'that it is only a new convention.' (BB, 23).

One reason Wittgenstein may have objected to Freud's thinking that he had discovered a new class of happenings—unconscious thoughts, feelings, etc.—is that those who do not explicitly recognize the conventional component in their discovery will forget its status and think there is some other way in which someone can have toothache than either his feeling it or having a decayed tooth. They will think that with the help of psychoanalysis he can eventually come to stand to his unconscious toothache—the toothache he does not feel at the moment—in the same relation in which he stands to his conscious toothache—that he can come to remember having had it, after all—thus enabling them to dispense with evidence that his tooth was in a state of decay, and even with clarifying the sense in which someone does not feel toothache and does not have a decayed tooth may nevertheless have toothache. ('The new expression misleads us by calling up pictures and analogies which make it difficult for us to go through with our convention' (BB, 23).)

But Wittgenstein seems to have a more absolute, less pragmatic, objection to the idioms in which Freud communicates his discoveries as to his patients' unconscious ('This ugly explanation makes you say you really had these thoughts whereas in any ordinary sense you really did not.') What has the dreamer been cheated into accepting about her thoughts when she agrees that she really had them though she was not aware of having them? We get a better grasp of the character of Wittgenstein's misgivings on this point if we ask ourselves how we are to imagine an unconscious thought. Suppose we begin with a conscious fantasy, what must we think away for it to be an unconscious fantasy? What can we subtract from our conception of it as conscious which, while rendering it unconscious, still leaves it thought or fantasy? We qualify our thoughts in all sorts of ways in which it makes no sense to qualify something of which we are not conscious. But to preclude any talk at all of unconscious thoughts would, in view of the extraordinary scope of the term 'thought', be peremptory as well as inconsistent with the permissiveness of the Blue Book: 'Should we say that there are cases where a man despises another man and does not know it; or should we describe such cases by saying that he does not despise him but unintentionally behaves towards him in a way, speaks to him in a tone of voice, etc. etc. which in general would go together with despising him? Either form of expression is correct . . . '(BB, 30).

Perhaps Wittgenstein felt that what he conceded of attitudes like despising does not apply to dream interpretations because we can imagine someone who was unaware of despising another nevertheless behaving 'in a way . . . which in general would go together with despising him.' (BB, 30). We do not know what it would mean to say of one of Freud's dream interpretations (much more elaborate than the dream itself) that the person whose dream it was behaved in a way which generally went along with dreaming dreams with that particular latent content. But suppose we simplify matters by restricting the interpretation to one dream image—that of the flowering branch. There is a famous case which is representative of a class of cases in which a literal mode of expression seems justified—Morton Prince's patient with a phobia for church bells of which she could give no account: 'While she was narrating some irrelevant memories of her mother the hand wrote rapidly as follows . . . "I prayed and cried that (my mother) would live and the church bells were always ringing and I hated them." This last sentence was accompanied by anguish and tears quite incongruous with her oral narration.' (Prince, 1913, 40). Do not we want to say of this kind of case that here the picture Freud encourages of unconscious thoughts as behind or alongside the conscious ones finds application? But can we transfer the natural implications of Prince's account to cases like that of the flowery dreamer and so say that while she dreamt that she was holding a flowering branch she was really grasping an erect phallus just as Agave was really holding her son's head? I am not sure.

In Prince's bell-phobia case there was accompanying 'expression-behaviour' appropriate to the unconscious thought—not so with the flowering branch. If we decide to forego such 'expression behaviour', it may involve us in commitments which, when we became aware of them, would cause us to backtrack and concede that we ought not to have said that, in those circumstances, someone had thoughts but did not know it, or believed they were thinking about one thing when they were really thinking about another, or thinking one thing about it when they were really thinking another thing about it. We are not clear as to when a new fact about a psychological state authorizes us to redescribe its intentionality. If I have understood Wittgenstein's objection then, 'An unconscious wish to have sexual intercourse caused you to dream of watering a garden', is unobjectionable ('connections not previously known'). Whereas 'Your dream of watering a garden was really about making love' amounts to cheating. But need it? 'Someone only thought that he was pointing out something to a companion but really was pushing him' is not, as Wittgenstein implies, cheating. We need not confine ourselves, as he would have us ('two entirely different games'), to 'His wish to push his companion into the water caused him to extend his arm at the first plausible pretext thus pushing him into the river but it is nevertheless true, as he himself believed, that he was pointing.' Can we assimilate the dream image to the pointing and hold that Wittgenstein was wrong about this too?

We see why it would be misleading to say that since the perfume was 'made from things having intolerable smells' it really stank, but the issues raised by Wittgenstein with respect to the flowery dream are much less clear. Suppose the dreamer was addressed as 'Violetta' (the name La Dame aux Camelias bears in Verdi's opera), would not that entitle us to something stronger than just a causal connection between the camellia-sprouting branch and 'La Dame aux Camelias'? Is not the stench breaking through? There are two closely related issues here, one as to what, if anything, would entitle us to speak of someone having unconscious thoughts, feelings, etc., and the other what this implies about the experience of which the analytically uncovered one was the unconscious substrate. When can I say not only that at some stage she had the unconscious thoughts of an erect phallus but that in entertaining the image of the flowering branch she was unconsciously entertaining a state of affairs involving an erect phallus—i.e. that the branch was really a phallus?

The latter issue may be like that which leads people to object to the statement 'Water is H_2O' (D. H. Lawrence, Michael Oakeshott and Wittgenstein himself). And the solution may be the same as that suggested by Lawrence in the case of water. Just as Lawrence concedes that 'alert science' is not reductionist and does not intend 'Water is H_2O' to be a denial of the reality of the phenomenal qualities of water, neither need an 'alert' psychoanalysis be reductionist. This still leaves the problem of the precise content of an imputation of unconscious thoughts stripped of reductionist implications. The presuppositions of Freud's theory of dreams is that in the course of the night the dreamer had such and such thoughts of which she was unaware and which when subjected to certain translations of which she was also unaware became the manifest dream which she relates on waking.

Suppose we get rid of the special epistemic difficulties attaching to the imputation of thoughts to a dreamer (Z, 71–72) and apply Freud's interpretation to the dreamer's associations instead. Let us suppose that, as often happens, the flowery dreamer had a vague sense of the significance of the blossoming branch but only after some hesitation and effort was able to formulate it in the words, 'It is as if I were the angel Gabriel in pictures of the Annunciation', or—in a way which is characteristic of dream-talk—'as if I were both the angel transmitting God's message to the Virgin and the Virgin receiving it as well as one of the white-clad little girls walking in the Corpus Christi procession.' This was the 'development of the ideas' with which the episode of the blossoming branch was 'pregnant' as Wittgenstein puts it in the 1948 entry on dream interpretation (BB, 68). Now let us replace Freud's causal story as to how the flowering branch image arose during the night and substitute a causal story as to why the association to the Annunciation scene arose during the dream narration—so: flowering branch (conscious)—erect phallus (unconscious)—lily stalk (and thus sexual purity) held by the Angel of the Annunciation, (conscious). Though the sequence I have described may not warrant the strong conclusion that in thinking of the lily stalk she was thinking of a phallus, surely it warrants the claim that at some stage she thought of a phallus?

How much of what we mean when we speak of someone having thoughts carries over into our talk of unconscious thoughts may be an issue too ambiguous or nuancé for resolution. It may be like that which arises when one Catholic feels from some turns of phrase used by another, together with his general attitude, that he is badly instructed and entertains misconceptions as to the sense in which the consecrated host is simultaneously the body and blood of Christ. Or like that between realists and idealists as to how best to speak of the furniture in deserted rooms[2].

III

Even if Wittgenstein were wrong in thinking that it is necessarily mistaken for Freud to describe himself as having literally discovered the existence of unconscious thoughts, feelings, volitions, etc., there is still a distinctive feature of Freud's account of the unconscious which warrants the charge of confusion. This is Freud's view that the agent's original account is to be superseded by the psychoanalytic account through some species of introspection in spite of the fact that complete subjective ignorance intervenes between the original occurrence of the unconscious thought and its recognition.

In the sixth of the Introductory Lectures Freud assimilates the anamnesis of an hypnotic subject for his experiences during the trance state to the dreamer coming to understand the meaning of her dream ('exactly similar'). But of course these cases are not even roughly similar. Those who come to accept a psychoanalytic interpretation of their dreams do not do so because they come to remember transforming the latent dream content into the manifest dream. And though they may recollect wishes corresponding to the latent dream thoughts, they do not locate them in the night during which they dreamt their dream but in their waking life.

The problem this raises is not that of reconciling explanations invoking unconscious motives with those in which we normally privilege the

---

[2] There are remarks in Freud which Wittgenstein might have found conciliatory had he known of them. In *New Introductory Lectures* Freud says of the unconscious processes which bring about symptom formation that he 'dare hardly call them thoughts' (Freud, 1933, 29). And in the *Outline* he says that the occurrence of unconscious thoughts is something of which 'we are totally unable to form a conception' (Freud, 1949, 66). On the other hand, he does intermittently phenomenalize the unconscious, implying that what we now see through a glass darkly, we may under favourable conditions see face to face. In *New Introductory Lectures* he also writes: 'certain practices of mystics may succeed in upsetting the normal relation between the different regions of the mind so that the perceptual system becomes able to grasp the relations in the deeper layers of the ego and the id which would otherwise be inaccessible to it' (Freud, 1933, 106).

subject's own account of matters, but of explaining how their unconscious antecedents can be out of reach of introspection at the time of their occurrence and yet, thanks to psychoanalytic technique, later recalled along with their causal role in the episode they explain. Freud cites in support of this possibility the phenomenon of post-hypnotic compliance. The fact that someone who has responded to a cue by obeying an hypnotically implanted suggestion denies he knows why, or gives a spurious reason for his action, can nevertheless later realize why, is said to be proof that someone may know something without knowing that he knows it (Freud, 1949, 84–85). But what is it that the post-hypnotic subject can be said to know? We have no subject protocols of what this knowing is like, i.e., on what the subject's conviction of understanding the behaviour which was formerly misunderstood or opaque to him is based. So let us ask instead what Freud thought was going on and whether we can make sense of it. Why did Freud think the subject was later entitled to say that he knew why he had earlier taken off his shoe, or whatever the hypnotically implanted order was? What Freud's argument in favour of the validating role of belated avowal requires is that the the subject finally recalls taking his shoe off in compliance with an order. But what sense can we make of someone now remembering something he truthfully denied being aware of at the time? What we can conceive the subject finally remembering is the occasion of the hypnotic order itself, thus enabling him to make sense of his formerly opaque or implausibly accounted for action, by *inferring* that it was due to the hypnotist's command and his expressing this by saying he 'now knew' why he did it.

This avoids the incoherence involved in remembering the never experienced—but at a cost—since Freud assimilates the production of dreams and symptoms to compliance with a post-hypnotic order. For even if there was some phenomenological equivalent to the recall of the post-hypnotic order in the case of dreams or symptoms, something essential would be lacking for them to be relevantly analogous. Our grounds for crediting the veridicality of the patients' anamnesis would be missing. In the case of the post-hypnotic order, we were there: we saw and heard. Nothing like this is available in the case of the dream work or the symptom work. Thus the justice of Wittgenstein's remark, 'We are likely to think of a person's admitting in analysis that he thought so-and-so as a kind of discovery which is independent of his having been persuaded by an analyst . . . this is not the case'. (LC, 27).

Freud's incoherent invocation of the 'ultimate' say-so of the subject is not a mere excrescence which could be removed by simply adopting a version of psychoanalysis which restricts the use of the subject's endorsement as a method of validation because the content of many of his most distinctive and characteristic imputations and explanations, e.g. the full statement of the latent dream thoughts, is too elaborate to be linked to behavioural criteria while at the same time being too elaborate to have lurked unnoticed at the back of our minds. They demand anamnesis and are yet incapable of it.

Consider Freud's surmise that though, at the time Dora slapped Herr K when sexually importuned by him, she thought it was from outraged propriety, it was really from affronted vanity and jealousy at her recognizing in Herr K's words, 'I get nothing from my wife', the same formula he had used when attempting to seduce their governess ('what, thought you, dare he treat me like a servant'). The reason that we can credit the confirmation of Freud's reconstruction by Dora's belated acknowledgement is that, in this case, at the time of the slap Dora had no opportunity to deny that these were her feelings. This is not the case with 'the scornful doubt and denial' of the bedtime ritual girl of Introductory Lectures 17, say, and it is this kind of case which is more representative of Freud's procedure (and which the conception of resistance was introduced to rationalize.)

In his unpublished University of Virginia lectures, John Wisdom deals with the shock produced by the notion that an explicit denial might intervene between the subject's recognition of a mental state of affairs and his initial obliviousness to it by arguing that Freud has merely shifted the subject's authority, in a way familiar to us from folk psychology, to a further point along what Wisdom calls the 'corrigibility scale'. But even if this were conceded it would not resolve the problem which many of Freud's instances of patient-avowal as a criterion of validation present— hatred such as the Rat Man was held to have felt for his father, for example. Should he ever have come to recall it after such persistent denial we would speak not of ignorance but of hypocrisy and, if precluded from speaking of hypocrisy, we would deny his admission any probative value at all. Sartre is among those who have pointed out the incoherence which results from combining Freud's objectivism with the validating role of the patient's acknowledgment: 'Though the testimony of the subject is precious for the psychoanalyst . . . the sign that he has reached his goal . . . nothing in his principles . . . permits him to understand or to utilize this testimony.' (Sartre, 1962, 56–57).

The question of the limits of corrigibility raises issues too particular for demonstration. There are no simple conceptual truths to be appealed to. We cannot issue a general proscription on the imputation of mind-states on the basis of the patient's later acceptance where these were earlier denied. We can only say that belated recognition is incompatible with a certain kind of denial, or with a certain kind of content, or with a certain kind of denial coupled with a certain kind of content. These distinctions are rooted in our practices which place unformalizable limits on what we can intelligibly say. We can only discover that we are being over-restrictive by denying it and seeing what happens. Thus I say that we can imagine Dora coming to realize that the big book she was reading in the dream was an encyclopaedia (as Freud maintains) but not that, though she dreamt that she read it calmly, she now remembers that she read it agitatedly (as Freud also maintains).

There is an additional limit on the appropriateness of self-validation and one which is stronger than the ignorance which is incoherently superceded by knowledge. It has to do with the nature of the explanandum rather than the subject's epistemic state with respect to it. Freud says of one patient:

> I was curious to discover whether [her facial neuralgia] would turn out to have a physical cause. When I began to call up the traumatic scene the patient . . . described a conversation with her husband and a remark of his which she had felt as a bitter insult. Suddenly she put her hand to her cheek, gave a loud cry of pain and said: 'It was like a slap in the face . . .' There is no doubt that what happened was a symbolization. She had felt as though she had really been given a slap in the face . . . the sensation of a slap in the face came to take on the outward form of a trigeminal neuralgia . . . afterwards it could be set going by associative reverberations from her mental life. (Freud, 1895, 178–179).

Here we have Freud addressing a question which calls for an hypothesis by advancing an hypothesis. Where then is the confusion? It does not lie in any incongruity between the question and the answer but only follows from Freud's commitment to self-intimation as a mode of validation. If Freud thinks that the causal relation of the simile ' . . . like a slap in the face' to the hysterical symptom it explains can be determined as its felicity as a 'further description' of the state of mind which prompted it can be determined then he *was* confusing reasons and causes. Those philosophers who have seen no anomaly in Freud's commitment to belated introspection as a mode of validation were momentarily amnesic for the fact that the concept of the unconscious grew out of attempts to explain non-intentionalist phenomena like pains, paraesthesias, contractures, paralyses and convulsions (Cioffi, 1974, 344–345).

The epistemic predicament of the flowery dreamer can be used to illustrate the contrast which Freud is accused of obscuring between hypothesis and further descriptions, between problems which require investigation and those which will yield to reflection. Consider the concluding portion of the dream in which the dreamer rebukes a young man for embracing her and he assures her that it is permissible. Might not an image from the sphere of sexual life stand to this episode in a more epistemically direct way than as the outcome of an inferred nocturnal transformation of the ideas of a courtesan and a phallus into that of a flowering branch? Might not the relation be rather the same as that in which the flowering branch stood to the Angel of the Annunciation—as an idea with which the dream was pregnant 'precisely in virtue of acknowledging it as such' (68e).

Even that portion of the dream which the dreamer associated with the Annunciation may well have been concerned with sexuality without its being the case that it was the causal connection between either the flowering branch and unconscious ideation pertaining to phalluses, or between the red camellias and the courtesan/heroine of Dumas fils' play which entitled us to say so, but a quite different consideration, one which locates the theme of sexual deprivation and temptation among the ideas with which the dream episode of the flowering branch was pregnant. For how could the dream 'express her joy at having passed through life immaculately' (Freud, 1954, 319)—loosely speaking, presumably she consummated her marriage—without simultaneously containing the theme of sexual dissoluteness or at least of a grand passion like that of La Dame aux Camelias? On this view Freud's fault would then have not been that he produced an ugly interpretation of a beautiful dream (which some have taken Wittgenstein's central objection to be), but that (at least with respect to the general theme of sexuality) he behaves like a dishonest taxi driver who takes one by a gratuitously long route to a destination which was round the corner. In general what Freud does which is 'immensely wrong' is to ignore the themes implicit in the manifest content of the patient's communications and to insist that the meaning of the dream is only to be found with the help of his theory of dream formation.

There is, thus, much this woman's dream could have taught her about herself and her relation to her sexuality without embarking on a causal investigation of the images it contained—'the whole thing could have been treated differently'. Psychoanalytic dream interpretation loses much of its interest if the preoccupations or wishes in whose service the dream is said to have been enlisted are accessible without these interpretations. (The empirical case for the dispensability of Freud's 'deep' interpretations is made in Fisher and Greenberg, (1977, 63–74).)

Of course such a procedure ignores the theme of guilt over infantile masturbation in which Freud finds the true meaning of the dream, but in doing so it ignores just that component in dream interpretation which Freud both asserts and denies is accessible to the dreamer, and whose veridicality we have no way of determining; that is, it evades the 'abominable mess'.

IV

Wittgenstein has a further reason for his charge of confusion. Freud was mistaken to proffer hypotheses at all and not just to misconstrue them as revelations as to what the patient was 'really' doing, thinking or saying. And if this encounters the objection that, when we are dealing with the kind of matters which bring people to analysts, hypotheses are precisely what we want, then a reply is possible along the following lines: the matters which bring people to analysts are epistemically miscellaneous and many of them, including many broached by Freud, are appropriately addressed by reflection. If we replace joke–laughter or dream–impression, for which Wittgenstein holds empirical explanation inappropriate, by the states of mental distress that neurotics typically give accounts of—feelings of helplessness, worthlessness, abandonment, isolation, rage—does Wittgenstein's notion that to advance hypotheses with respect to them is a sign of confusion necessarily lose its plausibility?

An ambiguity dogs the concept of self-understanding as it figures in enterprises such as attempting to understand the sources of our unhappiness, the nature of our aspirations, the precise content of our regrets, disappointments, apprehensions, remorse, self-felicitations, anger. These expressions can be understood in such a way that empirical inquiry bears on them, or so that it does not. In which of these senses is Freud deploying the notion? It is the diversity of answers that have been given to this question which suggests that we are dealing with a mess.[3]

Joseph Wortis was an American psychiatrist who had a short training analysis with Freud in 1933 and has left a record of the experience. One episode in particular is instructive for what it reveals about the epistemic character of the expectations aroused by Freud and his intermittent repudiation of these expectations. On one occasion Wortis had a dream in which he asks of someone who had had a psychotic breakdown whether they had manifested their latent homsexuality during it. Freud propounded an interpretation of this dream which Wortis found unconvincing and which moved him to offer his own: 'Why not say that it showed an anxiety that I would show homosexual traits if I ever became psychotic?' 'That is your idea,' said Freud. 'It would be nothing new. You knew that before. I was telling you something you did not know before because it was unconscious. You still have not learned the meaning of the term "unconscious".' On another occasion Freud remonstrates with Wortis for doubting an interpretation on the grounds that he 'did not in the least feel that way': 'The trouble is that you probably do not believe in the unconscious; you still expect to find an

---

[3] Freud himself invokes his aesthetic explanations as elucidatory of the character of his psychopathological ones. In the case history of the Rat Man he assimilates ellipsis as it occurs in obsessional thoughts to ellipsis in jokes (Cioffi, 1987, 345–346).

Frank Cioffi

agreement between a dream interpretation and your conscious thoughts.' (Wortis, 1954, 103). The conception of his task Freud evinces in this anecdote is remote from that which he expresses at other times and which is assigned him by his hermeneutic and humanist admirers and is unlike what Alan Bergin calls 'accurate empathy': 'responding to client affect just below the surface and labelling, identifying or emphasizing it' as contrasted with 'making connections between past and present, being diagnostic or theoretical, or telling the patient about feelings he 'really has' when he is not experiencing them.' And yet Bergin goes on to say that 'it is very difficult to distinguish between the technique of "accurate empathy" and what some analysts call "good interpretation" ' [Bergin, 1966, 241]. To the extent that this is so, 'good interpretation' is not properly psychoanalytic and is not even appropriate where the problem the patient presents calls for explanation rather than clarification.

To see how Wittgenstein's confusion thesis sets limits to psychoanalytic explanatory pretensions, while at the same time setting limits on the appropriateness of a procedure in which such pretensions were candidly abandoned, consider his remarks on dream interpretation in a notebook entry for 1948:

> We might think [of Freudian dream interpretation] in the following way: a picture is drawn on a big sheet of paper which is then so folded that pieces which do not belong together at all in the original picture now appear side by side to form a new picture . . . (This would correspond to the manifest dream, the original picture to the latent dream thought). Now I could imagine that someone seeing the unfolded picture might explain "Yes, that's the solution, that is what I dreamt, minus the gaps and distortions". This would then be the solution, precisely in virtue of his acknowledging it as such. What is intriguing about a dream is not its causal connection with events in my life but rather the impression it gives of being a fragment in a story . . . What's more if someone shows me that this story is not the right one: that in reality it was based on quite a different story, so that I want to exclaim disappointedly "Oh! So that's how it was!" it is really as though I have been deprived of something. The original story certainly disintegrates now as the paper is unfolded . . . but all the same the dream story has a charm of its own like a painting that attracts and inspires us. The dream affects us as does an idea pregnant with possible developments. (CV, 68).

Let us assume, as Freud enjoins us to, that it is a matter of great importance what is on this unfolded sheet because folded up in a different way, under different conditions, it results not in the surrealistically juxtaposed images and episodes of the manifest dream, but in an affliction—vaginismus, say, or anorexia, or hysterical migraines. For example, Dora, who Freud thinks limped because of an unconscious fantasy of bearing a child out of wedlock, might have dreamt of limping as well, in which case the successful deciphering of her dream would have yielded the secret of her limp. Would we not say that, in these circumstances, psychoanalysis had done Dora a service much more valuable than that of helping her to formulate 'the development of the ideas with which her dream had been pregnant'? There are occasions when, though an hypothesis is an inappropriate response to a desire for a further description, a desire for a further description may not be an appropriate desire.

Over forty years ago John Whitehorn, in an influential paper, 'Meaning and cause in psycho-dynamics' [Whitehorn 1974], remonstrated with psychanalysts for indulging in aetiological speculation and urged them to concentrate on 'the meaning implied in the patient's experiences' instead. Perhaps because his preoccupations were predominantly therapeutic, the epistemic character of this enterprise was left unclear. Were hypotheses relating past to present to be abandoned for hypotheses pertaining to the patient's current psychic state or, as Whitehorn's language suggests but does not entail, was he going further and recommending what Bergin called 'accurate empathy' and forgoing causal inquiry altogether?

A quarter of a century on we find comparable ambiguities in Roy Schafer's *Language and Insight*—the Sigmund Freud Memorial Lectures for 1975–76. Schafer tells us that he proposes to emancipate the practice of psychoanalysis from the mechanistic implications of Freud's metapsychology by replacing it with an 'action' language. But this turns out to perpetuate the traditional equivocations. On the one hand an attempt is made to distance the new approach, not merely from mechanism, but from causal categories altogether ('one is under no obligation to use a grammar that commits one to causal questions and answers'). For example, instead of saying 'the reason an analysand skipped an hour was to avoid a hostile confrontation with the analyst', we ought to say that 'the analysand avoided that hostile confrontation by skipping an hour', so that we 'will be speaking of one event not two and so will not be implying causal relations between reasons and actions . . . ' (Schafer, 1978, 191]. Yet in the same lecture we are told that among the 'actions' that the analysand comes to acknowledge are 'entering into the breast, explosively expelling bad objects, hiding a secret penis', etc., etc. But is it likely that the analysand's epistemic relation to these is that in which he stood to his reason for missing the analytic hour, as the use of the term 'recognition' implies? Are they internally and a-hypothetically related to their manifestations in the way that the source of the poignancy of the pealing church bells was?

Frank Cioffi

Or consider the introduction to a book of essays commemorating the twenty-fifth anniversary of the William Alanson White Institute. We are told that, by 1970, patients were presenting with complaints different from those they presented with in the early days of psychoanalysis. Instead of the hysterical symptoms which were then so common, there were 'character problems, feelings of ennui, alienation, meaninglessness. Difficulties in living had supplanted paralyses and blindness.'(Witenberg, 1973, 5). It is plausible to construe this shift from blindness and paralyses to feelings of ennui and alienation as involving a radical change in the epistemic character of the understanding sought. But when the exposition combines a full-fledged dissociative conception of the unconscious in which 'the analyst's knowledge of the unconscious determinants is taken for granted', and the patient is asked 'to view himself as an object', with one in which he is asked to engage in 'a careful inquiry into his feelings and attitudes' and to 'relive his experience, attending to nuances previously ignored', we are entitled to suspect, as in the case of Schafer, that 'the abominable mess' was well and thriving. (Witenberg, 1973, 9).

What is it, then, that patients feel they have learned as to their propensities, susceptibilities and misconceptions in the course of the analysis? What grounds do they believe themselves to possess for their new-found understanding? Is the process like what John Wisdom described as 'coming to see more clearly the things they had felt creeping in the shadows', or rather like what he described as being enabled to read the invisible writing to which a re-agent has been applied (Wisdom, 1973, 90–103)? Until we are clearer as to what it is analysts claim to know in consequence of their patients' corroboration and what it is they feel entitled to impute to them without their concurrence, we will not be in a position to decide when they are being gullible (or overbearing), and when they have expedited illumination of a kind which can licitly dispense with extra-reflective support (or have quite properly overruled the patient on matters beyond his jurisdiction.)[4] In the same paper John Wisdom describes the task of the analyst

---

[4] More recent specimens of the confusion are to be found in those peer group comments on Grunbaum's *The Foundations of Psychoanalysis* (1984) which defend the relevance of the subjects' ultimate recognition of their motives or meaning, and in Grunbaum's denial of it (*Behavioural and Brain Research*, June 1986). Those who attempt to justify the patients' 'privileged cognitive status' claim too much and Grunbaum concedes too little. How can we be unqualified to judge whether episodes from our past which figure in our self-elucidations as 'psychological fixed stars' have not also exerted a causal influence over us? How can I come to realize that throughout my life I have felt like an unprepared schoolboy praying that the period would end before he was called upon, while not at the same time

as that of 'bringing to light those (unconscious) models from the past which powerfully influence our lives in the present' (Ibid., 96). There are both therapeutic and epistemic purposes for which it is not necessary to construe these models as occult causes waiting for the analyst to summon them from beyond the veil of appearances.

The past can figure in psychoanalytic discourse in a way other than that of a speculative causal antecedent of a current proclivity. It may stand to the present not just as a putative influence determining or conditioning it, but as that which confers on our current anticipations, apprehensions and demands that which makes them what they are. We may call attention to the relation between past and present with the same aim with which in Wittgenstein's analogy, attention is drawn to the relation between an ellipse and a circle—not to speculate that this particular circle evolved from that ellipse but 'to sharpen our eyes to a formal connection'.

An evocative account of the subjective side of this enterprise has been given by William James:

> Whenever we seek to recall something forgotten, or to state the reason for a judgement which we have made intuitively (the) desire strains and presses in a direction which it feels to be right but towards a point which it is unable to see . . . What we are aware of in advance seems to be its relations with the items we already know . . . we know what we want to find out beforehand in a certain sense . . . and we do not know it in another sense. [James, 1950, vol. 1, 585, 588].

having come into possession of the answer to many questions that present themselves to an outside narrator as explanatory puzzles? Of course there are truths reflection alone could not bring to light—facts 'beyond the truth of immanence' in Merlau-Ponty's phrase. But is our epistemic relation to 'the expectant libidinal impulses we bring to each new person' (Freud, 1924, 313), or to the hidden teleology behind the repeated self-frustrating relationships that Freud describes, like that in which we stand to an undiagnosed cancer (Hanly)? As for the issue that Grunbaum poses of avoiding the *post hoc propter hoc* error when imputing a patient's improvement to the therapeutic sessions, his way of putting the matter homogenises the phenomena excessively. Precisely what improvements? Why is it reasonable for a man who takes to weight lifting to attribute his expanding pectorals to his work on them, or for someone to attribute his increasing proficiency in a foreign language to his exercises in it, or the improvement in his game to the coaching of a golf or tennis pro, but not reasonable for a patient to attribute his improved mental state to the therapeutic sessions? The answer to this question will depend on the particular character of the changes explained. The problem cannot be resolved in the abstract terms in which Grunbaum poses it.

Frank Cioffi

When Rush Rhees says that a man 'bewildered at the sort of person he finds himself to be' may feel a need to talk to someone 'who could help formulate what was in [his] mind', the need he refers to is not to be appeased by properly psychoanalytic accounts whether they were like the stale cigarette smoke to which Rhees unkindly compares them or not (Rhees, 1971, 23–26). As a recent account of Wittgenstein's views puts it, 'Freud seeks to offer explanations where . . . what is required is not explanation but clarification' (Johnston, 1989, 50)[5].

In conceiving of his inquiry as one into the causes of his patients' condition Freud may sometimes have misconstrued his own questions and not merely theirs (Habermas's 'scientistic self-misunderstanding'). Consider the epistemic character of the hidden teleology Freud imputes in the following passage:

> We have come across people all of whose relationships have the same outcome; the benefactor who is abandoned in anger after a time by each of his proteges . . . the man whose friendships all end in betrayal by his friend; the man who time after time in the course of his life raises someone else to a position of great authority . . . and then, after a certain interval, himself upsets that authority and replaces him; the lover each of whose amorous relationships passes through the same stages and reaches the same conclusion.' (Freud, 1959, 44).

Does Freud mean us to assimilate these to the predicament, poignantly described by Dr Johnson, of the epileptic who 'tumbles and revives and tumbles again and all the while he knows not why'? Must we accept this assimilation?

Despite Freud's occasional equivocations and tergiversations, funda-mental to psychanalysis is a conception of lived life as epiphenomenal to processes which must be laboriously excavated and could have been otherwise, just as the cause of pain of a certain locale, quality, duration and periodicity is only laboriously to be determined and could have been otherwise (referred pain). But life-pain need not be entirely like that. Its complete understanding may require two distinct enterprises, one employing reflection and the other investigation. What we have instead is, for the most part, the Freud-inspired hodgepodge with one hitching a ride on the back of the other and which is doing the epistemic and therapeutic work only to be guessed at—'an abominable mess'.

[5] Van den Bergh, a phenomenological therapist, describes the Freudian unconscious as 'a second reality behind the phantoms of healthy and neurotic life' (and holds it to be the mistaken result of 'the premature cessation of psychological analysis') (Van den Bergh, 1960, 83).

Wittgenstein and Psychology: on our 'Hook Up' to Reality

JOHN SHOTTER

> We must do away with *explanation*, and description alone must take its place. And this description gets its light, that is to say its purpose, from . . . philosophical problems. These are, of course, not empirical problems; they are solved, rather, by looking into the workings of our language, and that in such a way as to make us recognize those workings: *in spite of* an urge to misunderstand them. The problems are solved, not by giving new information, but by arranging what we have already known. Philosophy is a battle against the bewitchment of our intelligence by means of language. (PI, I, 109)

My task in this paper is to discuss Wittgenstein and psychology. Now central to an understanding of anything psychological is, I think, an understanding of the role of language in human affairs. But what *is* the part it plays? As we know, Wittgenstein thought of it in his earlier and later work in two distinctly different ways: In the *Tractatus* [TR] its role was representation—language functions to provide 'pictures' of states of affairs in the world; while in the *Philosophical Investigations* its role is communication—it is *used* within certain, circumscribed ways, within the confines of certain *language-games*, to 'move' people to relate themselves to one another in particular *forms of life*—if in this view it still seems that words *are* used to represent things, then that is only because 'representation' is one of the (many) 'games' one can 'play' with language in sustaining the forms of life in question.

At the moment in the landscape of modern psychology, there are a number of different movements of importance, which relate to these two phases in Wittgenstein's work. The mainstream is following through all the implications of what it calls 'the cognitive revolution': the idea that everything intelligent we do involves a 'cognitive process' working in terms of 'inner' *mental representations* of the 'external' world, and that the way to study such processes is by modelling them in computational terms (e.g. Boden, 1982; Johnson-Laird, 1983). But there are also, in fact, quite a number of other movements in opposition to this approach. Among them are: the *ecological approach to perception* of the Gibsonians (Gibson, 1979); the *rhetorical approach to social psychology* being pioneered in this country by Michael Billig (1987); while, along with Kenneth Gergen in America, I am myself attempting to fashion a whole *social constructionist* approach to psychology (Gergen, 1985; Shotter, 1984; Shotter and Gergen, 1989).

Wittgenstein's philosophical investigations are, I feel, relevant at a number of points in this landscape: first, they offer good reasons for thinking that the current 'cognitive' orientation in psychology is radically misconceived, and the idea, that computer models are relevant to the understanding of human activities, will eventually lose its credibility; whilst at the same time, they also offer helpful hints towards the development of all the new movements I have just mentioned—as I shall show below.

In developing my argument, let me begin with a quotation, not from Wittgenstein, but from someone who had a major influence upon him (Janik and Toulmin, 1973; CV), the great nineteenth-century physicist Heinrich Hertz—the discoverer (or should we say: inventor?) of radio waves. Right at the beginning of his *The Principles of Mechanics* (orig. German edition, 1894), in introducing an important analysis of certain problems, to do with the use of symbolic representations in science, Hertz described their role thus:

> In endeavouring . . . to draw inferences as to the future from the past, we always adopt the following process. We form for ourselves images or symbols of external objects; and the form that we give them is such that the necessary consequents of the images in thought are always the images of the necessary consequents in nature of the things pictured. In order that this requirement may be satisfied, there must be a certain conformity between nature and our thought. (Hertz, 1954, 1)

In other words, we say our theories are true theories if the *predictions* we derive from them match or 'picture' the *outcomes* of the processes we study. So: although we can bring off some quite spectacular results in the sciences, it is just *in terms of such results*, not the whole structure of a theory, that we think of a theory as a *true* theory. Our knowledge, as Quine [1953] said later, 'is a man-made fabric which impinges on experience only along the edges'.

This 'instrumental' criterion of truth, as I shall call it, however, allows for a considerable degree of loose-jointedness in the relations between our theories and the character of our surroundings—what we uncritically call, our reality.[1] 'As a matter of fact,' says Hertz (1954, 2),

> we do not know, nor have we any means of knowing, whether our conceptions of things are in conformity with [the things themselves]

[1] In the paper I shall oscillate between talk of 'reality' and talk of 'surroundings' or 'circumstances'. While in the *Tractatus* Wittgenstein thought of 'reality' as grounding our talk, in the *Remarks on the Philosophy of Psychology* he came to talk of it as grounded in its 'surroundings'.

in any other than this *one* fundamental respect. The images we may form of things are not determined without ambiguity by the requirement that the consequents of the images be the images of the consequents.

Now this lack of a *direct* 'hook-up' between theory and reality may not worry most natural scientists, but given the political and moral climate that emerged in the late 1960s, and the then mounting criticisms of the demeaning images of persons promoted by mainstream psychology,[2] as a psychologist, it came to worry me. For in studying people, I came to be concerned, not just with truth in an 'effective' or 'instrumental' sense, achieved by the use of *models*, but with the 'adequacy' of such models, with whether they do justice to *the being* of a person. But to be able to judge that, we must know what a human being 'is'. And that problem, as Hertz makes perfectly clear, cannot be solved (without undecidable ambiguities to do with 'appropriateness') by formulating models and looking for 'conformities' between their products and human products. The discovery of what something 'is' for us, can only be discovered from a study, not of how we talk about it in reflecting upon it, but of how 'it' necessarily 'shapes' those of our everyday communicative activities in which it is involved, *in practice*; an influence which is only revealed in the 'grammar' of such activities. Hence Wittgenstein's claim that: 'Grammar tells us what kind of object anything is . . . (PI, I, 373)

To some extent then (but only to an extent), the problem of *what it is for us to be a human being*, is a philosophical problem, and in Wittgenstein's terms, there are two interlinked aspects to its philosophical study: Besides (1) an investigation of the (in fact very many different) ways in which our *image*(s) or *concept*(s) of ourselves are implicitly involved in our everyday activities and practices; (2) we must also study the degree to which our explicit *formulations* or *accounts* of them actually accord, or not, with our practices (RPP, I, 548). For it is there, Wittgenstein felt, in the formulations we use to specify the nature of our knowledge, that misunderstandings of the 'link' between them and the reality they are meant to represent arise. Indeed, to point straightaway to what might be argued *is* just such a misunderstanding: In the Preface to the *Tractatus*, Bertrand Russell states the then standard philosophical view of language: 'The essential business of language is to assert or deny facts' (TR, x). But is it? Does such a claim represent, i.e. accord with, what 'are' in fact the nature of our linguistic practices?

---

[2] Indeed, criticism at that time was quite strong—as the following example illustrates: 'That modern psychology has projected an image of man which is as demeaning as it is simplistic, few intelligent and sensitive non-psychologists would deny' (Koch, 1964, 37).

The view that Wittgenstein later came to hold, which I now believe is the correct view, is the one which I have already mentioned: that, if it does seem that words can be used to *represent* things, to 'picture' facts, then that is just *one* of the uses of language possible for us from within a form of life *already constituted* by the language-games in which such words are used.

Hence the interlinked nature of the two aspects of Wittgenstein's study: (1) On the one hand, by being content merely to describe rather than to explain the nature of our mental activities, he shows how indefinitely various their nature is. For example: many instances of what we call 'remembering', or what we call 'recognizing', are all in fact very different from one another. While they may all *in their context* be called cases of remembering or recognizing, when they are examined in themselves, we find they have no properties in common among them at all. And on the other, (2) by exposing the temptation we feel to *explain* so-called 'mental processes', he shows how we fall victim to the need to find a single *basic* process in each case, which will show us 'how' remembering or recognizing occurs, or is done. For instance, about 'recognizing', he says:

> It is easy to have a false picture of the processes called 'recognizing'; as if recognizing always consisted in comparing two impressions with one another. It is as if I carried a picture of an object with me and used it to perform an identification of an object as the one repre-sented by the picture . . . (PI, I, 604)

Surely, recognizing a voice, a smell, a feeling, an emotion, or a person's legal rights, is done in some other way than by comparing a state of affairs with a picture.

> A main cause of philosophical disease—a one-sided diet: one nour-ishes one's thinking with only one kind of example. (PI, I, 593)

In coming to this view of philosophy, as entailing an analysis of lan-guage use, Wittgenstein was again deeply influenced by Hertz's com-ments to do with a special set of problems in science: those which arise, not out of any lack of empirical knowledge, but out of 'painful contra-dictions' in our ways of *representing* such knowledge to ourselves. About such problems, Hertz [1956, 8] had said:

> It is not by finding out more and fresh relations and connections that [they] can be answered; but by removing the contradictions between those already known, and thus perhaps by reducing their number. When these painful contradictions are removed . . . our minds, no longer vexed, will cease to ask illegitimate questions.

And this was the method Wittgenstein turned to when, in the Preface to the *Philosophical Investigations*, he was to write of the 'grave mistakes' in 'my old way of thinking' that talks with friends had forced him to recognize.

As it is Wittgenstein's 'old way of thinking', which is currently at the heart of mainstrain psychology, before turning to the relevance of his later work for a new psychology, let me first just say a little more about the view of the relation between language and reality which it incorporates, the view which he later came to think of as 'a grave mistake'. In psychology, the view in question is attributed by many cognitive psychologists to Kenneth Craik, who in his very influential 1943 book stated it thus:

> My hypothesis is that thought models, or parallels, reality—that its essential feature is not 'the mind', 'the self', sense-data', nor propositions but symbolism, and that this symbolism is largely of the same kind as that which is familiar to us in mechanical devices which aid thought and calculation. (Craik, 1943, 57)

Thus, for instance, Johnson-Laird (1943, 2) in his book *Mental Models*, explicitly follows Craik in suggesting that 'the psychological core of understanding . . . consists in your having a "working model" of the phenomenon [in question] in your mind'. Margaret Boden (1982, 224) also makes essentially the same claim: '[Artificial intelligence research (AI)] studies not the world itself, but the way representations of the world can be constructed, evaluated, compared, and transformed.'

This is 'the old way of thinking' central to Wittgenstein's approach in the *Tractatus*. There, he made such claims as: 'We make to ourselves pictures of facts' (TR, 2.1), and 'The picture is a model of reality' (TR, 2.12). Further, such a model is 'linked with reality' (TR, 2.1512) by being 'like a scale applied to reality' (TR, 2.1512). And 'What every picture, of whatever form, must have in common with reality in order to be able to represent it at all—rightly or falsely—is the logical form, that is, the form of reality' (TR, 2.18).

But what is that form?[3] What counts as *appropriateness* here? What is the character of the 'link' or the 'hook up' between phenomena and their

---

[3] Even before Wittgenstein, others began to express a degree of unease about the nature of scientific theories, and to grant that the mathematically expressed axioms and theories of physics were not necessarily truths about the physical world. One such is Einstein. Indeed, about such propositions, he said: 'Insofar as the propositions of mathematics give an account of reality they are not certain; and insofar as they are certain they do not describe reality . . ' (quoted in Kline, 1980, 97). A theory is, he said, a 'free invention of the mind'. 'It is a work of pure reason; the empirical contents and their mutual relations must find their representation in the *conclusions* of the theory' (Einstein, 1979,

representations. Here is a central weakness, for the trouble is, as Wittgenstein says in the *Tractatus*: 'The picture . . . cannot represent its form, of representation . . .' How can we get to know its form then? Well, the model itself '*shows it forth*,' he says (TR, 2.172; my emphasis); thus, to the extent that its *form* is *shown* in its structure, its correspondence to reality is something which one must 'just see'. As Lewis Carroll realized (in the tale of Achilles and the Tortoise), we cannot be cognitively (or physically) coerced through irrefutable reasoning to accept it. In other words, as Wittgenstein realized, the fact is, as he put it in his book *On Certainty*, 'the idea of "agreement with reality" does not have any clear application' (OC, 215). But if we do not always check our claims to truth by a procedure of formally comparing theory and reality in terms of their 'pictured shape', how can they be checked? For sooner or later, one's claims have to be publicly accepted or not by others, and for that to be possible, others have to be able to apply the same kinds of procedures and criteria in judging them as oneself. Thus, 'if language is to be a means of communication,' says Wittgenstein, then, 'there must be agreement not only in definitions but also (queer as this may sound) in judgments . . . (PI, I, 242).

Indeed, whatever kind of utterance one makes, one must be able to judge the nature of its relation to its surroundings; how it is linked to the world. And in particular, if it is a claim to knowledge, then one must ask: 'How might such a claim be "rooted" or "grounded"?' For, although Wittgenstein rejected 'picturing' as the only way in which representing was done, this did not mean to say that he rejected the whole idea of being able to justify one's claims to knowledge in some way or other: they must be such that they are 'permitted', 'allowed', or 'afforded' as representations of reality, of *our* circumstances.

> Giving grounds . . . ., justifying the evidence, comes to an end:—but the end is not certain propositions striking us immediately as true, i.e., it is not a kind of *seeing* on our part; it is our *acting*, which lies at the bottom of the language-game (OC, 204).

No matter how we might twist and turn, and attempt to find somewhere, a fundamental, 'naturalistic', or 'logically necessary' founda-

---

311). It is *not*, as classical empiricist philosophers claimed (and many empiricist psychologists still claim), deduced from experience 'by abstraction'. Indeed, 'a clear recognition of the erroneousness of [the classical empiricist view] really only came,' says Einstein (1979, 312), 'with the general theory of relativity, which showed that one could take account of a wider range of empirical facts . . . on a foundation quite different from the Newtonian one'. So: although both views may be 'permissible'—as Hertz (1954, 2) put it—'two permissible and correct models of the same external objects may yet differ in respect of appropriateness'.

tion—which can be explicitly formulated in stable, unequivocal, formal terms, we always run up against the question: 'How can you justify your claim to others?' This, however, always occasions the prior problem of how one can make one's claims intelligible to others. In other words, the 'grounds' for our claims to knowledge ultimately are to be found in who we 'are', in our forms of life. For it is in our socialization into a certain way of being, that we learn how to do such things as making claims, raising questions, conducting arguments, sensing disagreements, recognizing agreements, and so on. These *ontological skills*—these ways of being a certain kind of socially competent, first-person member of our society—are necessary for there to be any questions, or arguments, at all [Shotter, 1984].

> 'So you are saying that human agreement decides what is true and what is false?'—It is what human beings *say* that is true and false; and they agree in the language they use. That is not agreement in opinions but in form of life. (PI, I, 241)

What this means then, to repeat, is that in actual fact, there are an indefinite number of ways in which the connection between an utterance and its circumstances is, or can, literally, be 'made', and, if a claim to knowledge, be justified. Indeed, if we ask, how many kinds of uses for our utterances there might be, the reply we receive is:

> There are *countless* kinds: countless different kinds of use of what we call 'symbols', 'words', 'sentences'.[4] And this multiplicity is not something fixed, given once for all; but types of language, new language-games, as we say, come into existence, and others become obsolete and get forgotten . . . (PI, I, 23)

The 'logical' form used in a 'picturing' relation to our supposed 'reality', is thus only one such way; other ways of formulating claims to knowledge about one's circumstances, such as narrative, metonymic, or even ironic forms, are possible also. Indeed:

> It is interesting to compare the multiplicity of the tools in language and of the way they are used . . ., with what logicians have said

---

[4] Someone else who takes a similar view is Garfinkel (1967, 31): 'Not *a* method of understanding, but the immensely various methods of understanding are the professional sociologist's proper and hitherto unstudied and critical phenomena. Their multitude is indicated in the endless list of ways that persons speak. Some indication of their character and their differences occurs in the socially available glosses of a multitude of sign functions as when we take note of marking, labelling, symbolizing, emblemizing, cryptograms, analogies, anagrams, indicating, minaturizing, imitating, mocking-up, simulating—in short, in recognizing, using, and producing the orderly ways of cultural settings from "within" those settings.'

about the structure of language. (Including the author of the *Tractatus-Logico-Philosophicus*.) (PI, I, 23)

The trouble is, in science as in logic (as also in psychology), because we mistakenly '*compare* the use of words with games and calculi which have fixed rules . . .' (PI, I, 81), we always think that words *must* have stable, unequivocal, already determined *meanings*. But in the openness of ordinary everyday life, in comparison with the closed world of logic, this is precisely *not* the case.

To state now explicitly the well-known Wittgensteinian slogan: in everyday life, words do not in themselves have a meaning, but a *use*, and furthermore, a *use only in a context*; they are best thought of, not as having already determined meanings, but as *means*, as tools, or as instruments for use in the 'making' of meanings—'think of words as instruments characterized by their use,' he says in *The Blue Book* (BB, 67). For, like tools in a tool-box, the significance of our words remain open, vague, ambiguous, until they are used in different particular ways in different particular circumstances. 'When we say: "Every word in language signifies something" we have so far,' says Wittgenstein (PI, I, 13), 'said *nothing whatsoever*; unless we have explained exactly *what* distinction we wish to make . . .,' and we make different distinctions (with the same word) in different situations—'our talk gets its meaning from the rest of our proceedings,' he says (OC, 229). This is utterly to repudiate the assumption that words in language *already* have a meaning independently of the circumstances of life in which they are used.

Here, then, we have a very different view of the nature of language and of the function of words and symbols from that still held by psychologists (and by most scientists in general, for that matter). How did Wittgenstein ever come to this view of words as 'instruments' and of meaning as 'always situated'? What was his 'method' or 'methods', so to speak. First, as I have already remarked, he resists the temptation to rush to an explanation or understanding of something too early; we must first be clear about *what* is it that really puzzles us. Indeed, every time he hears the claim that something *must* have a certain character to it, he says (and you can almost hear him *shout* it in anger): 'Don't think, but look!'—do not think of what *must* be hidden, within us somewhere, but look at the *circumstances* of our talk. This is because our ways of talking 'tempt' us into thinking that what we say *must be justified* by reference to what the talk is about; it tempts into thinking that because we talk of certain 'things', the things we talk of '*must*' actually exist.

For example in psychology: If we were to observe a person A writing down a series of numbers 1, 5, 11, 19, 29, watched by a person B who then tries to continue the series. If B succeeds, and exclaims: 'Now I can go on!', we say that B has *understood* the series, and we are tempted to try to discover the mental process of understanding which seems to be hidden behind what B has done. But as Wittgenstein points out, in solving the series B may do any one of a number of different things: (1) tell of inventing and confirming a general formula; (2) tell of discovering the sequence of differences (4, 6, 8, 10); (3) simply say that the series is one already familiar to them; or (4) in fact, say nothing, and simply continue the series. Behind all these different activities, we are tempted to say that there *must be* a single, essential process of understanding, and it is our job as psychologists to discover its nature.[5] But, says Wittgenstein:

> If there is any thing 'behind the utterance of the formula' it is *particular circumstances*, which justify me in saying I can go on—when the formula occurs to me.
>
> Try not to think of understanding as a 'mental process' at all.—For *that* is the expression which confuses you. But ask yourself: in what sort of case, in what kind of circumstances, do we say, 'Now I know how to go on', when, that is, the formula *has* occurred to me? (PI, I, 154)

And he *continues*:

> That way of speaking is what prevents us from seeing the facts without prejudice . . . *That* is how it can come about that the means of representation produces something *imaginary*. So let us not think we *must* find a specific mental process, because the verb 'to understand' is there and because one says: Understanding is an activity of the mind. (Z, 446)

We have here, then, an example of his method at work. But because of all the temptations to which we fall victim, it is not easy to implement. For the trouble is, if one does just 'look' at everyday human social activity, all one sees is its 'bustle' (RPP, II, 625, 626), its variability; indeed, 'variability itself is a characteristic of behaviour without which behaviour would be to us as something completely different' (RPP, II, 627).

That then is the task he set himself: simply to describe what actually 'are' our everyday linguistic practices. And if there is a key to Wittgenstein's later philosophy, then I think that it is this: the raging determination to renounce all theory, and 'to put all this indefiniteness, correctly and unfalsified, into words' (PI, I, 227). Where, as he said, 'The difficulty of renouncing all theory: One has to regard what

---

[5] 'Idiot savants', as we know, say that they instantly 'just see' the solution to the most complex of arithmetic problems, leaving us totally puzzled as to the 'processes' involved.

appears so obviously incomplete, as something complete' (RPP, I, 723).

Indeed:

> Mere description is so difficult because one believes one needs to fill out the facts in order to understand them. It is as if one saw a screen with scattered colour-patches, and said: the way they are here, they are unintelligible; they only make sense when one completes them into a shape.—Whereas I want to say: Here *is* the whole. (If you complete it, you falsify it.) (RPP, I, 257)

So: if we take it that one of Wittgenstein's major insights in his later philosophy is that the idea of 'agreement with reality' lacks any clear application, then I think this counts as another: that everyday human activities do not just *appear* vague and indefinite because we are still as yet ignorant of their true underlying nature, but that they are *really* vague. 'We are under the illusion that what is peculiar, profound, essential, in our investigation, resides in its trying to grasp the incomparable essence of language. That is, the *order* existing between the concepts of proposition, word, proof, truth, experience, and so on' (PI, I, 97). But the fact is, there is no order, no already determined order, just an '*order of possibilities*,'[6] an order of possible orderings which it is up to us to make as we see fit. And this, of course, if we are to act in the world and be able really to influence what happens there, is exactly what we require of language as a means of communication: we require the words of our language to give rise to vague, but not wholly unspecified 'tendencies', which permit a degree of further specification *according to the circumstances of their use*, thus to allow the 'making' of precise and particular meanings appropriate to those circumstances.

We are tempted in the example above to put the coloured patches into an order, because only that seems to give them a meaning. But that is not the case. What they then take on is not so much a meaning as *intelligibility*, i.e., they become capable of being grasped reflectively and intellectually, i.e., represented as having a place within a closed and orderly language-game. But in such circumstances, as we know from works of science fiction, it is possible for syntax to masquerade as meaning to such an extent that it is possible to create a 'sense' of a 'reality' that does not in fact exist. And the fact is, in their *incomplete* state, within a particular context of action, they possess a perfectly clear meaning, according to the particular exigencies of that context; 'the

---

[6] Here Wittgenstein makes contact with his views about language in the *Tractatus*, where he sees propositions as determining a place in a space of possibilities (TR, 3.4 to 3.442). See also Janik and Toulmin (1973, 142–144) for an account of Hertz's and Boltzman's influence here.

circumstances decide whether, and what, more detailed specifications are necessary' (PI, 199). They take on their meaning according to how they are used in the context. Because of this, though:

> The *facts* of human natural history that throw light on our problem, are difficult for us to find out, for our talk *passes them by*, it is occupied with other things. (In the same way we tell someone: 'Go into the shop and buy . . .'—not: 'Put your left foot in front of your right foot etc. etc., then put coins down on the counter, etc. etc.' (RPP, I, 78)

Mostly we talk with the aim of creating and sustaining various forms of life, with the aim of 'going on', and not with stopping to contemplate its 'facts'. For the really important knowledge for us in all of this, is to do with us 'knowing our way about'[7] within the indefiniteness of our ordinary, everyday human affairs.

What then does all this mean for psychology, and for our attempts to improve our understanding of remembering and recognizing, of thinking, perceiving and acting? What actually should we investigate, in wanting to say something sensible about feelings, about emotions, and about motivation, and in what way should try to communicate our results? It means that we should 'take the various psychological phenomena: thinking, pain, anger, joy, wish, fear, intention, memory etc.,—and compare the behaviour corresponding to each'. But, he asks:

> What does behaviour include here? Only the play of facial expression and the gestures? Or also the surrounding, so to speak, the occasion of this expression? . . . (RPP, I, 129)
> the word 'behaviour' as I am using it, is altogether misleading, for it includes in its meaning the external circumstances. (RPP, I, 314)

But it is precisely these circumstances—our shared practices, our embodied ways of judging, discriminating, and reacting, our ontological skills at being who we 'are'—which are not amenable to systematic description.

This does not mean, however, that we should give up psychology and turn to a study of computer models of either the brain, or of supposed 'mental processes'. Far from it. Indeed, about the resort to such approaches he made comments like the following: About thinking:

> No supposition seems to me more natural than that there is no process in the brain correlated with associating or with thinking . . .
> [W]hy should the *system* continue further in the direction of the

---

[7] 'A philosophical problem has the form: "I don't know my way about"' (PI, I, 133).

centre? Why should this order not proceed, so to speak, out of chaos? . . . (RPP, I, 903)

Or about remembering:

Why must something or other, whatever it may be, be stored up [in one's nervous system] *in any form*? Why *must* a trace have been left behind? Why should there not be a psychological regularity to which *no* physiological regularity corresponds? If this upsets our concepts of causality then it is high time they were upset. (RPP, I, 905)

Now it is not that Wittgenstein wants to deny that there is any process at all involved in thinking and remembering, and such like; only that an orderly 'picturing' process lies at the bottom of it.[8] In other words, as Wittgenstein sees it, what we as human beings seem able to do (and here I am theorizing!), is to take vague and unformulated, possible forms of order, and to 'give' or to 'lend' them a socially intelligible and legitimate order, hence to assign them a *use* or *significance* within the contexts belonging to one or another of our forms of life.

Within the sphere of remembering, someone who has studied the process in exactly these terms, was Sir Frederic Bartlett in his classic book *Remembering*. There he says this about people attempting to remember a complex situation:

In all ordinary instances he [the person] has an overmastering tendency simply to get a general impression of the whole; and, on the basis, of this, he constructs the probable detail. Very little of his construction is literally observed and often, as was easily demonstrated experimentally, a lot is distorted or wrong so far as the actual facts are concerned. But it is the sort of construction which serves to justify his general impression. (Bartlett, 1932, 206)

If asked to characterize this nature of the *general impression* functioning as the origin of the process, as he says, the word which is always cropping up is 'attitude';

---

[8] As he comments in (PI, I, 304), 'How does the philosophical problem about mental processes and states and about behaviourism arise?—We talk of processes and states and leave their nature undecided. Sometime perhaps we shall know more about them—we think. But that is just what commits us to a particular way of looking at the matter. For we have a definite concept of what it means to learn to know a process better. (The decisive movement in the conjuring trick has been made, and it was the very one we thought quite innocent.)—And now the analogy which was to make us understand our thought falls to pieces. So we have to deny the yet uncomprehended process in the yet unexplored medium. And it now looks as if we had denied mental processes. And naturally we don't want to deny them.' 'We have only rejected the grammar which tried to force itself upon here.' We want only to say that whatever their nature is, it is indeterminate.

> Attitude names a complex psychological state or process which is very hard to describe in more elementary psychological terms. It is, however, as I have often indicated, very largely a matter of feeling, or affect. We say that it is characterized by doubt, hesitation, surprise, astonishment, confidence, dislike, repulsion and so on. Here is the significance of the fact, often reported in the preceding pages, that when a subject is being asked to remember, very often the first thing that emerges is something of the nature of an attitude. The recall is then a construction, made largely on the basis of this attitude, and its general effect is that of a justification of the attitude. (Ibid., 207)

In other words, the mental process in question is of a two-way kind: (1) in the agent–attitude direction, the act of recall 'constructs' the memory; but the agent cannot construct the memory just anyhow. Thus (2) in the other, attitude–agent direction, the attitude acts back upon the agent and determines the 'grounds' for the construction. The agent can only construct what the initial 'attitude' will permit or afford. Thus, in no way is remembering for Bartlett a matter of 'retrieving' an already well-formed memory trace from a 'memory-store'. Whatever is 'stored' in one as a result of one's past experiences need have no discoverable *order* in it at all; its order is something constructed during the process of remembering.

But we face a yet further task in our claims to be remembering something than being able to check 'within ourselves', so to speak, whether our formulations are permissible or not; we must also check them for their social function as intelligible and legitimate *accounts* —for verbally recounted 'memories' do not just occur in a social vacuum. Indeed, although Bartlett does not in fact reflexively explore the implications of his own theories for the gathering of his results, it is clear that people are not just providing neutral statements, but feel their conduct 'questioned' in some way. Thus, as he says,

> the confident subject justifies himself—attains a rationalization, so to speak—by setting down more detail than was actually present; while the cautious, hesitating subject reacts in the opposite manner, and finds his justification by diminishing rather than increasing, the details presented. (Ibid., 21)

In other words, not only are we working here within a framework of social accountability, such that we have a responsibility to others (and to ourselves) to formulate in our 'efforts after meaning' a justifiable memory-account—one which the circumstances 'affords' [Gibson, 1979]—but the accounting practices involved have a *rhetorical structure of (implied) criticism and justification*. It is just this topic—the expression of an attitude within a rhetorical context of argumentation—that has been studied by Michael Billig (1987).

John Shotter

Here then is where we make contact with some of the current approaches in psychology which are in opposition to the mainstream, cognitive, mental representations approach. Gibson (1979) in his *ecological* approach to perception, has emphasized—not unlike Hertz, in talking about 'permissible' formulations (see above note 3)—what particular behaviours an organism's surroundings or circumstances will *afford*, given the kind of organism it is. Like Wittgenstein—who, as we have seen, points out that it is not 'seeing' but our 'acting' which grounds our ways of talking—so Gibson also makes it clear that:

> Perceiving is an achievement of the individual, not an appearance in the theatre of his consciousness. It is a keeping-in-touch with the world, an experiencing of things rather than a having of experiences . . . [P]erception is not a mental act. Neither is it a bodily act. Perceiving is a psychosomatic act, not of the mind or of the body but of a living observer. (Gibson, 1979, 239–240)

In other words, Gibson provides the possibility for an account—similar to the two-way flow account I provided above—of a much closer form of 'hook up' between us and our surroundings than that provided in previous (merely causal) theories of perception. But what he clearly lacks in his theory of perception, is any account of how any checking or testing might occur as to whether one's perceptions not only made sense *within a form of life*, but can be evaluated as intelligible and legitimate. It is here that, I think, Michael Billig's (1987) work on a rhetorical approach to arguing and thinking becomes relevant.

Clearly, the major revolution in the analysis of human action introduced by Wittgenstein, Austin and Ryle: unlike the implicit assumption in modern scientific psychology, that ethics is an applied science based upon psychology and biology,[9] assumes that in anything intelligible we say about human conduct, we express or at least presupposes judgments of good/bad, appropriate/inappropriate, skilful/clumsy, etc., judgments which are grounded in reasons, which in turn may be grounded in one or another form of life. But what this means, is that one must be aware in all of one's behaviour, of its fittedness to its circumstances, especially if one wants to act in other than a routine manner: for although we are free to act as we please, as long as we make use of the ways of acting and speaking accepted in our society, we must apply

[9] For instance, Broadbent (1961, 9) says: 'It is a cliché nowadays to say that our mastery of the material world is outstripping our ability to control ourselves . . . It is urgent that our behaviour should be brought up to the standard of our knowledge . . . [P]erhaps the most hopeful road is to apply to behaviour itself the method of attack which has proved so useful in dealing with the material world . . .' See Argyle (1969) for an identical view.

them with care in negotiating with the others around us lines of action acceptable to them. Hence Billig's claim that all properly *social* contexts, are *contexts of argumentation*, that is, contexts structured by the possibility of the activities within them allowing criticism and/or requiring justification, perhaps interminably.[10]

But this view, to be quite explicit about it, leads to the following very radical claim: that our *psychological being* derives its nature from whatever 'rooting' we might have in various forms of life; with some forms having more historical continuity and social extent than others. And that we would not be 'us' except for the 'parts' we play in the language-games constituting them. Which means, that whatever misunderstandings there might be in our society's ways of talking, *philosophical analysis alone cannot disentangle us* from our involvement in them—hence my comment at the beginning of this paper, that the problem of what or who we 'are' is only *to an extent* a philosophical problem, other aspects of the problem are practical–ethical and political. Thus 'the sciences of man,' as Charles Taylor (1971, 51) called them:

> cannot be *wertfrie*; they are moral sciences in a more radical sense than the eighteenth century understood . . . [T]heir successful prosecution requires a high-degree of self-knowledge, a freedom from illusion, in the sense of error which is rooted and expressed in one's way of life; for our capacity to understand is rooted in our own self-definitions, hence in what we are. To say this is not to say anything new: Aristotle makes a similar point in Book I of the *Ethics*. But it is still radically shocking and unassimilable to the mainstream of modern science.

But this, I think, is *precisely* the relation of Wittgenstein's work to current psychology: for, the claim that understanding the nature of mind is *not* simply a 'scientific' matter of 'discovering' its properties, but *is* a moral and a political problem, to do with how we *should* relate ourselves to one another, *is* a radically shocking claim and unassimilable to psychology in its current guise as a modern science.

But gradually, views of this kind—that people's worlds cannot be understood in terms merely of abstract, decontextualized, non-social,

---

[10] A very important paper in this respect is Gallie (1955–56) on essentially contested concepts'. See also my own paper on rhetoric and the recovery of civil society (Shotter, 1989). It was because of the possibility of interminable argument s in ethics and morals, of course, that Liebniz sought his *Characteristica Universalis*, which if we had it, we should be able when confronted with such problems say: 'Let us take our slates and calculate.' Indeed, Broadbent (1961, 11) justifies the natural scientific approach along these lines too.

non-historical principles—must, I think, be assimilated and understood, for surely, their time has now arrived. For just as in Wittgenstein's 'dark' but 'interesting times' in Vienna, in which there was a loss
of confidence in the power of the intellect to help shape one's future; a
feeling that the conditions for honesty in social debate no longer
existed; and of a precariousness in both social and international relations. These feelings, which *some* of us feel now (for they are not
necessarily shared by all) were also, as Janik and Toulmin (1973) point
out, experienced by many in Wittgenstein's Vienna (1890–1919).
Then, just as now, attention came to focus upon an analysis of communication, upon a critique of language. And it is Wittgenstein's
achievement, (1) to have shown how the 'tools' we (and he) had
previously thought adequate to the conduct of meaningful discussion of
real and urgent problems fail us; and (2) to have provided the basis for
the fashioning of more adequate alternatives—alternatives which this
time, I think, *can* help us to face and to cope with the uncertainties and
fluidities of life in an 'open' and honest way, instead of trying once again
to defend ourselves against them by entrapping ourselves within one or
another 'closed' form of life, blind to what is going on about us.

Wittgenstein and Social Science

ROGER TRIGG

I

The work of the later Wittgenstein has had a vast influence in the field of social science. This is hardly surprising as the effect of that philosophy has been an emphasis on the priority of the social. Empiricist philosophy started with the private experience of the individual and from there built up an inter-subjective picture of the world. Wittgenstein, on the other hand, began with the rule-governed practices of a community. Both the nature of private experience, and of an objective world, was deemed to depend on concepts all could share. Society is the source of such concepts and thus becomes the key notion in our understanding of ourselves and our relation to the world.

Wittgenstein was preoccupied with the nature of concepts. How can we communicate with each other? How is it that we can obtain and use language? The natural picture of the situation did not find favour with him. That is the one according to which we can each think clearly and have determinate experiences apart from our ability to use language. The latter would then communicate facts about ourselves and the world that are themselves independent of language. We each can have a clear vision of many things before we are educated in the assumptions of a particular society. We come, if not fully formed, yet at least with definite characters, to a social world which is the product of the interaction of individuals like ourselves. Learning concepts may then seem to be a matter mainly of fitting them to a particular part of reality, whether a private experience or an object in the external world. Other people will have similar experiences and will understand by analogy what we mean when we talk of our feelings. They will see which part of the objective world we pick out. We each have access to objective reality, whether the subjective world of our own experience, or the public one to which everyone has access.

There is room in this picture for a strong conception of the self, existing in its own right as the subject of all experience and logically prior to it. There is also a clear vision of a self-subsistent reality, whatever its constituents may be. The point is that it is in no sense dependent for its existence on our interaction with it. We can discover it, but do not create it. There is an absolute distinction between the subject and the object of experience. Both are independent of each other. If I see a lion, I can assume that it has an independent existence, and is not the product in some peculiar way of my conceptual scheme. Similarly I myself have a real existence, and do not need to have been inducted into the practices of a society to see the lion for what it is and react accordingly.

All this, and in particular the radical distinction between subject and object, is questioned by the later Wittgenstein. Instead of the private he emphasizes the public, and instead of the individual he stresses the social. Concepts are not based on individual private experience, but are rooted in our social life which of its nature is shared publicly. Nothing I think or say about myself and the world is determinate until it has been mediated by the rule-governed practices of our shared life. His arguments against the possibility of a private language are particularly relevant in this connection. Our private experiences, such as pain, seem particularly good sources of concepts which are based on what we each alone have access to. Surely I know what a pain is by feeling it, and not by being taught in society the meaning of the concept of pain. Wittgenstein tackles this head on and argues against the possibility of 'private objects'. One of his main arguments rest on the possibility of undetected error. He says: 'Always get rid of the private object in this way: assume that it constantly changes but that you do not notice the change because your memory constantly deceives you' (PI, I, 207). We may not be experiencing the same sensation again even when we think we are. This only serves to demonstrate, Wittgenstein believes, that what is meant by 'the same sensation' must be derived from something other than what we think we feel. The rules for using the expression must have anchors in the public world. Otherwise, not only will we each mean something different when we talk of our sensations. Wittgenstein's point is that individuals will be liable to mean something different every time they use the same expression, even though they do not realize it. That, though, is to say that their use of words is in fact meaningless.

Wittgenstein deals with the concept of private sensation as a particularly difficult test case for his views on the public nature of concepts. If even the concept of pain is public property, then so must all concepts be. He couples his views on concepts, which he links closely with the use of words, with the idea of a rule. An idiosyncratic use of words leaves listeners wondering whether the speaker means what is said or fails to grasp a concept. There must therefore be a rule for the application of a concept, and moreover one shared by a community. Otherwise one could never distinguish between cases where a concept is being misapplied and those where it is being applied properly and something strange is being said. If we have to rely on an individual's identification of a sensation as pain, what happens when we hear him say that he has a pain but it is not unpleasant? (See Trigg, 1970) Wittgenstein would hold that we do not know how to react. If, on the other hand, the use of the word 'pain' is linked to the public expression of a sensation, there are public criteria for the use of the word, and we no longer have to worry about the possibility of private mis-identification. Even the use of words for private sensation is embedded in a public practice, which, in this case at least, is linked to very general facts about human nature connected with how we exhibit pain.

The example is a controversial one, since even if Wittgenstein is right that concepts are public and shared, it by no means follows that the pain itself is simply a public matter. Needless to say, the concept of pain and the sensation of pain cannot be identified. However that may be, Wittgenstein uses the unverifiability of a person's judgment about pain to insist that there can be no logical gap between the judgment and the pain. The judgment, or the verbal expression of pain, is simply to be viewed as part of our normal pain-behaviour. It is embedded in a normal human practice with public rules. As Wittgenstein points out, not only is recognizing a pain not a private matter, but neither is following a rule, for similar reasons. He says: '"Obeying a rule" is a practice. And to *think* one is obeying a rule is not to obey a rule' (PI, I, 202). As he goes on to point out, you cannot obey a rule privately. As in his argument against the possibility of a private language, he rests his case on the possibility of error. He claims that 'otherwise thinking one was obeying a rule would be the same thing as obeying it'. Thus his arguments against the possibility of private mis-identification of sensations, are also arguments for the public character of rules. An impression of a rule is not a rule. As Wittgenstein says on this point: 'The balance on which impressions are weighed is not the impression of a balance' (PI, I, 259). A game in which there could be no distinction between what an individual player considered the rules to be and the rule themselves would cease to be a game. Without some shared agreement about the matter, there could be no distinction between different individuals milling around a piece of grass doing what they pleased, and a properly organized game of football.

II

Wittgenstein's opposition to private concepts leads him to stress the public nature of rules, and the agreement on which that is based. Such an agreement need not, he maintains (PI, I, 241), involve an identity of opinions about what is true and false. It does however, stem from a shared 'form of life'. Thus the priority of the public over the private

Roger Trigg

forms the basis for a stress on the shared nature of our life together. Perhaps a 'form of life' is based on what Wittgenstein refers to as 'the natural history of human beings' (PI, I, 415), or perhaps forms of life are to be regarded as ultimate. He certainly says: 'What has to be accepted, the given, is—so one could say—a *form of life*' (PI, I, 226). This appears to point to his dislike of the continued quest for explanation. We should, he argues, look at a language-game as 'the *primary* thing' (PI, I, 656). Whether or not forms of life are derived from anything beyond themselves, they cannot be explained or justified. They are just there even if they are an expression of human nature. One cannot reason about them, because reasoning can only take place within a particular context. There could be no such thing as a detached, free-floating reason, unconstrained by the assumptions of any context.

Wittgenstein sums up the situation as he sees it when he says: 'Instinct comes first, reasoning second. Not until there is a language-game are there reasons' (PI, I, 689). Reasoning depends on concepts, which need language, and that depends on practices of one kind and another. These may be the results of the 'common behaviour of mankind' (PI, I, 206) which Wittgenstein claims is the system of reference by means of which we interpret an unknown language. Even if they are, however, reason is impotent, since it is always the product of a practice and could never be detached from one. Elsewhere, he takes more seriously the possibility of radical conceptual differences, saying:

I want to say: an education quite different from ours might also be the foundation for quite different concepts. For here life would run on differently. (Z, 387)

From one point of view, it is irrelevant how far Wittgenstein wishes to espouse conceptual relativism (see Trigg, 1973), however unpalatable its consequences. His attack on reason is devastating, whether some of our practices are based on the fact of our common humanity or whether they are always based on more local considerations. He is stressing that concepts, the very constituents of our thought, can only be acquired and understood within the context in which they have their life. The fact that they must be public property, and not a private indulgence of individuals, itself establishes the priority of the social. We can only learn to think within the confines of a social practice, and are the creatures of our society. We cannot abstract ourselves from it in order to reason about it. 'Practices', 'forms of life', and 'language-games' are all terms bearing witness to the intimate mutual dependence of language and other forms of acting. As Wittgenstein says in a famous sentence, 'the term "language-game" is meant to bring into prominence the fact that the *speaking* of language is part of an activity, or of a form of life' (PI, I, 23). It is through participation in a society that we learn to use language and hence to think. Even if we are not taught *what* to think, the concepts which enable us to make distinctions are closely allied to the way our life is lived. If our life was different, so would be our concepts. Indeed, to adopt a more clearly relativist way of putting the position, there would then be a sense in which we would be living in a different world.

The public nature of concepts and the priority of rule-governed social activity are, for Wittgenstein, two sides of the same coin. Rules are not idiosyncratic private creations but are woven into the pattern of our life. He stresses (PI, I, 199) that it is not possible that somebody should obey a rule on only one occasion. Like that of a game, the notion of a rule is linked to that of a custom. From this follows the importance of all kinds of social institutions, even of such a basic nature as making a report or giving an order. They all have to be based on a common understanding, which is itself the product of a common way of behaving. This embedding of thought and action in the functioning of a community leads also to a stress on the importance of context. The meaning of what we do inevitably then depends on it surroundings. Causes and effects can be identified independently of whatever happens to accompany them. Once attention is switched to meaning, it is apparent that lifting an occurrence from its surroundings will serve to destroy its significance. Emotions, for instance, Wittgenstein would claim, are meaningful because of their context. You cannot cut out one second of a deep feeling such as ardent love or hope from its surrounding, and expect it could remain the same. Unlike pain perhaps, it is much harder to argue that hope is hope whatever the context in which it occurs. As Wittgenstein says: 'The surroundings give it its importance.' He points out that the word 'hope' refers to a 'phenomenon of human life'. It could not be torn out of the fabric of that life and still be as it was. By illustration, he maintains that 'a smiling mouth *smiles* only in a human face' (PI, I, 583).

These points can be generalized from particular facets of human life to more complicated social institutions. Wittgenstein himself does this by pointing out (PI, I, 584) that in different surroundings, even the institution of money does not exist. He also gives the example of a coronation. One minute of a solemn ceremony in Westminster Abbey can be put in a different context somewhere else, and the whole significance of what is happening can change.

This emphasis on context has coalesced with the concerns of social anthropology. It can involve just a salutary reminder that no word or action should be seen in isolation from its surroundings. What appears strange to an outsider can be perfectly meaningful seen from the standpoint of the practices of a society. Field-work is not an optional extra to anyone who wishes to understand properly what is going on.

Roger Trigg

To understand the part you have to participate in the whole. We thus slip quickly to the position that participation is an absolute pre-condition for any understanding. Social scientists are then faced with a dilemma. If they 'go native' they are hardly fulfilling a scientific role. Yet the alternative appears to be an inevitable failure to grasp what is really going on inside a culture.

III

How far does the later Wittgenstein's theory of meaning help the practice of social science? At first sight the intertwined trinity of the public, the social, and the contextual, provides an important rationale for social science. When meanings are not just public property, but enmeshed in the nature of a society so that they cannot be understood apart from it, it seems to be the social scientist who may provide the key to such understanding. When society is given such prominence, social explanation is going to be of primary importance. Individuals derive their role from wider patterns of life and do not come to society pre-formed. We do not enter society with ready-made ideas or beliefs, or with any prior understanding of anything. Society made us. Thought apart from language is to be ruled out. Wittgenstein was highly suspicious of the recollections of a deaf-mute, as reported by William James, of complicated thoughts which he had before he was able to learn language (PI, I, 342). Wittgenstein demonstrated once again with this reaction his reluctance to accept claims about private mental processes detached from public behaviour. The private is to depend on the public, just as the individual has to be logically secondary to the social.

The social sciences are thus presented with the opportunity of seizing the high ground of intellectual endeavour. If I only think as I do because society is as it is, who better to throw light on the situation than a social scientist? It is perhaps not surprising that Marxists find much that is congenial in Wittgenstein's thought. They agree with his emphasis on the priority of social arrangements, and the desire for explanations at the level of society. The intimate link between concepts and society is, at the least, compatible with Marxism. Nevertheless, others have suggested that Wittgenstein should be seen as a genuinely conservative thinker. He accepts that language-games change with time, but it looks as if he envisages evolution rather than revolution. His emphasis on society can be seen in a more traditionalist light. There are many conservatives who would stress that we are each the product of the history of our society. We cannot therefore change society without attacking the very source of our being. This too is compatible with Wittgenstein's position.

However Wittgenstein is interpreted from a political standpoint, the scope of his views on the nature of concepts offer to social science seems enormous. He could even be seen as ruling out the possibility of other forms of explanation. His work has provoked much interest in the philosophy of psychology, but his pre-occupation with the public world leaves little scope for psychology as a discipline except as a branch of social science. When the presuppositions of society are reflected in all its concepts, only the social scientist is equipped to show us to ourselves.

Wittgenstein is concerned with concepts and meaning, not with hypotheses about causal origins. On this view genuine social science cannot get behind people's understanding of what they are doing, but can only lay bare the conceptual rules they do in fact follow. Yet what then is the difference between sociology and philosophy? If the function of each can only be to elucidate the nature of our concepts, embedded as they are in particular forms of social life, they would seem to merge. Peter Winch, following Wittgenstein, would in fact hold this. He says: 'The central problem of sociology, that of giving an account of the nature of social phenomena in general, itself belongs to philosophy' (Winch, 1958). For Winch, sociology and epistemology are closely linked.

There are two reasons why this is so. The search for meaning forces sociology away from the scientific ground. The emphasis is on the significance of activities in their social context, rather than the giving of some causal story. Events can thus only be identified through appeal to the concepts of participants in the society, rather than being causally linked in some scientific fashion quite apart from the understanding of the members of the society. At the same time philosophy is forced on to similar ground. Wittgenstein's stress that we must accept language-games as given involves a repudiation of any idea of justification, or of providing a rational foundation for activities and practices. Philosophy has to leave everything as it is. Wittgenstein says:

> Philosophy may in no way interfere with the actual use of language; it can in the end only describe it. For it cannot give it any foundation either (PI, I, 124).

The conservative tendency of Wittgenstein's thought may be apparent here, but what is more marked is the way in which he pushes philosophy towards the realm of sociological description. It is not to be understood as providing a rational justification or criticism of what we do. Reason is a matter that can only be internal to particular language-games. It cannot be wrenched apart from them so as to pass judgment from the standpoint of some contextless and external realm of truth.

Metaphysics was, it seemed, to be totally eschewed. Wittgenstein says: 'What we do is to bring words back from their metaphysical to their everyday use' (PI, I, 166). We must see how people actually use words in their ordinary lives. One of the prime philosophical vices is to assume that words always function in the same way and that because 'house' refers to one kind of object, it follows that 'pain' must refer to another, albeit a private one. Once such confusion in our thought has been exposed, the task of philosophy is, it seems, complete. Similarly a social scientist will have finished his work when he has shown how the concepts of a given society are actually used by a participant. There can be no further question as to whether they are right or wrong to view things as they do.

IV

The view of philosophy as the mere classification of concepts not only emasculates it as a discipline. It also removes the possibility of giving proper foundations to other parts of human intellectual endeavour. The role of human reason itself is downgraded when metaphysics is dismissed. There is no scope for upholding or criticizing language-games when they just have to be accepted and described. This could be accounted a virtue in the social sciences, since it removes the possibility of criticizing the members of other cultures as mistaken or ignorant. We can therefore avoid the charge of ethnocentricity, of assuming the rightness of our own conceptual scheme in dismissing others. Yet this gain, if such it be, is achieved at a fearful cost, since there is then nothing in principle left beyond our own society to which we can appeal and as a result learn that perhaps we ourselves are mistaken. Humility towards other cultures is all very well but the paradox of a Wittgensteinian approach is that such humility has to go hand in hand with a blind acceptance of one's own form of life. One may not be able to claim one is right, but the fear of being wrong is forever removed. This is because where language-games and forms of life as such are concerned, no room is left for the notions of truth and falsity.

What, too, according to Wittgenstein, could be the role of a prophet calling society to a proper vision of things? It looks as if anyone standing out against the rules of a given society is like someone wrecking a cricket match by refusing to play by the rules. They are not playing the game and that is all that can be said. There is no possibility of conceding that one person may be right and everyone else wrong. The rules of cricket cannot be judged against anything beyond themselves and Wittgenstein puts social practices on a similar footing. One person cannot see the truth when everyone else is blind, and condemn whole practices.

Reason is not allowed to detach itself in that way from its social context. The meaning of words is 'internally related' (to use a phrase beloved by the followers of Wittgenstein) to the social institutions in which they gain currency. They cannot be detached from their background and still be properly used, any more than they could be used in a totally fresh context, while retaining a shred of their original meaning. This may be a familiar recital of the later Wittgenstein's views about meaning, but when we couple them with his reluctance to separate thought and language, and the consequent identification of words and concepts, there is no room left for the employment of any rationality outside our normal form of life, or in repudiation of it.

Reason is viewed as a component of our way of life, which cannot be separated from it. The realist's belief in a reality independent of our conceptions of it sinks out of sight. According to Wittgenstein's account reality can only be shown us in the concepts we possess and the language we use. No sense can be given to it somehow existing in its own right and perhaps even being misunderstood by us. We can go wrong within a practice, just as a bowler can bowl a 'no ball' in cricket, but we cannot ever get outside it to judge it as a whole by appealing to reality. Similarly, beliefs held within a way of life cannot claim any truth which ought to be accepted by non-participants. For Wittgenstein truth cannot be separated from beliefs and the latter cannot be separated from the role they play in people's lives. Any metaphysical idea of reality, or of a truth bound up with it, has to be discarded. Whatever mystical inclinations Wittgenstein might have felt, when it came to question of reason and truth he kept his feet on the ground. Reasoning demands concepts and they are linked to the use of words. All questions of reason and truth must take into account the constraints of language. He held that the origin of language-games is a reaction, so that their basis is not a rational grounding but just a way of behaving. He says: 'Language—I want to say—is a refinement'. He adds that 'in the beginning was the deed' (CV, 31).

Christianity and its practice provides one example of Wittgenstein's approach. For him, religion could not be accepted as a metaphysical system, claiming (rightly or wrongly) some form of objective truth. He denied that it could even be based on historical truth. His point was it was not claiming anything, or was a doctrine, in the sense of being a theory about what has happened or will happen. It is, he claims (CV, 28), rooted in what takes place in human life. For him the meaning of religion cannot be connected with claims about the existence of God or the destiny of the human soul. Its roots rather lie in such experiences as consciousness of sin and despair. It is not even clear whether Christianity is an example of what Wittgenstein might have in mind as a 'form of life'. Apart from the fact that religion in general, or Catholicism in particular might be plausible candidates too, there is a worrying vagueness about the concept. No view which bases everything on the importance of context should avoid spelling out what might count as the proper context. Reference to communities, or societies, is useless if we are left wondering what might count as one community.

Human reactions as such, expressed in all societies, could form the basis for all our concepts. That is probably an over-generous interpretation of Wittgenstein but human life itself could be the context for the learning and teaching of concepts. Yet even if that position were accepted, there is still no room for the exercise of the kind of rationality which could detach itself from its context to inquire into what could be true. What is perhaps more plausible is that *some* concepts might be based on universal human reactions, such as the way we exhibit pain, while others are linked to more local ways of behaving, as for instance is the context of a particular religion. Whether the context is universal, as far as humans are concerned, or more restricted, the context gives meaning to assertion. For Wittgenstein metaphysics is the simple result of language being abstracted from the 'language-game which is its original home' (PI, I, 116). As such it strives to make claims which he believes cannot be made.

We can never get outside all language-games and talk rationally, just as it is never possible to reason properly beyond the limits of language. Even if what we say has its roots in the 'common behaviour of mankind', it still cannot be torn loose from that and aspire to metaphysical truth. In fact 'metaphysical' need imply nothing more than a claim to objective validity detached from any particular language-game. The metaphysical urge is precisely the desire to break free of language and speak of reality. Wittgenstein's own examples of words used metaphysically include 'knowledge', 'being', 'object', and 'I'. Each of these is important in the traditional picture of a subject, the self, trying to obtain knowledge of an objective reality. The traditional dichotomy between the subject and object of knowledge is under attack by Wittgenstein. Just as there can be no reality beyond that exhibited in the concepts of a form of life, the self cannot be abstracted from the form of life of which it is a product. There is no metaphysical subject (see Trigg, 1988) lurking behind the employment of language, with, for instance, clear non-linguistic thoughts that may not always be expressed adequately within language. There is no metaphysical object, as the goal of all our thoughts, existing apart from particular practices.

V

The refusal to distinguish between the subject and object of knowledge, the implicit attack on the possibility of unprejudiced reason, the removal of the possibility of truth as a standard—all of this adds up to a direct onslaught on the very possibility of rationality. It is not surprising that the application of Wittgenstein's ideas in the field of social anthropology has seemed to result in a paralysing relativism. The issue is not just that an anthropologist cannot make any distinction between rational and irrational behaviour. Anthropology itself can no longer claim truth, or even the right to be heard, since it too merely gains its meaning from particular practices (presumably those of twentieth-century academics in the Western World). No comparison of different societies is possible, and in fact ethnocentricity becomes inevitable. No claims about anything can be made unless they are put forward from the standpoint of some language-game or other. They can have no force except as a flourish of rhetoric beyond the confines of their game.

Social anthropology has been much discussed by supporters and detractors of Wittgenstein. It is however one example of a wider problem. No philosopher can take away with impunity the possibility of rational foundations for any intellectual activity and attack the possibility of an objective truth—of things being the case whether we recognize them to be so or not. It is vital for the pursuit of knowledge in any sphere that how we conceive things is not necessarily linked with the way things are. The raison d'être of any part of science depends on this insight (see Trigg, 1989). Otherwise progress is an illusion and our first thoughts are always going to be as good as our last. There would be no point in further investigation, in rational criticism, in experiments or any other activity which has made Western science appear as an exemplar of rationality. Without a distinction between the subject and object of knowledge. I need never be mistaken, since there is no target for my beliefs. For Wittgenstein deviation from the norms of a society would be the only form of error. He thereby establishes meaning by anchoring it to public standards. Yet one can surely turn one of his dicta against himself. If whatever is going to seem right to the members of a society is right, does not mean 'that here we can't talk about right'?

The attack on reason coupled with the acknowledgment of the primacy of instinct, and the breakdown of the distinction between subject and object, provide echoes of the position of Nietzsche. This may be more than accidental, and there could be an historical influence, even if an indirect one. Whether or not that is so, the philosophical dangers are acute. Relativism and its close relation, nihilism, are the inevitable result of the undermining of the power of human rationality.

Wittgenstein's stress on the public, the social and the contextual seemed of immense importance to social science. It appeared to give it a whole new scope. With the blurring of the distinction between the epistemological and the sociological, it could even appear as if social science would take over the former role of philosophy. Yet an attack on metaphysics is also an attack on any rational foundation for social science. An absolute precondition for understanding any society must be a distinction between the person understanding and what is being understood. There is a difference between knowledge and reality. The latter is the proper object of knowledge but the subject of knowledge, the person who knows, must remain distinct. A philosophical attack on the very distinction between subject and object goes with an attack on the meaningfulness of the notion of an objective reality and the possibility of truth.

For knowledge to be possible in the field of social science, the nature of a society, or social reality, has to be regarded as distinct from the investigator. An analogous situation is necessary in the physical sciences, and the inability of an observer to be sufficiently separate from the physical system under investigation would undermine the possibility of knowledge. That is why there are philosophical difficulties about quantum mechanics (see Trigg, 1989, chapter 6). An observer who is continually interacting with a system cannot observe it in the detached way necessary for the acquisition of knowledge. This is a perpetual problem in social science, since we are all members of a society. No-one, even in the name of science, can step outside every society and abandon every presupposition. Nevertheless the claim of human relationality would be that it is possible, even if difficult, to examine the workings of society, whether one's own or another, with some detachment. The practice of social science, indeed, should enable us to stand back from our own society and see it with new eyes. We will no longer take its assumptions for granted, or uncritically apply its concepts. For this reason some may be deeply suspicious of social science as a destabilizing influence within a given society. It could, some fear, lessen commitment to the tacit assumptions of a community, and itself encourage the downward path to nihilism. Yet rational criticism need not be destructive, and it might serve to strengthen the institutions of a community, assuming there are good grounds for their existence. The unforeseeable changes of tampering with customs that have evolved over a long period can themselves perhaps be demonstrated by the work of social science.

This view of social science as a source of knowledge could not be shared by Wittgenstein. It assumes the ability to grasp the concepts of a society and simultaneously to distance ourselves from them. It takes for granted that we can study another society without being genuine participants. Full participation of the kind envisaged by Wittgenstein as necessary for the acquisition of concepts is contrary to any scientific approach. It implies that the only way to understand a cannibal society is to *be* a cannibal. The inevitable result of adopting such a policy is for social scientists, simply to 'go native'. The more, though, that they participate in an alien society, the less they can be said still to be members of their own and still be deemed scientists. Wittgenstein's views also imply that a proper comparison between societies is impossible as their concepts are going to be strictly incommensurable. The most, perhaps, that we could hope to achieve would be an ability to switch speedily from seeing the society as a Western social scientist to seeing it as a participant. Since the two could not be put together, any more than we can see a duck-rabbit simultaneously as a duck and as a rabbit, social science becomes impossible. The attack on the distinction between subject and object ensures that we can never see a society as it is, and be sufficiently detached.

The problem is not just that understanding demands participation. The issue is how far we can think of a society, however defined, as constituting an independent reality. Whatever a form of life or a language-game might be, the task of social science becomes opaque unless they are possible objects of investigation. We should, for instance, be able to see how different societies attempt to meet the same human needs, but in so doing we are assuming that social reality exists in its own right. The possibility may also exist that the real workings of a society may not be properly perceived by its members. By assuming that people's actions in a society have to be defined by their shared understanding, Wittgenstein cannot allow for this. They could never, for instance, be accused of possessing a 'false consciousness', any more than a society could be criticized for failing to match its understanding with the way the world actually is. At neither level, whether that of social reality, or of physical and even metaphysical reality, can gaps be opened up between understanding and reality. We cannot distance ourselves from what we think we know, since subject and object are merged.

Reference to social reality does, of course, beg the question whether there is such a thing. A strongly individualist view may well wish to query the notion. What kind of reality do social institutions, and indeed societies as such, possess as opposed to that of individuals? Wittgenstein is no individualist but it is significant that he would find it difficult even to pose the question. The issue is in part, whether sociology even has a subject-matter. Is it actually *about* anything? Wittgenstein seemed to guarantee it a role with his emphasis on the central importance of social context. Yet he cannot regard individuals and society as having any genuine existence independent of each other. For similar reasons he cannot allow the sociologist an independence from the society under investigation. The latter cannot be understood as having a reality apart from the understanding of the sociologist. Either the latter shares the concepts which help to constitute the society and is not properly detached from it, or there can be no engagement with the society at all. Wittgenstein's emphasis on the social character of concepts may make society more important, but it makes the task of social science in uncovering the workings of that society an impossible one.

Anyone viewing the complexities of society and the unintended consequences, good and bad, of the mutual interaction of many people, must realize that the understanding of participants may not tell the whole story. Otherwise, everything would be apparent at the surface of society and there would be little need for social science. Social scientists have to be able to do more than describe how people see things or express the assumptions of particular form of life. They claim to be talking about something, and to do that they must use a reason unconstrained by the factors of a particular language-game. Unless social science is an example of the exercise of human rationality about the nature of society, it is nothing. Our ability to reason about reality lies at the root of our intellectual endeavour. Yet it is an ability put in grave doubt by the later Wittgenstein. In rooting our reason in society, he made it impossible to reason about society.

Certainty and Authority

PETER WINCH

> So is this it: I must recognize certain authorities in order to make judgments at all? (OC, 493)

1. Introduction

I want in this paper to consider Wittgenstein's great posthumous work *On Certainty* in a different perspective from the usual: from the point of view of certain deep questions in political philosophy. These questions concern the nature of the state's authority and the citizen's obligation to it; the notion of legitimacy and the role of consent in this context. Such issues have many dimensions; but they arise in part out of difficulties in reconciling the application of such concepts with our understanding of human rationality, especially practical rationality. I think it has been, and remains, characteristic of the main tradition of discussion of such issues to leave certain important questions about the nature of practical rationality unasked. I believe that these questions *are* asked, though in a different context, in Wittgenstein's *On Certainty*.

2. 'Practical Reason'

I want first to sketch a model of positions that have been characteristic of writers in the social contract tradition from, say, Hobbes to Rawls. The model has seldom been explicitly articulated and not all its elements are common to all the writers I have in mind.

Acting is bringing about (or refraining from bringing about) a change in the world by an agent. An agent acts for reasons, which are a special sort of cause. An action is an event caused in this way. Reasons for acting are a combination of the agent's desires and beliefs in the sense that the action is a *logical conclusion* from these. Where what happens does not follow in this way from desires and beliefs there is no action, no 'will'. The 'beliefs' spoken of here constitute the agent's (rational) assessment of the current situation in which he or she is situated and the causal possibilities of that situation relevant to his or her desires. So an agent acts only where he or she tries to bring about (or refrains from bringing about) a change believed, in the light of an assessment of the current situation, to further the agent's desires. It is important to notice that the rationality of the *action*, according to this conception, depends on the rationality of a prior *belief* and of the conclusion drawn from that belief (in conjunction with a desire).

3. Hobbes: Command and Counsel

Consider in this light a famous pair of definitions given by Hobbes:

COMMAND is, where a man saith, *do this* or *do not this* without expecting other reason than the will of him that says it. From this it followeth manifestly, that he that commandeth, pretendeth thereby his own benefit: for the reason of his command is his own will only, and the proper object of every man's will, is some good to himself. COUNSEL, is where a man saith, *do*, or *do not this*, and deduceth his reasons from the benefit that arriveth by it to him to whom he saith it. And from this it is evident, that he that giveth counsel, pretendeth only, whatsoever he intendeth, the good of him, to whom he giveth it. (Hobbes, 1840)

It is striking that, in the case of command, Hobbes cuts off the 'action' from any consideration of reasons by the ostensible 'agent', whose own beliefs and projects are to be thought of as irrelevant. The difficulty raised by his definition is how the *will* of another person, the one who commands, can be thought of by the one commanded as *on its own* a reason for acting, given the account of such reasons, and of their relation to the will, that I have sketched (and that Hobbes accepts).

I am not going to discuss here Hobbes's own interesting attempts to deal with the difficulty. Considered quite generally, it looks as though it may perhaps be overcome, at least temporarily, in cases where the person has *consented* to be subject to someone's authority for the sake of long-term concerns of his or her own. The social contract tradition attempts to assimilate the authority of the state over its citizens to this sort of case: to represent it as something that originates in the consent of each citizen, consent which has been given for this sort of reason.[1]

4. Hume on authority and consent

4.1. *The citizen and the press-ganged seaman*

However, all such attempts run foul of the difficulty expressed with characteristic panache by Hume:

[1] Different writers have, for their own purposes, given very various accounts of the nature of these 'reasons', but these differences need not detain us in the present context.

Should it be said that, by living under the dominion of a prince which one might leave, every individual has given a *tacit* consent to his authority and promised him obedience, it may be answered that such an implied consent can only have place where a man imagines that the matter depends on his choice. But where he thinks—as all mankind do who are born under established governments—that by his birth he owes allegiance to a certain prince or certain form of government, it would be absurd to infer a consent or choice which he expressly in this case renounces and disclaims.

Can we seriously say that a poor peasant or artisan has a free choice to leave his country when he knows no foreign language or manners and lives from day to day by the small wages which he acquires? We may as well assert that a man, by remaining in a vessel, freely consents to the dominion of the master, though he was carried on board while asleep and must leap into the ocean and perish the moment he leaves her. (Hume, 1951)

4.2. 'A more philosophical refutation'

In this same essay Hume offers what he calls 'a more regular, at least a more philosophical, refutation of this principle of an original contract, or popular consent'. It is idle, he argues, to base political obligation on a contract, since the obligation to keep a contract is subject to exactly the same difficulties. These difficulties, differently stated, are once again the difficulties of reconciling an obligation with a conception of practical rationality as acting in pursuit of one's projects in the light of one's present assessment of one's situation. To be 'bound' by something one has said in the *past* seems incompatible with that.

Now as G. E. M. Anscombe has noted (Anscombe, 1981), Hume's point has a much wider application than he realizes, since it applies to *all* cases of, or analogous to, acting in accordance with a rule; and hence affects our understanding of all our 'practices of reason', to use her felicitous phrase. The relation of such practices to reason does *not* lie in the fact that everything we do in their context is 'rational' according to the criteria of the model we have been assuming. Perhaps this is brought out as graphically as anywhere in *Philosophical Investigations*, where, without of course having Hume in mind, Wittgenstein in fact attacks head-on the conception that gives rise to Hume's problem.

Would it be correct to say that it is a matter of induction, and that I am as certain that I shall be able to continue the series, as I am that this book will drop to the ground when I let it go; and that I should be no less astonished if I suddenly and for no obvious reason got stuck working out the series, than I should be if the book remained hanging

225

in the air instead of falling?—To that I will reply that we don't need any grounds for *this* certainty either. What could justify the certainty *better* than success? (PI, I, 324)

'The certainty that I shall be able to go on after I have had this experience—seen the formula, for instance,—is simply based on induction.' Does this mean that I argue to myself: 'Fire has always burned me, so it will happen now too?' Or is the previous experience the *cause* of my certainty, not its ground? Whether the earlier experience is the cause of the certainty depends on the system of hypotheses, or natural laws, in which we are looking at the phenomenon of certainty.

Is our confidence justified?—What people accept as justification is shewn by how they think and live. (PI, I, 325)

We expect *this*, and are surprised at *that*. But the chain of reasons has an end. (PI, I, 326)

It is important to notice that Wittgenstein does not directly *answer* any of the major questions he raises here: Is the certainty that I can go on when I am following a rule *inductive*? Is my previous experience *the cause or the reason* of, for example, my certainty that this fire will burn me? Is my certainty that I can continue the series, or my certainty that I shall get burned by this fire, *justified*? More particularly, is our certainty in such cases justified by *success*? Instead, in each case he asks further questions designed to persuade us that the sense of the questions we were initially inclined to ask is not as clear as we thought. More particularly, he tries to persuade us that our asking of these questions stems from confusions about the notions of *justification, reason*. We think of 'induction' as a form of reasoning; but many of the cases that are most fundamental to the philosophical problems about induction do not, in any clear sense, involve reasoning. Hence any analogy we may see between these 'inductive' cases and cases of certainty in following a rule would take us no further in establishing that this latter sort of certainty is 'rationally justified'.

At the end of the quoted passage Wittgenstein is suggesting, I believe, that we are inclined to ask the questions we do because we think of *justification* as involving a perspective *independent* of 'the way we think and live', when in fact it characterizes and arises out of this. We cannot ask (without a good deal of further explanation) whether the way we think and live is itself justified. If we were not certain about these things under normal circumstances the flow of our lives would not be what it is. So our certainty *is* justified, is it? Wittgenstein does not answer this question either, but asks another: 'What could justify the certainty *better* than success?'! (I.e. the successful pursuit of our lives.) This is not to say that our certainty *is* justified by its 'success'. We live our lives and these certainties play their part; but we are not certain *in order to* live our lives as we do. If we did find our certainties constantly leading us into difficulties, no doubt some justification would be required for us to retain them. But none of this is to say that, in present circumstances, their 'success' *is* their 'justification'. More importantly, I think Wittgenstein is suggesting that, things being as they are, any question of justification here has no clear sense.

4.3. *Consent and the Habit of Obedience*

I now return to Hume's 'Of the Original Contract', in which we find the observation, remarkable in the light of the foregoing:

> Obedience or subjection becomes so familiar that most men never make any inquiry about its origin or cause, more than about the principle of gravity, resistance, or the most universal laws of nature.

People do not normally accept the state's authority because they have inquired into the reasons for so doing; in particular, not because they have previously consented to it; and if they did, that would not solve the problem that the contractarian tradition has set itself, since it is no *more* puzzling that people should accept the authority of the state than that they should in any other way behave in ways contrary to what they see will further their interests and concerns in the situation they are presently in, as may for instance be the case when they act so as to fulfil their own earlier promises; or, more generally, as may be the case whenever they act as they do 'merely' out of some *commitment* to which they feel themselves subject by virtue of what has happened, been done, or been the case in the past.

Hume asks us to consider the case of a hereditary prince, deposed by an unpopular usurper who never succeeds in winning the real support of the people; the original prince returns victorious after some years and is greeted with enthusiasm by the people as their legitimate ruler. In such a case, Hume notes, the people who welcome back their prince, think of his title to legitimacy not as depending on their consent, but rather on his birth. 'They consent', as he interestingly expresses it, 'because they perceive him to be already by birth their lawful sovereign.' I.e. consent does indeed play a role in the relations between citizens and ruler in this case, but not the role described by social contract theorists. It is not the *source* of their sense of the ruler's legitimacy; rather, their recognition of his legitimacy is expressed in the role played by the thought of his royal birth in the way they consent to his rule, and the importance they attach to this is of course rooted in the hereditary institutions which belong to their form of political life. It goes without saying that this form of life involves certain ingrained habits of obedience towards people occupying certain positions within it. Equally, if these habits are to be *challenged*, as of course they sometimes are, a basis will still have to be found for the challenge *in* the life of the community. There will have to be some context within which those who support the traditions and those who oppose them can identify what they are disagreeing about. The reasons that may be offered on either side get their bite from the background of habits against which they are offered; not from any independent combination of present concerns and beliefs about the present environment. Something analogous holds for the notion of *consent*. What consent amounts to in any particular case again depends on the context of relationships, institutions, traditions etc. within which it is accorded or withheld. What, for instance, will count as consent in intimate relations between friends, would not do so where someone assumes a legal obligation like adopting a child. *A fortiori* this holds for consent in a *political* context. Whether or not a person is to be regarded as having given his or her consent to a particular régime is not something that can be decided without looking at the background of that citizen's behaviour and the forms of justification that belong to it. This I take to be the important point concealed in Hume's throwaway line: 'They consent, because they perceive him to be already by birth their lawful sovereign'.

5. On Certainty and Practical Rationality

In order to make proper sense of this we need to look at the conception of practical rationality (reasons for action) afresh. I believe that Wittgenstein's *On Certainty* provides us with a fruitful perspective. I cannot here even begin to examine as they deserve all the components of the positive picture he paints. I shall confine myself to sketching what I take to be essential to the whole composition before highlighting the features most important for my own purposes.

Wittgenstein challenges the twin assumptions (a) that *reasonable* belief is belief that is *justified*:

> My having two hands is, in normal circumstances, as certain as anything that I could produce in evidence for it.
>
> That is why I am not in a position to take the sight of my hand as evidence for it. (OC, 250)

and (b) that reasonable *action* is action based on reasonable *belief*:

> As if giving grounds did not come to an end sometime. But the end is not an ungrounded presupposition: it is an ungrounded way of acting. (OC, 110)
>
> Our talk gets its meaning from the rest of our proceedings. (OC, 229)

He also questions the traditional opposition between *form* and *content* in logic. Logic is indeed formal:

everything descriptive of a language-game is part of logic. (OC, 56)

But it is neither contentless nor characterizable independently of the language games within which it is applied:

I want to say: We use judgments as principles of judgment. (OC, 124)[2]

A corollary might be provocatively expressed as follows: the *reasonable person* is not defined by reference to logic; logic is defined by reference to what the kind of person we take to be 'reasonable' does or does not accept.[3]

There cannot be any doubt about it for me as a reasonable person.— That's it.— (OC, 219)
The reasonable man *does not have* certain doubts.
These practices which define 'reason' have to be *learned*. (OC, 220)[4]
From a child up I learned to judge like this. *This is* judging. (OC, 128)
This is how I learned to judge; *this* I got to know as judgment. (OC, 129)

In mastering them I became certain of many things, though not all these attendant certainties can themselves strictly be said to be 'learned'.

[2] Cf. too: 'The *truth* of my statements is the test of my *understanding* of these statements' (OC, 80). 'That is to say: if I make certain false statements, it becomes uncertain whether I understand them' (OC, 81). 'The *truth* of certain empirical propositions belongs to our frame of reference' (OC, 83). 'Can't an assertoric sentence, which was capable of functioning as a hypothesis, also be used as a foundation for research and action? I.e. can't it simply be isolated from doubt, though not according to any explicit rule? It simply gets assumed as a truism, never called in question, perhaps not even ever formulated' (OC, 87). 'It may be for example that *all enquiry on our part* is set so as to exempt certain propositions from doubt, if they are ever formulated. They lie apart from the route travelled by enquiry' (OC, 88).
[3] Cf. too: 'Is it wrong for me to be guided in my actions by the propositions of physics? Am I to say I have no good ground for doing so? Isn't precisely this what we call a "good ground"?' (OC, 608).
[4] Cf. too: But I did not get my picture of the world by satisfying myself of its correctness; nor do I have it because I am satisfied of its correctness. No: it is the inherited background against which I distinguish between true and false' (OC, 94). 'The propositions describing this world picture might be part of a kind of mythology and their role is like that of rules of a game; and the game can be learned purely practically, without learning any explicit rules' (OC, 95).

Peter Winch

I do not explicitly learn the propositions that stand fast for me. I can *discover* them subsequently like the axis round which a body rotates. The axis is not fixed in the sense that anything holds it fast, but the movement around it determines its mobility. (OC, 152)

No one ever taught me that my hands don't disappear when I am not paying attention to them. Nor can I be said to presuppose the truth of this proposition in my assertions etc. (as if they rested on it), while [in so far as] it only gets its sense from the rest of our procedure of asserting. (OC, 153)

It is a feature of the manner in which we acquire these practices that we do not, as a matter of fact, doubt their reliability.[5]

This is how calculation is done, in such circumstances a calculation is *treated* as absolutely reliable, as certainly correct. [OC, 39]

But furthermore this absence of doubt is a requirement for the intelligibility of the practice or practices within which it is embedded. And it is the practice that determines when an apparent expression of doubt is understandable as such and when it is not.

There are cases such that, if someone gives signs of doubt where we do not doubt, we cannot confidently understand his signs as signs of doubt.

I.e.: if we are to understand his signs of doubt as such, he may give them only in particular cases and may not give them in others. (OC, 154)

A specially important case is the trustworthiness[6] of our informants and teachers.

A child learns there are reliable and unreliable informants much later than it learns facts which are told it. (OC, 143)

The child learns by believing the adult. Doubt comes *after* belief. (OC, 160)

Here too Wittgenstein's first aim is to remind us of familiar facts; but the reminder is for a particular purpose.[7] The purpose, or at least *one*

[5] Cf. too: *This* is how one calculates. Calculating is *this*. What we learn at school for example. Forget this transcendent certainty, which is connected with your concept of spirit [*Geist*]' (OC, 47).

[6] See Lars Hertzberg, 'On the Attitude of Trust', *Inquiry*, 31, 307–322. Hertzberg suggests that we should distinguish between trustworthiness and reliability in this context.

On Certainty contains very many important observations on this topic, all of which I cannot hope to discuss adequately here. See, for instance, OC, 143, 159–162, 167, 170–172, 187–188, 233, 263, 310–317, 600.

[7] 'The work of the philosopher consists in assembling reminders for a particular purpose' (PI, I, 127).

purpose, is to persuade us that without this primitive trust a child would never learn enough to be able to ask questions we would regard as 'sensible', in particular, questions about who is a reliable informant and who is not, and questions about what can be regarded as an established fact and what cannot.

5.1. *The Authority of Teachers and Informants*

I am now getting close to the point that is most central to my own discussion. The relation of the child to its adult informants here described can quite naturally be called one of accepting the adult's *authority*; it is moreover quite continuous with other kinds of relation between children and adults within the context of which children will quite naturally do what adults tell them to do, a response which cries out to be called an acceptance of adult authority. But before I explore this further, there are some important aspects of Wittgenstein's discussion in *On Certainty* that I have not yet mentioned.

First, although the case of children is particularly important in that it has to do with the ways in which our most fundamental concepts are formed, this acceptance of informants as trustworthy is characteristic of adult life too. As adults we can, it is true, as small children cannot, in many cases raise questions about the reliability of certain people, newspapers, books, etc. But there are limits to this.

> I believe what people transmit to me in a certain manner. In this way I believe geographical, chemical, historical facts etc. That is how I learn the sciences. Of course learning is based on believing.
>
> If you have learnt that Mont Blanc is 4,000 metres high, if you have looked it up on the map, you say you *know* it.
>
> And can it now be said: we accord credence in this way because it has proved to pay? (OC, 170)
>
> Perhaps someone says 'There must be some basic principle on which we accord credence', but what can such a principle accomplish? Is it more than a natural law of 'taking for true'? (OC, 172)

Of course the things we learn in this sort of way do hang together; and we tend to reject things we are told, or read, which do *not* hang together with the big picture we have acquired. But to say this is a very long way from saying that we believe as we do on the basis of evidence. It is only within the context of the big picture that we can evaluate evidence.

> Now one might say that it is experience again that leads us to give credence to others. But what experience makes me believe that the anatomy and physiology books don't contain what is false? Though

it is true that this trust is *backed up* by my own experience. (OC, 275)

5.2. *'A community which is bound together by science and education'*

However, the role of 'giving credence to others' in the development of our rational capacities has to be handled with great caution as is shown by the following ironic exchange:

Do you *know* that the earth existed then?—Of course I know that. I have it from someone who certainly knows all about it. (OC, 187)
It strikes me as if someone who doubts the existence of the earth at that time is impugning the nature of all historical evidence. And I cannot say of this latter that it is definitely *correct* (OC, 188)

This is important. Both the question and the answer in 187 sound off-colour, but it is the answer that most interests me now. First, as already remarked, it is very unlikely that I *did*, as a matter of fact, learn, for example, that the earth has existed for at least a couple of hundred years from any particular person. Second, the idea that some special expertise is involved here ('someone who certainly knows all about it') is ludicrous. We are not dealing here with knowledge individuals may or may not have, but (for example) with 'the nature of all historical evidence'; and in order to describe this we have to refer to the life of a community: for instance to the existence of documents and the ways they are treated by scholars, the kind of intellectual authority exercised by these scholars in the wider community; and so on.

'We are quite sure of it' does not mean just that every single person is certain of it, but that we belong to a community which is bound together by science and education. (OC, 298)

Children grow into the life of this community and in so doing come to exercise the rational powers that go with their being recognized as fellow members of the community by others.[8] A condition of their doing so is that they react, as individuals, in certain ways rather than others to the doings and sayings of other individuals who are already part of that community. But we describe those doings and sayings and the nature of the reactions of children to them in terms of concepts which themselves have sense only in the context of the life of that community.[9] They have the significance they do for us by virtue of their connection with that life.

[8] Swift's Yahoos bring this point out.
[9] There is an important parallel here with Wittgenstein's insistence in the *Tractatus* that the limits of logic can be explored only from *within* our language.

This point applies of course to, amongst much else, the way in which we use the term 'authority' in this sort of context. We speak of children responding to the authority of adults; of the authority of text-books and of scholars. I remarked earlier that children's responses to adults comprise not merely acceptance of the adult's authority in the imparting of information, but also reactions of obedience when told to do something. In both cases of course greater maturity brings with it an ability to *question* such authority in particular cases; but we would hardly understand what it meant to ascribe such an ability to very young infants from the outset. And the terms of any later 'questioning' would make use of concepts belonging to a context in which a great deal was *not* questioned.

6. Hobbes: Unity in Multitude

I started with a problem raised by Hobbes' definition of 'command' and I have now reached a point where I can return to Hobbes with another quotation expressing something central to his position and touching on an issue which is very fundamental to the notion of political authority.

> A multitude of men, are made *one* person, when they are by one man, or one person, represented; so that it be done *with the consent of every one of that multitude in particular*. For it is the *unity* of the representer, not the *unity* of the represented, that maketh the person *one*, and it is the representer that beareth the person, and but one person: and *unity*, cannot otherwise be understood in multitude. And because the multitude naturally is not *one*, but *many*; they cannot be understood for one; but many authorize everything their representative saith, or doth in their name; every man giving their common representer, authority from himself in particular . . .[10]

This position is very deeply embedded in Hobbes' thinking. The reason why a multitude cannot be regarded as a unity unless by way of a representative lies in Hobbes' conception of reason as the faculty through which an individual pursues his or her own interests. It is the rational pursuit of those interests on the part of each individual that is responsible, on Hobbes' view, for the 'state of war' as mankind's 'natural condition', i.e. the impossibility of any mutual trust or agreement. *On Certainty* on the other hand turns the tables on Hobbes by showing that the conception of *reason* requires as its background precisely a community in which there is such trust and agreement. The

[10] *Leviathan*, ch. 16 (Hobbes, 1840).

same goes for the notions of *authorizing* and *authority* on which Hobbes relies for establishing a 'representer'. Certainly a man may give a representer authority 'from himself in particular', but only in a community in which such relations of authority are already recognized, i.e. a community which already has the sort of 'unity' which Hobbes takes to be achievable only *through* such an individualistic conferring of authority.

7. The State and 'the Natural Condition of Mankind'

There is something else here too. If one looks at the relation of the individual citizen to the government and, more fundamentally, to the state within which this government operates, it is obvious that, normally or characteristically at least, what we may call the 'will' of the citizen plays a crucial part. In paying taxes for instance, *the citizen applies the concept* of taxation; he or she would not pay the money, or not pay it in the same spirit or for the same reason, if it were extorted by a Mafia-like protection racket.[11] Now this concept that is applied is not the citizen's own invention; it has its sense only within the context of the institutions of the state. And when I speak of these 'institutions' I include not merely their, as it were, official aspect but also, very importantly, their role in the whole life of the community: in the attitudes of citizens to each other and to officials for instance.

Our concern here is with *the kind of description* of political life needed to make the relation between a citizen and the state intelligible. And this is inseparable from the question of the point of view someone wishing to offer such a description needs to adopt.

The idea of a 'natural condition of mankind' or of a 'state of nature' is important not so much in its character as a historical hypothesis but as an attempt to view our political life 'from the outside', that is, from a point of view which does not already take for granted the concepts characteristically deployed in the course of such a life. There have been great and important differences between writers concerning what is 'outside' and what 'inside'. Hobbes lies at an extreme point on the scale. For him there is *no* communal point of view which does not involve the state. That is the point of the passage about a multitude being 'one' only when represented (by a sovereign). So for Hobbes one reaches a point 'outside' only with *individuals* in their 'natural condition', described, that is, without the use of concepts depending for their sense on a settled communal life in which they participate. Hence the importance of Hobbes' attempts to give purely individualistic accounts of language,

[11] This is not to deny that the line may sometimes be difficult to draw!

thought and so on: attempts which fail for reasons which *On Certainty* brings out.[12]

8. 'What Right He has to Order Him'

But these attempts are essential to Hobbes's project. He does not write as a political sociologist (if I may be permitted an anachronistic concept here). He is not merely concerned to describe relations of power; he wants to recommend a certain attitude to us, his readers, as citizens; i.e. he wants to offer us *reasons* for adopting such an attitude. This is expressed very clearly in the following:

> You may perhaps think a man has need of nothing else to know the duty he owes his governor, and what right he has to order him, but a good natural wit; but it is otherwise. For it is a science, and built upon sure and clear principles, and to be learned by deep and careful study, or from masters that have deeply studied it.[13]

This aspect is not peculiar to Hobbes' project; it is characteristic of the whole tradition and is evident in recent times in the work of such disparate writers as Rawls and Nozick. The project requires clarity about what could *count* as a 'reason' in such a context and hence raises difficulties in the 'philosophical' rather than the 'sociological' dimension. Hobbes needs to show his reader that the sovereign has legitimate authority over him ('what right he has to order him'), and he has to address the reader as though he or she were still in mankind's 'natural condition'[14] and to represent such a right, ultimately, in terms of some good that accrues to the reader in the context of his or her own interests and concerns.

9. Conclusion

The most important point that, leaning on certain discussions in *On Certainty*, I have wanted to make is this. Amongst the many diffi-

---

[12] This is not, alas, to say that *On Certainty* has put an end to such attempts. Nowadays, under the label of 'artificial intelligence', they receive large funding.

[13] *Behemoth*, Dialogue IV (Hobbes, 1840).

[14] In this respect his stance is just like that of Rawls, who asks his reader to adopt 'the original position'. The 'veil of ignorance' that characterizes this 'position' runs foul of Wittgenstein's point that what is 'reasonable' cannot be characterized independently of the *content* of certain pivotal 'judgments'. Of course this needs showing in detail in a way I cannot attempt here.

culties, not all of them philosophical, that the notion of the state's 'authority' has been thought to give rise to, is a puzzle about how it is to be reconciled, as it demands to be, with the notion of agency. By barring the putative 'agent' from acting according to his or her own reasons the notion of authority seems to threaten to make the notion of the 'agent's' will inapplicable and thereby drain away the status of agency into the one exercising authority. Forms of authority other than the political may be thought to connect in an acceptable way with the agent's own deliberations; the difficulty about the state is that the authority it seems to claim, and that is widely acknowledged, is *not* seen to depend in this way on the agent's will.

What Wittgenstein shows is that, so far from its being the case that all recognition of authority derives from the exercise of practical reason on the part of the recognizer, the notion of practical reason itself requires at many points a recognition of the authority of others that is *primitive*. Once this is accepted the notion of the state's authority is freed from the requirement to satisfy conditions that are in fact unsatisfiable.

Of course I am not saying that is the end of the matter. Rather, by clearing away an illusory problem we may be better able to face real problems: concerning for instance, the various roles that the state plays in our lives and thinking, the relations between its authority and other forms of authority with which we are familiar, the maintenance of social order, etc.

Is anything left corresponding to the questions asked by Hobbes, Locke, Hume, Rousseau and others, of the form 'Why should I obey?' Well, there clearly are and will continue to be situations giving rise to such questions: as currently in East Germany, Czechoslovakia, South Africa, Rumania. Such questions will characteristically involve evaluating an existing situation against a norm, a norm, that is, of political *legitimacy*. Such an evaluation takes place within the general conceptual framework of political authority. It does not involve questioning that whole concept.

Am I then maintaining that such a wholesale questioning of the concept is impossible? No. Am I setting the *status quo* in concrete as is well known to be the sneaky practice of 'Wittgensteinian conservatives'? No. To say: 'this is a way in which people think' is not to say 'You, or we, should, or must, think like this.' It is to say: there is more than one way of thinking and it takes more than the bare concept of 'rationality' to decide between the sense of these. It is to point out some of our conceptual resources and to try to dissipate certain confusions about those resources. No one is enjoined by this to *use* those resources in any particular way, or at all. Anyone is at liberty to set him or herself against a whole way of thinking and proceeding; to resolve to do things without invoking the state. Of course anyone else is equally at liberty to point out any inconsistencies there seem to be in such a person's behaviour. And it remains to be ascertained what exactly a consistent life along these lines will look like. Perhaps this is not as easy as might first appear. But I am *not* saying that no such life is possible.

Fools and Heretics

RENFORD BAMBROUGH

'Where two principles really do meet which cannot be reconciled with one another, then each man declares the other a fool and a heretic.' This sentence from Wittgenstein's *On Certainty* (OC, 611) is the source of my title. A passage in George Orwell's *Shooting an Elephant* might have prompted the same choice: 'The Catholic and the Communist are alike in assuming that an opponent cannot be both honest and intelligent. Each of them tacitly claims that "the truth" has already been revealed, and that the heretic, if he is not simply a fool, is secretly aware of "the truth" and merely resists it out of selfish motives' (Orwell, 1950, 177).

The word 'heresy' is most at home in religion, where we also find the Psalmist and St Anselm confronting the *fool* who hath said in his heart that there is no God. The passions of the orthodox and the heterodox may express themselves in physical as well as in logical conflict. Besides religious debates there have been religious wars. T. E. Hulme remarked that the point of all creeds is to draw 'a peculiarly complicated but quite definite line which will mark you off finally and distinctly from the people you can't stand.' He had a solid brass knuckleduster designed for him by Gaudier-Brzeska, and when a critic made disrespectful comments on some Epstein statues he declared that 'the most appropriate way of dealing with him would be a little personal violence'.

W. H. Auden's understanding of heresy, besides associating it with public conflict, also hints that part of the purpose of othodoxy is to bolster the individual's shaky faith: 'Dogmatic theology is designed to exclude heresy rather than to define orthodoxy' (Auden, 1973, 51–52). Politicians are another pugnacious breed, and their fighting, literal and metaphorical, is associated with much waving of banners and affixing of labels, much crying of folly and hunting of heresy. And for good or ill—for good *and* ill—even philosophers form parties, coin slogans, and attach labels to each other if not to themselves: logical positivists, Wittgensteinian Fideists, Swansea Wittgensteinians, and other badges of folly or heresy.

In all these fields the role of dogma is much the same: to help us to preserve some sense of security and some conviction of certainty in the face of what we recognize to be the almost intolerable complexity of the issues we struggle with in morals and politics, philosophy and religion.

Renford Bambrough

The metaphors of *frameworks* and of *foundations* are commonly used when there is talk of conflicts of principle and of the quest for certainty, and these pictures are in place here just because of their suggestion of fixity amid the flux of opinion.

The work that provides my title also treats my theme. Wittgenstein intervenes in the conflict between G. E. Moore and the sceptic of the senses about the existence of an external world; a conflict, he implies, in which each party can only declare the other to be a fool and a heretic. He invents (OC, 92) the example of a king who has been brought up to believe that the world began with him: 'I do not say that Moore could not convert the King to his view, but it would be a conversion of a special kind; the king would be brought to look at the world in a different way.'

Similar conflicts are common outside the sphere of academic philosophy. Bertrand Russell refers in *An Outline of Philosophy* (Russell, 1927) to an inner conflict in the mind of Edmund Gosse's father. The elder Gosse was a believer in the literal inspiration of Holy Scripture, but he was also well read in the scientific writings of his day. As a fundamentalist reader of the Bible he thought he knew that the world was created in 4004 B.C., but he knew from his reading of modern science that the work of biologists and geologists provided strong evidence for a much more distant date. Since he had a general confidence in the methods of scientific investigation, and a close familiarity with the evidence, he was in a dilemma between two apparently well attested but mutually contradictory beliefs.

Here it will be useful to introduce the notion of a *pivot* in thought, of which I shall be making use later. It is akin to Wittgenstein's ideas of the axis and the hinge:

> I do not explicitly learn the propositions that stand fast for me. I can *discover* them subsequently like the axis around which a body rotates. This axis is not fixed in the sense that anything holds it fast, but the movement around it determines its immobility.' (OC, 152)

> . . . the *questions* that we raise and our *doubts* depend on the fact that some propositions are exempt from doubt, are as it were like hinges on which those turn. (OC, 341)

When we find ourselves in a dilemma between two incompatible opinions we may move in either of two directions. We may turn on the pivot either to reject one of them because it conflicts with the other, or to reject the other because it conflicts with the first. Most of those who shared Gosse's knowledge of science, on noticing a conflict between geology and a literal understanding of the scriptures, rejected or reinterpreted the meaning of the scriptures. Gosse turned in the other direction on the pivot: he rejected or reinterpreted the results of geology. The fossil record, taken by itself, strongly suggested that the world had existed for many millennia before the scripturally authenticated date of 4004. It followed that the fossil record was misleading. God had created the world in 4004, but had created a world in which there were misleading indications of its age and origin, designed to ensnare unbelievers and to try the faith of God's children.

The mechanism of the pivot comes into operation wherever there is such a stark dilemma, whatever its subject matter. Parmenides thought he could prove by pure reason, by reflection on the nature of *being*, that all variety and all plurality is an illusion; that time and change and motion and differentiation are all alike impossible. He was driven by the force of inescapable argument to deny the actuality of all the movements and changes, colours and sounds, that we perceive in the world around us. His follower Zeno produced his notorious paradoxes in support of the same conclusion. Achilles can never catch the tortoise, the arrow does not move through the air, the athlete never reaches the turning post in the stadium. When we are presented with the same arguments we turn them to another purpose. We take the obvious falsehood of the conclusions as showing that there is something wrong with the arguments, and seek to locate and expose and rectify the misunderstandings of the nature of being and motion and change that are the sources of the inspiration that Parmenides attributed to his patron goddess.

The structure repeats itself in all the contexts of controversy. Again and again, in ethics, politics, philosophy and religion, we choose between opposed views or pictures by using one of them as our ground for rejecting the other. And again and again we find that others choose differently, rejecting our view just because it conflicts with another to which they are more deeply attached. In all such cases we may ask the questions asked by Wittgenstein: '*What* is to be tested by *what*? (Who decides *what* stands fast?)' (OC, 125). We hold fast, hang on with a stubborn resolve that Wittgenstein is thinking of when he asks whether it would be '*unthinkable* that I should stay in the saddle however much the facts bucked' (OC, 616).

To many philosophers and many others it seems clear that conflicts about values are specially likely to take this form. Two men may share a loyalty to a particular conception of society, embodying what they see as an ideal of justice. They may then come to see and to agree that only a powerful and determined authoritarian government could impose on society the pattern that they both find attractive. This is one of the best known forks in the political road, a juncture at which one of them may be impelled to sacrifice liberty to justice and equality and the other to sacrifice equality to liberty and justice.

Renford Bambrough

Often a controversial thinker or prophet is the focus of dissension, as in some picturesque instances from the history of the University of Sydney, where the Department of English divided into two over arguments about Leavis, and the Department of Philosophy divided into two over arguments about Marx, and where the Department of Economics came to the brink of a similar division over Marx and Keynes.

W. H. Auden, in the essay from which I have quoted, gives a good example of the operation of the pivot in theology and religion, the natural home of heresy and dogma. The Gnostic philosopher or theologian argues that Christ was *God*, and therefore *cannot* have been crucified. The Crucifixion must therefore be an illusion. Another, whom Auden describes as a liberal humanist, argues: 'He *was* crucified, and therefore he was not God.' The opponents share a premise, as those whose disagreement turns on a hinge or pivot always do: that the concept of God and the concept of crucifixion are incompatible. Simone Weil rotates on a different axis, but illustrates the operation of a similar mechanism in the same context, when she declares that it is the *Resurrection* that is the stumbling block; the Crucifixion is enough.

In considering such conflicts of principle as these, we are raising the chief questions of epistemology. How are we to resolve our deepest disagreements? On what foundations can we build our system of knowledge or belief? Where are we to find the *archai*, the *principia*, the beginnings or sources of our understanding? Must all reasoning be founded upon an unreasoned choice? If not, is there any alternative to founding it upon unreasoned intuition, declaring that some things are self-evident, and that he who will not drink this health is not to be *answered*, but just anathematized as a fool and a heretic?

These are accordingly the questions that Wittgenstein considers in *On Certainty*. But it is not so clear what answers he wants to give. In some places he speaks of the possibility of making a *decision* that something is so or not so (OC, 362 and 368). And some of his talk of *persuasion* is in line with this way of thinking: 'At the end of reasons comes *persuasion*' (OC, 612; see also 262). Here there seems to be an implication that persuasion is to be contrasted with reason, to be thought of as beginning only when reasoning has already come to an end. But there are other and more numerous places where Wittgenstein puts the matter quite differently:

> In certain circumstances a man cannot make a *mistake*. ('Can' is here used logically, and the proposition does not mean that a man cannot say anything false in those circumstances.) If Moore were to pronounce the opposite of those propositions which he declares certain, we should not just not share his opinion, : we should regard him as demented. (OC, 155)

Similar language is used in other passages. The man who supposes that *all* our calculations are uncertain may be described as *crazy*. One who doubts whether he has a body will be taken to be a half-wit. There are some cases where doubting would seem to amount to a form of *madness*, or at least to raise the question whether it is the doubter or the confident majority that is of sound mind (OC, 217, 257, 281, 420). The same point is put positively: 'The reasonable man does *not have* certain doubts' (OC, 220).

Wittgenstein's remarks in these passages have a clear relevance to the topic known as the ethics of belief. Sometimes, he says (OC, 495), one might *admonish* the doubter rather than reply to him. And certainly heresy, like folly, is often *rebuked*, treated as a perversion of the will rather than a failure of the understanding. It is natural that Orwell should speak of self-deception here, or of deliberately concealing an apprehension of the truth. One of the questions at issue is where the line is to be drawn, if a line *can* be drawn, between the ethics of belief and the pathology of belief; between madness, some infection of sickness in the understanding, and failure or perversity of the will. This leads in turn to questions about the relation between the active and the passive in understanding and in action, and hence about the nature and extent of our responsibilities for our thoughts and beliefs as well as for our actions. Can we, by taking thought, alter either our theoretical beliefs or our practical attitudes? 'Is it maybe in my power what I believe? or what I unshakeably believe?' (OC, 495). If we cannot choose any of our beliefs it is hard to see how it could be our *duty* to believe something, and yet the notion of heresy seems to require that it might be our duty to modify our beliefs. The notion of folly, analogously, seems to imply that a suitably directed and supported rebuke should be able to change a man's mind, cause him to give a different answer to a question, and yet remain sincere.

J. H. Newman, in one of his *Parochial Sermons*, raises this problem and gives some indication of where we might look for a solution:

> Which of our tastes and likings can we change at our will in a moment? Not the most superficial. Can we then at a word change the whole form and character of our minds? Is not holiness the result of many patient, repeated efforts after obedience, gradually working on us, and first modifying and then changing our hearts? (Newman, 1835, 12)

Collingwood recognizes that the adoption of a theory or a thesis is an *act*, undertaken by an agent, when he remarks in *The New Leviathan* that somebody who is below the level of free will is below the level of rationality (Collingwood, 1942, 274). We ordinarily recognize that we and others bear some responsibility for our beliefs as well as for our characters and actions. It is not just that we bear a straightforward moral responsibility for the amount and kind of effort we devote to the consideration of a question. In propounding a belief, just as much as in adopting a practical attitude, we endorse the belief as something that *we* are prepared to defend and to take responsibility for. My beliefs are part of what constitutes my identity, what makes me who I am. That is part of the reason why it is so natural to speak of a *commitment* to a view or a theory, as well as to a programme or a policy.

I believe that we can cast some new light on our familiar conflicts about conflict if we think of the special case of *inner* conflict, and in particular of the case where inner conflict is resolved by the *conversion* from one side to another of the person who is the scene and subject of the conflict.

Wherever there can be conflict between one person and another, there may be conflict between a person and himself. Wherever there are two opinions or doctrines or dogmas that are the lines of division between two people or two parties, there may be an individual human being who is divided against himself, who halts between those two opinions. And it often happens that a person changes sides, becomes what until then he would have called a fool or a heretic. The structure of such inner conflict is parallel to the structure of external conflict, of dissension between the two parties between which an individual thinker may find his allegiance divided. There are ex-Marxists and future Marxists as well as Marxists, and the same applies to Christians and positivists, liberals and levellers, Baconians, bimetallists and vegetarians.

The kinship between inner conflict and outer conflict is implicitly recognized in the modes of expression that are naturally adopted for the conduct of inquiry and debate about philosophical and religious and moral ideas. There have always been philosophical manifestos, ancient and modern—from Gorgias of Leontini to *Radical Philosophy*—but much of the thinking of philosophers and moralists has been recorded in *meditations* and *confessions*. Heraclitus declared '*edizēsamēn emauton*'—'I searched within myself'—but he also denounced the folly of those whose wide learning had not taught them understanding, those whose eyes and ears were bad witnesses because their souls were not dried by the light of reason. Even when philosophers write treatises they usually give them the structure of conversations, a structure that is found equally in the exchanges of one thinker with another and in that dialogue of the soul with itself that is, according to Plato, the form of all human thought. The Seventh Letter scarcely goes far enough to stand by Plato's own principles: what is fundamental is not the duologue of master and individual pupil: when we go right down to the root of any matter what we find is a philosopher arguing with himself, like

Augustine, Descartes and Wittgenstein. And these examples confirm what the case of Heraclitus illustrates, that the philosopher who is alone in his room, meditating, confessing, engaging in criticism and self-criticism, can at the same time be in contact and in conflict with others in the Academy, in the Agora, in the Temple.

To think of conversion is to think again of inner and outer conflict, and hence of the central themes of the theory of knowledge. A conversion is commonly either a reaction against an upbringing or, as Evelyn Waugh puts it in *Brideshead Revisited*, 'a twitch on the thread', a return to an upbringing; and no topic is more germane to the problems in this field than this notion of upbringing, training, initiation into the thoughts and customs of a community. We might remark of Gosse, as Wittgenstein remarks in a parallel case, that in order to have such a strange belief, one needs to have 'grown up in quite special circumstances' (OC, 262). He is again noting a remarkable fact about human beings, a feature of our natural history that is of great significance for the theory of knowledge, when he reminds us that 'one can instruct a child to believe in a God, or that none exists, and it will accordingly be able to produce apparently telling grounds for the one or the other' (OC, 107).

Wittgenstein may seem here to be supporting the suggestion that there can be no rational means of resolving conflicts of principle. Even if we refrain from branding each other as fools or heretics, are not some of our disagreements so profound and intractable that we cannot hope to reconcile them, and must simply agree to differ? When Hume derides the monkish virtues, when Boswell grieves at Hume's deathbed unbelief, it seems to many that there is necessarily nothing more to be done. Upbringings differ from time to time and place to place, and understandings change with them. There are different practices, opinions, beliefs. That is a plain fact and we must reckon with it. Wittgenstein notes that 'what men consider reasonable or unreasonable alters', and he asks 'But is there no objective character here?' As he points out, '*Very* intelligent and well-educated people believe in the story of creation in the Bible, while others hold it as proven false, and the grounds of the latter are well known to the former' (OC, 336).

In the passage from which I take my title (OC, 609–612), he speaks of *fighting* an opposed belief; if there is a conflict between our trust in physicists and some other people's trust in oracles, and we say that they are *wrong*, 'aren't we using our language-game as a base from which to *combat* theirs?' If we do give reasons, they end in persuasion, as when missionaries convert pagans. Two impressive examples are given earlier (OC, 239):

I believe that every human being has two human parents; but Catholics believe that Jesus only had a human mother. And other people might believe that there are human beings with no parents, and give no credence to all the contrary evidence. Catholics believe as well that in certain circumstances a wafer completely changes its nature, and at the same time that all evidence proves the contrary. And so if Moore said 'I know that this is wine and not blood', Catholics would contradict him.

All this is perfectly true. But it is also true that the same applies in every sphere of human inquiry. There is nothing here that is special to religion and ethics and philosophy. Even in physics, there are orthodoxies that live and die. Even in physics, people believe and understand in accordance with their education and training, so that as Planck said, new ideas in physics are accepted only when old physicists die. He presumably did not imply that there is no objective validity or invalidity in the ideas of physicists. Nor do I think that Wittgenstein wished us to draw any such consequences from his remarks about his own examples.

Stark conflicts plausibly tempt us to think of them as irresoluble, but there is one natural step from the present position that takes us in the opposite direction. I have argued that inner conflict and outer conflict share a common structure. There is one element in that shared structure that is easily forgotten or demeaned. In order for a change to be recognized as a *conversion*, it is necessary that it should be an event in the history of a single identifiable person. Paul the Apostle is a new man, but this new man *is* nevertheless the man who *was* Saul the persecutor. Logan Pearsall Smith, in his introduction to a selection of passages from Donne's Sermons, traces the continuity between a rakish poet and an ascetic divine:

> Donne was in the habit of drawing a distinction, in his letters, between the Jack Donne of his earlier life and Dr Donne, the Dean and grave divine and preacher. But, as he himself said, men do not change their passions, but only the objects of them. . .
>
> So Donne retained his old passions and ways of thought; but whereas he had formerly, as he himself says of St Augustine, made sonnets of his sins, he now made sermons of them. Dr Donne was still Jack Donne, though sanctified and transformed, and those who have learned to know the secular poet will find in the writer of religious prose the same characteristics, the subtle, modern self-analytic mind moving in a world of medieval thought, the abstract, frigid scholastic intellect and the quickest senses, the forced conceits and passionate sincerity, the harsh utterance and the snatches of angel's music—in fact all that has attracted or perhaps repelled them in the author of the 'love-songs and satiric weeds', the sensual elegies

and rugged verse-letters of his earlier period. (Smith, 1922, xxxi–xxxii)

A man cannot disown responsibility for things he said or did or believed before his conversion by pointing out how great a conversion he has undergone since he said or did or believed them. He is the man who said or did or believed those things. Many a justified sinner, recognizing this, is inclined to harp on the evil days and doings of his life before he saw the light.

This requirement of personal identity before and after conversion must include some continuity of beliefs, and that continuity provides an analogue in the case of inner conflict for something that I have long urged to be a requirement for the occurrence of external conflict, namely that the two parties to the conflict should share some beliefs and understanding that are relevant to the making of a decision, to the determination of the question on which they are divided. Wittgenstein is attending to this point when he refers to a conviction that is 'anchored in all my *questions and answers*, so anchored that I cannot touch it' (OC, 103). He goes on to speak of a *system* as a necessary environment for the confirmation and disconfirmation of any hypothesis: 'And this system is not a more or less arbitrary and doubtful point of departure for all our arguments: no, it belongs to the essence of, what we call an argument. The system is not so much the point of departure, as the element in which arguments have their life' (OC, 105). He points out that a man cannot even make a mistake unless he already judges in conformity with mankind (OC, 156).

Two men who quarrel about the truth or falsehood of a belief can refer their dispute to the system that is the element in which their arguments have their life. My disputes with myself take place in the same element. A divided self must also be a united self. What I had initially regarded as an alien creed must come to have some appeal for me before I can be in conflict about it. However deeply divided I may be, I remain an identifiable individual person, answerable for what I say and do and believe and doubt. When I stand at the fork in the road, halting between two opinions, my indecision or inner conflict is intelligible, to others and to me, only by reference to a unity and a continuity that it does not call in question; and it will be resolved, if at all, by the achievement of a reintegration of my thoughts, and of my feelings, and of my thoughts with my feelings, that is to say by the restoration of that state of *harmonia* that is for Socrates and Plato the fruit of self-knowledge: the integration of mind and heart, each with itself and each with the other.

Self-knowledge is still knowledge. The search for it, described and enacted in dialogue after dialogue, is at one and the same time a search for a resolution of intellectual conflict and perplexity and a search for the achievement or restoration of wholeness and harmony of life. The old and the new self, like other parties to other disputes, share most of their understanding. They have followed the same road to this point. They share the upbringing that confers a core of understanding that persists and must persist in spite of those differences of upbringing and influence that arise from and lead to the disputes that call for resolution. Too often we are content with a static picture of conflict, of trench-mortar fire directed from and at prepared positions. To look at cases of inner conflict is to be helped to remember the *dynamic* of conflict, external and internal alike. Every enquiry that is of any interest or value has this dynamic character; it moves on. Such movement is illustrated by the theology and the geology of the elder Gosse. The collocation of those two sciences recalls to me a visit I paid many years ago to a house near Dublin where George Bernard Shaw had lived in his youth. On a plaque at the gate was inscribed a quotation from Shaw: 'The men of Ireland are mortal, but the hills of Ireland are immortal.' My host and guide, Professor W. B. Stanford of Trinity College, was caustic: 'Altogether typical,' he said. 'It's not just bad *the*ology, it's bad *geo*logy.' What Gosse needed was better theology. Perhaps, like Planck's physicists, he had to die so that others could give birth to the better theology that would preserve what was central in Gosse's inheritance, and show that what had to be sacrificed to good geology was not good theology but bad geology in theological disguise. What was needed was a proper and necessary *shift of ground*, a turning in one direction rather than the other on the pivot. It happened, and it led, at least for a time, to changes in upbringing by which later generations were guided through or round Gosse's fork in the road.

Parmenides was a pioneer of philosophical logic, and his logic led him to his dilemma, spiked him to the turning spit. What he needed was even better logic. With a better understanding of existence and predication we do not now think that we must choose between our respect for logical necessities and our trust in our five senses. Eyes and ears, as Heraclitus said, are bad witnesses for men who lack understanding. But they are invaluable witnesses when they give evidence before an intelligent judge.

No conflict can be total. Every conflict is between something that we have come to believe and something else that we have come to believe, and both beliefs will need to be compared again with what we have throughout this process continued to believe. There is therefore inexhaustible scope for further enquiry, both to separate one question and one kind of question from another and to answer one by one the questions that we can understand and handle. But the dynamic of enquiry is conducted against a stable background, against what Wittgenstein calls 'the inherited background against which I distinguish between true and false' (OC, 94). If someone who shares this inherited background tries or pretends to believe something that the background excludes, we shall notice that his *life* shows that he knows or is certain of things that his attempt or pretence would require him to question: 'My *life* consists in my being content to accept many things' (OC, 344). 'His conduct *exhibits* exactly that which he denies' (OC, 427; see also 7).

These quotations at once remind us of a famous sentence from the *Philosophical Investigations*: 'What has to be accepted, the given, is—so one could say—*forms of life*' (PI, 226). The same expression occurs in *On Certainty* itself:

> One might say: '"I know" expresses *comfortable* certainty, not the certainty that is still struggling.' (OC, 357)
> Now I would like to regard this certainty, not as something akin to hastiness or superficiality, but as a form of life. (That is very badly expressed and probably badly thought as well.) (OC, 358)

It is admirably thought, but dangerously expressed. Yet it is less dangerous than the parallel sentence from the *Investigations*, since it uses the singular rather than the plural—*a* form of life. There is a clear implication that there are many other forms of life, but no suggestion, such as people have felt able to read into the *Investigations* passage, that there is a variety of *alternative* forms of life, between which we may be represented as *choosing*: having different ones at different times, or different ones in different generations or continents. That is not what Wittgenstein means. He is talking about *the* life of human beings, of all of us, as being that upon which that human understanding is based, by reference to which we settle what is a heresy and what is a piece of folly. I draw strong support for this interpretation from other passages in *On Certainty*. Immediately after using the phrase 'forms of life' (OC, 359). Wittgenstein goes on: 'But that means I want to conceive it as something that lies beyond being justified; as it were, as something animal.'

That last word strengthens my confidence that Wittgenstein is here doing what he calls elsewhere 'natural history'. The nature of the beast is the key to the nature of the beast's understanding. ('If a lion could talk, we could not understand him' (PI, p. 223)). It is not that some upbringing peculiar to our tribe or sect or society blinds us to what we might have seen if we had been brought up differently elsewhere—true and important though that can be—but that there is a *human* understanding, the understanding of a *human* animal in any society, in any time or place, in which some particular forms of doubt can secure no foothold.

My conclusion is that there are *no* conflicts of principle so profound that there is nothing left for the parties to do except to cry out against folly and heresy. I am not saying that folly and heresy do not occur. I am not even saying that it is never suitable to cry out against them. I am saying only that there are always other and better ways of dealing even with the most intractable of conflicts.[1]

---

[1] This paper is a revised version of the text of the J. R. Jones Memorial Lecture, University College of Swansea, 1979.

References

1. References to words or reported words of Wittgenstein are given as follows:

BB   *The Blue and Brown Books* (Oxford: Blackwell, 1958)

CV   *Culture and Value,* ed. von Wright, G. and Nyman, H. (Oxford: Blackwell, 1980)

LC   *Lectures and Conversations on Aesthetics, Psychology and Religious Belief,* ed. Barrett, C. (Oxford: Blackwell, 1966)

LW   *Last Writings on Philosophy and Psychology,* ed. von Wright, G. and Nyman, H. (Oxford: Blackwell, 1982)

NB   *Notebooks 1914–1916,* ed. von Wright, G. and Anscombe, G. (Oxford: Blackwell, 1961)

OC   *On Certainty,* ed. Anscombe, G. and von Wright, G. (Oxford: Blackwell, 1969)

PG   *Philosophical Grammar,* ed. Rhees, R. (Oxford: Blackwell, 1974)

PI   *Philosophical Investigations,* tr. Anscombe, G. (Oxford: Blackwell, 1953)[1]

PR   *Philosophical Remarks,* ed. Rhees, R. (Oxford: Blackwell, 1964)

PTR   *Tractatus Logico-philosophicus Protractatus,* ed. McGuinness, B., Nuberg, T. and von Wright, G. (Oxford: Blackwell, 1971)

RC   *Remarks on Colour,* ed. Anscombe, G. (Oxford: Blackwell, 1977)

RFM   *Remarks on the Foundations of Mathematics,* ed. von Wright, G., Rhees, R. and Anscombe, G. (Oxford: Blackwell, revised edition, 1978)

RPP   *Remarks on the Philosophy of Psychology,* ed. Anscombe, G. and von Wright, G. (Oxford: Blackwell, 1980)

TR   *Tractatus Logico-philosophicus,* tr. Pears, D. and McGuinness, B. (London: Routledge and Kegan Paul, 1961)

WLA   *Wittgenstein's Lectures, Cambridge, 1932–35,* ed. Ambrose, A. (Oxford: Blackwell, 1979)

WLL   *Wittgenstein's Lectures, Cambridge, 1930–32,* ed. Lee, D. (Oxford: Blackwell, 1980)

Z   *Zettel,* 2nd edn, ed. von Wright, G. and Anscombe, G. (Oxford: Blackwell, 1981)

2. Other references:

Anscombe, E. 1981. 'The source of the authority of the state', in *Collected Philosophical Papers,* vol. III *Ethics, Religion and Politics* (Oxford: Blackwell)

[1] References of the form (PI, I, –) are to *Remarks* in Part I; those of the form (PI, p. –) are to *pages* in Part II.

References

Argyle, M. 1969. *Social Interaction* (London: Methuen)

Auden, W. 1973. *Forewords and Afterwords,* selected by Mendelson, E. (London: Faber)

Ayer, A. J. 1954. 'Can there be a private language?', Aristotelian Society, *Supp. Proc.,* vol. 28

Baker, G. and Hacker, P. 1986. *Wittgenstein, Rules, Grammar and Necessity: An Analytical Commentary on the Philosophical Investigations,* vol. II (Oxford: Blackwell)

Bartlett, F. 1932. *Remembering: A Study in Experimental Psychology* (London: Cambridge University Press)

Berghahn, W. 1963. *Robert Musil,* in *Selbstzeugnissen und Bilddokumenten* (Reinbek bei Hamburg: Rowohlt Verlag)

Bergin, A. 1966. 'Some implications of psychotherapy research for therapeutic practice', *Journal of Abnormal Psychology,* 71

Billig, M. 1987. *Arguing and Thinking: A Rhetorical Approach to Social Psychology* (Cambridge: Cambridge University Press)

Blackburn, S. forthcoming 'Wittgenstein's Irrealism', paper presented at the XIVth International Wittgenstein Symposium held at Kirchberg-am-Wechsel, Austria, 1989, and to appear in the associated volume of conference proceedings

Boden, M, 1982. 'Formalism and fancy', *New Universities Quarterly,* 36

Boghossian, P. 1989. 'The rule-following considerations', *Mind,* 98

Bousma, O. 1986. In *Wittgenstein, Conversations 1959–51,* ed. Craft, J. and Hustwit, R. (Indianapolis: Hackett)

Broadbent, D. 1961. *Behaviourism* (London: Methuen)

Buber, M. 1965. 'The word that is spoken', in *The Knowledge of Man* (London: Allen & Unwin)

Church, R. 1955. *Over the Bridge* (London: Heinemann)

Cioffi, F. 1974a (ed.) *Freud* (London: Macmillan)

Cioffi, F. 1974b. 'Symptoms, wishes and actions', Aristotelian Society, *Proc.,* vol. 48

Cioffi, F. 1987. 'Explanation, understanding and consolation', *New Literary History,* XIX

Coleridge, S. T. 1983. *Biographia Literaria* (London: Routledge and Kegan Paul)

Collingwood, R. 1942. *The New Leviathan, or Man, Society, Civilization and Barbarism* (Oxford: Clarendon Press)

Craik, K. 1943. *The Nature of Explanation* (Cambridge: Cambridge University Press)

Diamond, C. (ed.) 1976. *Wittgensteins Lectures on the Foundations of Mathematics* (Hassocks: Harvester)

Diamond, C. 1989. 'Rules: Looking in the right place', in *Wittgenstein: Attention to Particulars, Essays in Honour of Rush Rhees,* ed. Phillips, D. and Winch, P. (London: Macmillan)

Einstein, A. 1979. 'On the method of theoretical physics', in *Einstein: a Centenary Volume,* ed. French, A. (London: Heinemann)

Engelmann, P. 1967. *Letters from Ludwig Wittgenstein, with a Memoir* (Oxford: Blackwell)

Fann, K. (ed.) 1967. *Ludwig Wittgenstein: The Man and his Philosophy* (New York: Dell)

Findlay, J. 1975. *Wittgenstein: A Critique* (London: Routledge and Kegan Paul)

Fisher, S. and Greenberg, R. 1977. *The Scientific Credibility of Freud's Theory* (Sussex: Harvester)

Flew, A. 1955. 'Theology and falsification', in *New Essays in Philosophical Theology,* ed. Flew, A. and MacIntyre, A. (London: SCM Press)

Fodor, J. 1987. *Psychosemantics* (Cambridge, Mass.: M.I.T. Press)

Freud, S. 1895. *Standard Edition, vol. 2* (London: Hogarth Press, 1953–74)

Freud, S. 1924. *Collected Papers, vol. 2* (London: Hogarth Press)

Freud, S. 1933 *New Introductory Lectures on Psychoanalysis* (London: Hogarth Press)

Freud, S. 1949a. *Introductory Lectures on Psychoanalysis* (London: Allen & Unwin)

Freud, S. 1949b. *Outline of Psychoanalysis* (London: Hogarth Press)

Freud, S. 1954. *The Interpretation of Dreams* (London: Allen & Unwin)

Freud, S. 1959. *Beyond the Pleasure Principle* (New York: Bantam)

Gaita, R. 1990. *Good and Evil, an Absolute Conception* (London: Macmillan)

Gallie, W. B. 1956. 'Essentially contested concepts', Aristotelian Society, *Proc.,* vol. 56

Garfinkel, H. 1967. *Studies in Ethnomethodology* (Englewood Cliffs, NJ: Prentice-Hall)

Gergen, K. 1985. 'The social constructionist movement in modern psychology', *American Psychologist,* 40

Gibson, J. 1979. *The Ecological Approach to Visual Perception* (London: Houghton Mifflin)

Gillet, G. 1989. 'Perception and neuroscience', *British Journal for the Philosophy of Science,* 40

Gödel, K. 1947. 'What is Cantor's Continuum Problem?' in *Philosophy of Mathematics: Selected Readings,* 2nd. edition, ed. Benaceraff, P. and Putnam, H. (Cambridge: Cambridge University Press, 1983)

Goodman, N. 1972. 'The new riddle of induction', in *Problems and Projects,* pp. 371–388 (Indianapolis: Hackett)

Grayling, A. C. 1988. *Wittgenstein* (Oxford: Oxford University Press)

Grunbaum, F. 1984. *The Foundations of Psycho-Analysis* (Berkeley: California University Press)

Haecker, T. 1920. 'Revolution', *Der Brenner*

Hanfling, O. 1989. *Wittgenstein's Later Philosophy* (London: Macmillan)

Hanly, C. 1972. 'Wittgenstein on psychoanalysis', in *Ludwig Wittgenstein: Philosophy and Language* ed. Ambrose, A. and Lazerowitz, M. (London: Allen & Unwin)

Harding, D. 1941. *The Impulse to Dominate* (London: Allen & Unwin)

Heidegger, M. 1972. *Was heisst denken?* (London: Harper and Row)

Hertz, H. 1954. *The Principles of Mechanics* (New York: Dover Press)

Hobbes, T. 1840. *Leviathan and Behemoth: The History of the Causes of the Civil Wars in England,* in *Collected Works* vol. III and vol. VI (London: Bohn)

References

Hume, D. 1888. *A Treatise of Human Nature,* ed. Selby-Bigge, L. A. (Oxford: Clarendon Press)

Hume, D. 1951. 'Of the Original Contract' in *Hume: Theory of Politics,* ed. Watkins, F. (Toronto: Nelson)

Ichheiser, G. 1970. *Appearances and Realities* (San Francisco: Jossey-Bass)

Isenberg, A. 1973. *Aesthetics and the Theory of Criticism* (Chicago University Press)

James, W. 1950. *The Principles of Psychology* (New York: Dover)

Janik, A. and Toulmin, S. 1973. *Wittgenstein's Vienna* (London: Wiedenfeld & Nicholson)

Johnson-Laird, P. 1983. *Mental Models* (Cambridge: Cambridge University Press)

Johnston, P. 1989. *Wittgenstein and Moral Philosophy* (London: Routledge)

Jones, S. 1968. *Treatment or Torture* (London: Tavistock Press)

Kenny, A. 1984. *The Legacy of Wittgenstein* (Oxford: Blackwell)

Kivy, P. 1980. *The Corded Shell* (Princeton: Princeton University Press)

Kivy, P. 1990. *Music Alone: Philosophical Reflections on the Purely Musical Experience* (Cornell: Cornell University Press)

Kline, M. 1980. *Mathematics: The Loss of Certainty* (Oxford: Oxford University Press)

Koch, S. 1964. 'Psychology and emerging conceptions of knowledge as unitary' *Behaviorism and Phenomenology,* ed. Wann, T. (Chicago: Chicago University Press)

Koehler, W., 1947. *Gestalt Psychology* (New York: Liveright)

Kraus, K. 1980. 'Apokalypse (Offener Brief an das Publikum)', in *Untergand der Welt durch schwarze Magie,* reprinted in Paperback-Ausgabe, vol. 7 (Munich: Kösel-Verlag)

Kraus, K. 1909. 'Die Entdeckung des Nordpols', *in Die chinesische Mauer,* reprinted in Paperback-Ausgabe, vol. 9 (Munich: Kösel-Verlag)

Kraus, K. 1914. 'In dieser grossen Zeit', in *Weltgericht,* reprinted in Paperback-Ausgabe, vol. 10 (Munich: Kösel-Verlag)

Kraus, K. 1974. *Beim Wort genommen,* reprinted in Paperback-Ausgabe, vol. 1 (Munich: Kösel-Verlag)

Kripke, S. 1981. 'Wittgenstein on rules and private language', in *Perspectives in the Philosophy of Wittgenstein,* ed. L. Block, pp. 238–312 (Oxford: Blackwell)

Kripke, S. 1982. *Wittgenstein on Rules and Private Language, an Elementary Exposition* (Oxford: Blackwell)

Locke, J, 1967. *Two Treatises of Government* (Cambridge: Cambridge University Press)

Locke, J. 1975. *An Essay Concerning Human Understanding,* ed. Nidditch, H. (Oxford: Clarendon Press)

Lodge, D. 1988. *Nice Work,* (London: Secker & Warburg)

Macdowell, J. 1984. 'Following a rule', *Synthèse,* 58

Mackie, J. L. 1982. *The Miracle of Theism* (Oxford: The Clarendon Press)

Maddy, P. 1980. 'Perception and Mathematical Intuition', *Philosophical Review,* 89

Malcolm, N. 1958. *Ludwig Wittgenstein: A Memoir* (London: Oxford University Press)

Malcolm, N. 1986. *Nothing is Hidden, Wittgenstein's Criticism of his Early Work* (Oxford: Blackwell)

Malcolm, N. 1989a. 'Language game (2)' in *Wittgenstein: Attention to Particulars, Essays in Honour of Rush Rhees,* ed. Phillips, D. and Winch, P. (London: Macmillan)

Malcolm, N. 1989b. 'Wittgenstein on Language and Rules', *Philosophy,* 64

McGinn, C. 1984. *Wittgenstein on Meaning* (Oxford: Blackwell)

McGuiness, B. (ed.), 1967. *Wittgenstein und der Wiener Kreis, Shorthand notes recorded by F. Waismann,* (Oxford: Blackwell)

McGuinness, B. (ed.) 1982. *Wittgenstein and his Times* (Oxford: Blackwell)

McGuiness, B. 1988. *Wittgenstein: a Life, Young Ludwig (1889–1921)* (London: Duckworth)

Moore, G. 1966. *Philosophical Papers* (New York: Collier Books)

Musil, R. 1978a. *Der deutsche Mensch als Symptom,* reprinted in *Gesammelte Werke,* ed. Frise, A. (Reinbeck bei Hamburg: Rowolt Verlag), vol. 8

Musil, R. 1978b. *Der Mann ohne Eigenschaften,* reprinted in *Gesammelte Werke,* ed. Frise, A. (Reinbeck bei Hamburg: Rowort Verlag), vol. 1

Newman, J. H. 1935. *Parochial Sermons* (London: Rivington)

Nietzsche, F. 1979. 'Aus dem Nachlass der achtiger Jahre', in *Werke,* ed. Schlecta, K., vol. IV (Frankfurt/M-Berlin-Wien: Ullstein Bücher)

Nisbett, R. and Wilson, R. 1977. 'Telling more than we know', *Psychological Review,* 84

Nyiri, J. C. 1982. 'Wittgenstein's Later Work in Relation to Conservatism', in *Wittgenstein and His Times* ed. McGuiness, B. (Oxford: Blackwell)

Nyiri, J. C. 1989. 'Tradition and freedom: Austrian Conservatism from Eotvos to Musil', *Salisbury Review* (March)

O'Hear, A. 1980. *Karl Popper* (London: Routledge and Kegan Paul)

O'Hear, A. 1984. *What Philosophy Is* (Harmondsworth: Penguin)

Orwell, G. 1950. *Shooting an Elephant and other essays* (London: Secker and Warburg)

Pears, D. 1970. *Wittgenstein* (London: Fontana)

Pears, D. 1987. *The False Prison,* 2 vols. (Oxford: Clarendon Press)

Pettit, P. and McDowell, X. (eds.) 1986. *Subject, Thought and Context* (Oxford: Clarendon Press)

Phillips, D. 1970. *Death and Immortality* (London: Macmillan)

Phillips, D. 1986. *Belief, Change and Forms of Life* (London: Macmillan)

Phillips, D. 1988a. *Faith after Foundationalism* (London: Routledge)

Phillips, D. 1988b. 'Grammarians and guardians', *The Logic of the Heart,* ed. Bell, R. (London: Harper & Row)

Potter, D. 1983. *Brimstone and Treacle* (London: Methuen)

Prince, M. 1913. 'The psychopathology of a case of phobia – a clinical study', *Journal of Abnormal Psychology*

Putman, H. 1981. *Reason, Truth and History* (Cambridge: Cambridge University Press)

Quine, W. 1953. 'Two dogmas of empiricism', in *From a Logical Point of View* (Cambridge, Mass.: Harvard University Press)

References

Rhees, R. 1970. *Discussions of Wittgenstein* (London: Routledge and Kegan Paul)

Rhees, R. 1971. 'The tree of Nebuchadnezzar', *The Human World*, No. 4

Rhees, R. (ed.) 1981. *Ludwig Wittgenstein: personal recollections* (Oxford: Blackwell)

Rogers, C. 1964. 'Towards a science of the person', in *Behaviourism and Phenomenology*, ed. Wann, T. (Chicago: Chicago University Press)

Russell, B. 1927. *An Outline of Philosophy* (London: Allen & Unwin)

Ryle, G. 1949. *The Concept of Mind* (London: Hutchinson)

Sartre, J-P. 1962. *Existential Psychoanalysis*, ed. May, R. (Chicago: Chicago University Press)

Schafer, R. 1978. *Language and Insight* (New Haven and London: Yale University Press)

Shotter, J. 1984. *Social Accountability and Selfhood* (Oxford: Blackwell)

Shotter, J. 1989. 'Rhetoric and the recovery of civil society', *Economy and Society*, 18

Shotter, J. and Gergen, K. 1989. *Texts of Identity* (London: Sage)

Spengler, O. 1972. *Der Untergang des Abendlandes, Umrisse einer Morphologie der Weltgeschichte*, (Munich: Deutsche Taschenbuch Verlag)

Stolnitz, J. (ed.) 1965. *Aesthetics* (London: Macmillan)

Sutherland, S. 1984. *God, Jesus and Belief* (Oxford: Blackwell)

Taylor, C. 1971. 'Interpretation and the Science of Man', *Review of Metaphysics*, 34

Travis, C. (ed.) 1986. *Meaning and Interpretation* (Oxford: Blackwell)

Travis, C. 1989. *The Uses of Sense* (Oxford: Clarendon Press)

Trigg, R. 1970. *Pain and Emotion* (Oxford: Clarendon Press)

Trigg, R. 1973. *Reason And Commitment* (Cambridge: Cambridge University Press)

Trigg, R. 1988. 'The metaphysical self', *Religious Studies*, 24

Trigg, R. 1989. *Reality at Risk* (London: Harvester, 2nd Edition)

Tylor, E. B. 1920. *Primitive Culture* (London: Murray)

Van der Bergh, J. 1960. *The Phenomenological Approach to Psychiatry* (Springfield)

Vesey, G. (ed.) 1973. *Philosophy and the Arts* (London: Macmillan)

Weil, S. 1957. *Intimations of Christianity among the Ancient Greeks* (London: Routledge and Kegan Paul.

von Wright, G. 1982. *Wittgenstein* (Oxford: Blackwell)

von Wright, G. 1984. 'Rule following, meaning and constructivism', in *Meaning and Interpretation*, ed. Travis, C. (Oxford: Blackwell)

Whitehorn, J. 1974. 'The concept of 'Meaning' and 'Cause' in psychodynamics', *American Journal of Psychiatry*

Winch, P. 1958. *The Idea of a Social Science* (London: Routledge and Kegan Paul)

Winch, P. 1987. *Trying to Make Sense* (Oxford: Blackwell)

Wisdom, J. 1973. 'Philosophy, metaphysics and psychoanalysis: extract' in *Freud: Modern Judgements*, ed. Cioffi, F. (London: Macmillan)

Witenberg, E. 1973. *Interpersonal Explorations in Psychoanalysis: New Directions in Theory and Practice* (New York: Basic Books)

Wortis, J. 1954. *Fragments of an Analysis with Freud* (New York: Charter Books)

Wright, C. 1968. 'Two-valuedness, Meaning and Intuitionism', unpublished Ph.D. thesis, University of Cambridge

Wright, C. 1980. *Wittgenstein on the Foundations of Mathematics* (London: Duckworth)

Wright, C. 1984. 'Kripke's account of the argument against private language', *Journal of Philosophy*, LXXXI, 759–778

Wright, C. 1986a. 'Does *Philosophical Investigations* I, 258–260 suggest a cogent argument against private language?' in Pettit and MacDowell, 1986

Wright, C. 1986b. 'Rule following, meaning and constructivism, in Travis, 1986.

Wright, C. 1986c. 'Inventing Logical Necessity' in *Language, Mind and Logic,* ed. Butterfield, J. (Cambridge: Cambridge University Press)

Wright, C. 1989a. 'Wittgenstein, Rule-following Considerations and the Central Project of Theoretical Linguistics' in *Reflections on Chomsky,* ed. George, A. (Oxford: Blackwell)

Wright, C. 1989b. Critical notice of McGinn's *Wittgenstein on Meaning, Mind,* p. 303

Wright, C. 1989c. 'Necessity, Caution and Scepticism', Aristotelian Society, *Supplementary Proceedings,* vol. LXIII

Wright, C. and Boghossian, P. forthcoming, 'Meaning – Irrealism and Global Irrealism'

Wuchterl, K. and Hübner, A. 1979. *Wittgenstein,* in *Sebstzeugnissen und Bilddokumenten* (Reinbek bei Hamburg: Rowolt Verlag)

Zweig, S. 1943. *The World of Yesterday* (London: Cassell)

Notes on Contributors

Professor G. E. M. Anscombe of the University of Cambridge was a pupil and executor of Wittgenstein's. As will be seen from the bibliography, she is a translator of much of Wittgenstein's published work. Her *Introduction to Wittgenstein's* Tractatus was published in 1959 and her *Collected Papers* in 3 volumes were published in 1981. She was a contributor to volume 18 of this series.

Renford Bambrough, a Fellow of St. John's College, Cambridge, is the editor of *Philosophy*, and a contributor to a number of volumes in this series. He is the author of *Reason, Truth and God*, 1969 and *Moral Scepticism and Moral Knowledge*, 1979.

Professor Jacques Bouveresse of the University of Paris I is the foremost writer in France on the philosophy of Wittgenstein. His works (ed. de Minuit) include *Le Mythe de l'interiorité. Expérience, signification et langage privé chez Wittgenstein*, 1976, *Rationalité et cynisme*, 1984, *La force de la règle. Wittgenstein et l'invention de la necessité*, 1987, and *Le pays des possibles. Wittgenstein, les mathématiques et le monde réel*, 1988.

Michael Brearley is a practising psychoanalyst. His 'Psychoanalysis and Philosophy' was published in Ilham Dilman (ed.) *Philosophy and Life* in 1984.

Frank Cioffi, who recently retired as Professor of Philosophy at the University of Essex, previously contributed to volumes 4 and 16 in this series. His 'Wittgenstein on Making Homeopathic Magic Clear' was published in Gaita (ed.) *Value and Understanding*, 1980 and 'Wittgenstein and obscurantism' in the Aristotelian Society Supplementary *Proceedings*, 1990.

Raimond Gaita, of King's College, University of London edited *Value and Understanding: Essays in Honour of Peter Winch* in 1980 and his *Good and Evil: An Absolute Conception* was published in 1990.

A. C. Grayling is a Fellow of St. Anne's College, Oxford. His last book was *Wittgenstein* in the Past Master series (1988), and his *The Question of Realism* is soon to be published by the Oxford University Press.

Oswald Hanfling of the Open University is the author of *Wittgenstein's Later Philosophy* (1989), among other books. He has been a frequent contributor to *Philosophy*. His 'Hume and Wittgenstein' appeared in volume 9 and 'Ayer, Language and Truth and Logic' in volume 20 of this series. He is a member of the Council of the Royal Institute.

Notes on Contributors

Anthony O'Hear is Professor of Philosophy at the University of Bradford and a member of the Council of the Royal Institute. His books include *Karl Popper* (1980), *Experience, Explanation and Faith*, 1984, *What Philosophy Is* (1985), *The Element of Fire* 1988 and *Introduction to the Philosophy of Science* 1989. He is a contributor to *Philosophy* and to volume 18 of this series.

D. Z. Phillips is Professor of Philosophy at University College, Swansea. His books include *The Concept of Prayer*, 1969, *Religion without Explanation*, 1976, and *Faith After Foundationalism* (1988). He is a contributor to *Philosophy* and to volumes 6 and 17 of the present series.

Professor John Shotter is currently Cornall Visiting Professor in Psychology, Swarthmore, Philadelphia, while on leave from the Rijksuniversitet of Utrecht. He is the author of *Images of Man in Psychological Research*, 1975, and *Social Accountability and Selfhood* (1984). His *Human Action and its Psychological Investigation* published in collaboration with Alan Gauld in 1977 is particularly relevant to the present volume.

Professor Roger Trigg of the University of Warwick is a contributor to *Philosophy* and to volume 17 of this series. He is the author of several books, the most recent being *Understanding Social Science*, 1985 and *Ideas of Human Nature*, 1988.

Peter Winch, sometime Professor of Philosophy at King's College, London, is now at the University of Illinois, Urbana-Champaign. He is the translator of Wittgenstein's *Culture and Value* (CV), and the author of *The Idea of a Social Science* (1958), *Ethics and Action*, 1972, *Trying to Make Sense* (1987) and *Simone Weil, 'the just balance'*, 1989.

Crispin Wright is Professor of Philosophy at the Universities of St. Andrews and Michigan, Ann Arbor. His *Wittgenstein on the Foundations of Mathematics* (1980) was followed by *Frege's Conception of Numbers as Objects* in 1983 and *Realism, Meaning and Truth* in 1986.

Index of Names

261

Index of Names